Expressing America

A Critique of the Global Credit Card Society

THE PINE FORGE PRESS SOCIAL SCIENCE LIBRARY

What Is Society? Reflections on Freedom, Order, and Change by Earl Babbie

Adventures in Social Research: Data Analysis Using SPSS by Earl Babbie and Fred Halley

Adventures in Social Research: Data Analysis Using SPSS with WINDOWS by Earl Babbie and Fred Halley

Crime and Everyday Life: Insights and Implications for Society by Marcus Felson

Sociology of Work by Richard H. Hall

Race, Ethnicity, Gender, and Class: The Sociology of Group Conflict and Change by Joseph F. Healey

The Production of Reality: Essays and Readings in Social Psychology by Peter Kollock and Jodi O'Brien

Sociological Snapshots: Seeing Social Structure and Change in Everyday Life by Jack Levin

Aging: Concepts and Controversies by Harry R. Moody, Jr.

The McDonaldization of Society by George Ritzer

Expressing America: A Critique of the Global Credit Card Society by George Ritzer

Sociology: Exploring the Architecture of Everyday Life by David M. Newman

Sociology: Exploring the Architecture of Everyday Life (Readings) by David M. Newman

Worlds of Difference: Structured Inequality and the Aging Experience by Eleanor Palo Stoller and Rose Campbell Gibson

The Pine Forge Press Series in Research Methods and Statistics
edited by Richard T. Campbell and Kathleen S. Crittenden

Investigating the Social World: The Process and Practice of Research by Russell K. Schutt

A Guide to Field Research by Carol A. Bailey

Designing Surveys: A Guide to Decisions and Procedures by Ron Czaja and Johnny Blair

How Sampling Works by Caroline Persell and Richard Maisel

Sociology for a New Century
A Pine Forge Press Series edited by Charles Ragin, Wendy Griswold, and Larry Griffin

How Societies Change by Daniel Chirot

Cultures and Societies in a Changing World by Wendy Griswold

Crime and Disrepute by John Hagan

Gods in the Global Village by Lester R. Kurtz

Constructing Social Research by Charles C. Ragin

Women and Men at Work by Barbara Reskin and Irene Padavic

Cities in a World Economy by Saskia Sassen

Expressing America

A Critique of the Global Credit Card Society

George Ritzer

The University of Maryland

PINE FORGE PRESS
Thousand Oaks ◆ London ◆ New Delhi

For information, address:

 Pine Forge Press
A Sage Publications Company
2455 Teller Road
Thousand Oaks, California 91320
(805) 499-4224
E-mail: sales@pfp.sagepub.com

Production: Scratchgravel Publishing Services
Designer: Lisa S. Mirski
Typesetter: Scratchgravel Publishing Services
Cover: Lisa S. Mirski
Production Manager: Rebecca Holland

Printed in the United States of America

95 96 97 98 99 10 9 8 7 6 5 4 3 2

Library of Congress Cataloging-in-Publication Data

Ritzer, George.
    Expressing America : a critique of the global credit card society
  / George Ritzer
        p.   cm.
    Includes bibliographical references and index.
    ISBN 0-8039-9044-8 (pbk. : alk. paper)
    1. Credit cards—Social aspects—United States.   2. Credit cards—
Social aspects.   3. Consumer credit—United States.   I. Title.
HG3756.U54R56   1995
332.7'65'0973—dc20   94-38142
                                                              CIP

for Sue

to whom my indebtedness (and my love) is endless

About the Author

George Ritzer is an acknowledged expert in the field of social theory and sociology of work and has served as Chair of the American Sociological Association's Sections on Theoretical Sociology and Organizations and Occupations. A distinguished Scholar-Teacher at the University of Maryland, Professor Ritzer has been honored with that institution's Teaching Excellence award. Two of his most recent books include *Metatheorizing in Sociology* (Lexington Press) and *The McDonaldization of Society* (Pine Forge Press). His books have been translated into many languages, including German, Russian, and Spanish.

About the Publisher

Pine Forge Press is a new educational publisher, dedicated to publishing innovative books and software throughout the social sciences. On this and any other of our publications, we welcome your comments and suggestions.

Please call or write to:

Pine Forge Press
A Sage Publications Company
2455 Teller Road
Thousand Oaks, California 91320
(805) 499-4224
E-mail: sales@pfp.sagepub.com

Contents

Preface / xi

1 The Credit Card: *Private Troubles and Public Issues / 1*
A Window on Society / 2
The Advantages of Credit Cards / 3
A Key Problem with Credit Cards / 5
Who Is to Blame? / 7
    The Individual / 7
    The Government / 8
    Business / 9
    Banks and Other Financial Institutions / 9
An Indictment of the Financial System / 11
Case in Point: Getting Them Hooked While They're Young / 12
A Sociology of Credit Cards / 15
    Mills: Personal Troubles, Public Issues / 16
    Marx: Capitalist Exploitation / 18
    Simmel: The Money Economy / 19
    Weber: Rationalization / 21
    Globalization and Americanization / 22
    Micro-Macro Relationships / 22
Other Reasons for Devoting a Book to Credit Cards / 23
    Something New in the History of Money / 23
    A Growing Industry / 25
    A Symbol of American Values / 27
Debunking Credit Card Myths / 28

2 Socio-History of the Credit Card: *We Probably Won't
    Recognize the Credit Card Field by the End of the Century / 31*
A Brief History / 33
    The Rise of the Universal Credit Card / 34
    The Entry of "Nonbanks" / 38

Co-Branded Cards / 39
The Decline of the "Charge" Card / 41
Credit Bureaus / 42
Industry Dynamics: Expand or Die / 42
Finding New Business / 43
The Competitive Environment in the 1990s / 50
Credit Legislation / 51
Future: Increasingly Incredible CREDEBELS / 53

3 Credit Card Debt: *Beware the Plastic Loan Shark / 59*
The Temptation to Imprudence / 60
Credit Cards / 60
Debit Cards / 62
Electronic Funds Transfers / 63
Consumer Debt as a Public Issue / 64
Consumer Debt as a Personal Trouble / 65
Who Is Responsible for High Credit Card Debt? / 68
Consumers / 68
Credit Card Companies / 69
How to Overcome the Temptation to Imprudence / 71
Be Aware of the Danger Signs / 72
Stop Credit Card Abuse / 73
Reduce the Costs of Credit Card Debt / 76
Getting Outside Help / 78
What Government Can Do / 81
What the Credit Card Industry Could Do / 81

4 Credit Card Fraud: *Screw You, Mac—I Got Mine / 83*
Fraud Against the Card Companies and Users / 85
Stolen Cards / 85
Stolen Credit Information / 86
Counterfeit and Altered Cards / 88
Fraudulent Credit Card Applications / 89
Abuses by Telemarketers / 90
Fraudulent Credit "Repair" / 91
Mean Machinations by Card Companies / 92
Excessive Interest Rates and Fees / 93
Exploitive Billing Tactics / 94
Mean Machinations by Card Users / 97

Weapons Against Credit Card Fraud / 98
  Protecting Credit Card Firms and Merchants / 98
  Protecting Consumers: Self-Preservation / 101
  Protecting Consumers: Government Action / 103
  Protecting Consumers: Proposals for Industry Action / 104
Fraud, Private Troubles, and Public Issues / 106

5 Secrecy, Privacy, and Credit Cards: *Who Isn't*
in Their Files? / 107
Secrecy Problems / 109
  Nondisclosure of Credit Terms / 109
  Erroneous Credit Records / 109
  Nondisclosure of Affinity Card Terms / 113
Privacy Problems / 114
  Excessive Data Collection / 116
  Illegitimate Access to Credit Records / 117
  Sale of Credit and Lifestyle Information / 119
  Computerized Databases / 121
Ways of Coping with Secrecy Problems / 123
Ways of Protecting Privacy / 125

6 Credit Cards, Fast-Food Restaurants,
and Rationalization: *All You Need Is 42 Digits*
to Make One Long-Distance Phone Call / 129
Similarities Between the Credit Card and Fast-Food
  Industries / 129
  Lack of Innovativeness / 129
  Reliance on Advertising / 130
  Expansion / 132
Rationalization / 133
  Calculability: The All-Important Credit Report / 137
  Efficiency: The Faster the Better / 142
  Predictability: Avoiding Those Painful Lulls / 144
  Nonhuman for Human Technology: No Visitors, No Staff / 146
  Irrationality of Rationality: Caught in the Heavy
    Machinery / 149
Personal Troubles, Public Issues, and Rationalization / 151
Ways of Coping with the Rationalized Credit Card
  Industry / 155

7 An American Express: *The Culture That Conquered
    the World / 157*
The Global Spread of Credit Cards / 159
Americanization and the Credit Card / 162
      Acceptance of American Exports / 165
      Rationalization / 165
      Modernism / 167
      Consumerism / 170
Anti-Americanism and the Credit Card / 171
Summing Up / 175

Appendix
Those Other CREDEBELS: *Debit Cards, Electronic Funds
    Transfers, and Automated Clearinghouses / 179*
Debit Cards / 179
Electronic Funds Transfers / 184
Automated Clearinghouses / 188
Personal Troubles, Public Issues, and the Other
    CREDEBELS / 192

Endnotes / 197

Index / 231

Preface

This is a sociological analysis and critique of the role of credit cards (and other forms of the transfer of funds electronically) in the contemporary world. But in another, even more important, sense it is about a more general process—"the American express"— a term I use to describe a range of related phenomena that are sweeping across, and dramatically altering, North America and, increasingly, a large portion of the rest of the world. While many other American icons mentioned in the pages of this book (the fast-food restaurant, the theme park, the shopping mall, and so on) are important components of this "express," the credit card may well be the linchpin that holds it all together. The credit card, therefore, is of particular significance because it is not only an expanding presence around the world but also an increasingly important means to all the other components of the American express.

The credit card is also the premier symbol of an American lifestyle that much of the rest of the world is rushing to emulate. While there is much to recommend such a lifestyle, there is another side to it that is largely ignored. That other side is the rampant expansion of the consumer culture and its attendant problems—consumerism and indebtedness, fraud, invasion of privacy, rationalization and dehumanization, and homogenization stemming from increasing Americanization. The objective of this book is to use a sociological perspective to spotlight the dark side of the increasingly global presence of the credit card, the American express more generally, and the accompanying lifestyle.

There are many dangers associated with the widespread and indiscriminate use of credit cards, and innumerable Americans have personally experienced the devastating effects of these hazards. Such difficulties are largely unknown to other, especially younger, Americans, as well as to the hundreds of millions in the rest of the world who are eager to embrace the credit card, the consumer society, and the American style of life that comes with them. A book devoted largely to the problems Americans have had with credit cards can serve to caution those who have not yet experienced such problems, both in the United States and in the rest of the world.

Another motivation behind this book is that credit cards, and the problems they pose, cry out for sociological, rather than the more customary psychological, analysis. In our society, preoccupied with individual-level analyses of social phenomena, there is a tendency to think about the problems associated with credit cards, and many other problems as well, as the result of individual deviance. In contrast, this book employs a more sociological approach that deals with the relationship between individual behavior and larger social forces. Thus, instead of thinking about credit card fraud as traceable only to individual criminals, we will also link it to the structure of the credit card industry. Instead of tracing credit card debt simply to individuals "addicted" to debt, we will also address the role played by the credit card industry in encouraging debt, even among college and high school students. Rather than arguing merely that evil individuals are invading our privacy, we will also trace that invasion to the day-to-day operations of the credit card industry. This kind of sociological perspective is needed to offer a corrective on the tendency to individualize and even medicalize the problems of the credit card industry (for example, in applying the idea of addiction to credit card abuse).

This book uses the analysis of credit cards as a "window" on society. Credit cards are a key feature of modern society, and an examination of them allows us to see clearly some of the essential features of the modern world. In the end, this study of credit cards leads us to some of the most essential problems in modern society—crime, debt, threats to privacy, rationalization, dehumanization, and homogenization. Thus, the credit card is both a key component of the modern world and a marvelous window into it.

As in an earlier book of mine entitled *The McDonaldization of Society*, *Expressing America* uses sociological theory to illuminate important social issues. Rather than relying on the work of a single social theorist (Max Weber) as I did in *McDonaldization*, I found it useful to employ a number of theoretical perspectives in *Expressing*

America, including the theories of C. Wright Mills, Georg Simmel, Karl Marx, and Max Weber, as well as micro-macro, agency-structure, and Americanization theories. Although this book is guided by theory, it, like its predecessor, is accessible and aimed at the general reader. This is not a theoretical treatise, but an effort to use sociological theory to inform a wide readership about the dangers of credit cards and the need to take a variety of reform-oriented and self-protective actions.

Credit cards (like fast-food restaurants) are everyday economic phenomena that are of great significance to people both materially and symbolically. These mundane economic phenomena, and the problems they pose, cry out for sociological analysis. Yet, ironically, sociologists have not devoted much attention to such seemingly "insignificant" social phenomena. Instead, they have preferred to deal with much grander issues, such as capitalism and socialism, or industrial and postindustrial society. In their rush to deal with such grand abstractions, sociologists have tended to ignore the more mundane issues that are of far greater significance to people on a day-to-day basis. Yet it is abundantly clear that the seemingly insignificant credit card (as well as the fast-food restaurant and similar phenomena) is profoundly changing the social world.

I would like to thank a number of people who reviewed earlier drafts of this manuscript: Gerri Detweiler (consultant and former director of Bankcard Holders of America), David Frisby (University of Glasgow), Mike Gatti (National Automated Clearing House Association), Tahira Hira (Iowa State University), Sean Kennedy (Electronic Funds Transfer Association), Peter Kollock (University of California, Los Angeles), Gianfranco Poggi (University of Virginia), John Walsh (University of Illinois, Chicago), and Cynthia Woolever (Midway College). I would also like to thank the Pine Forge Press staff—Rebecca Holland, Mary Sutton, and Sherith Pankratz—as well as manuscript editor Rebecca Smith. Also to be thanked are my invaluable assistants, Allan Liska and Rita Wood; Jeremy Ritzer, for his skills as an indexer; and a number of my undergraduate students, especially Michael Saks and Meghan Lee.

However, the most important person in helping to shape this book has been Steve Rutter, editor and president of Pine Forge Press. Steve is something of a throwback to an earlier era in academic publishing, when editors actually read the books they published. In fact, Steve read several iterations of this book and offered useful comments on each. Most important, when I began to lose sight of what I was trying to accomplish in these pages, Steve helped me to get back on track. Steve even assisted in the creation of the title of this book, with its rich multifaceted meanings. Clearly, Steve has helped to make this a far better book than it otherwise might have been. I owe him a deep debt.

George Ritzer

Acknowledgments

We gratefully acknowledge the following for permission to reprint quotes:

American Banker for Jeanne Dugan Cooper, "Burger King Program in Oregon Allows Customers to Pay by Credit Card or Check," *American Banker*, October 4, 1989, p. 10; Barton Crockett, "Banks Unlikely to Find a Bonanza in Debit-Card Supremacy," *American Banker*, August 26, 1992, pp. 1, 9; "EFT Experts Look Ahead With Costs on Their Minds," *American Banker*, May 20, 1991, p. 22A; Stephen Kleege, "Privacy a Concern with Marketing Based on Card Data," *American Banker*, March 14, 1994, p. 15; Jeffrey Kutler, "Visa Seals Debit Strategy by Purchasing Plus," *American Banker*, November 2, 1993, p. 3; Robert L. Pierce, "Seeking New Opportunities in Tomorrow's Payment-Systems World," *American Banker*, May 20, 1991, p. 22A; Karen Gullo, "Electronic Bill Payment Low-Cost Systems Explored," *American Banker*, January 27, 1992, p. 3; Jeffrey Kutler, "Is Banking Finally Ready for Smart Cards?" *American Banker*, March 14, 1989, pp. 26-27. Reprinted with permission of American Banker.

American Bankers Association for Mark Arend, "Card Profits: How Far Will They Slide?" *ABA Banking Journal*, September 1992, p. 82, and "Easing Borrowers Off the Road to Bankruptcy," *ABA Banking Journal*, February 1990, p. 42. Reprinted by special permission from the February 1990 and September 1992 issues of *ABA Banking Journal*, copyright © 1990 and 1992 by the American Bankers Association; for *Bank Card Fact Book*, Washington, D.C., 1990:23, © 1990 American Bankers Association. Reprinted with permission from *Bank Card Fact Book*. All rights reserved.

Associated Press for Robert Naylor, Jr., "House May Tighten Credit Report Rules," *Los Angeles Times*, September 24, 1991: D2; "Road to Cashlessness Paved With Plastic," *Los Angeles Times*, September 20, 1993. Reprinted with permission.

Business Week for Suzanne Woolley, "The Dawn of the Debit Card, Well, Maybe," *Business Week*, September 21, 1992, p. 79.

Computer Decisions for Edward J. Joyce, "Tales of EDI Trailblazers," *Computer Decisions*, February 1989, p. 65.

Consumer Reports for "Hello, Central, Get Me 18005551696 0348583 6939416 3859050 4887659 876," Copyright 1992 by Consumers Union of U.S., Inc., Yonkers, NY 10703-1057. Reprinted by permission from *Consumer Reports*, August 1992.

S. J. Diamond for "Credit Bureau's Tardy Rush to Aid Consumer," *Los Angeles Times*, October 11, 1991, p. D12. Reprinted with permission of the author.

Dow Jones & Company, Inc., for Steve Lipin, Brian Coleman, and Jeremy Mark, "Visa, American Express and MasterCard Vie in Overseas Strategies," *Wall Street Journal*, February 15, 1994, pp. A1, A10; G. Bruce Knecht, "American Express Embraces Co-Brands," *Wall Street Journal*, February 17, 1994, p. B1; Dana Milbank, "Hooked on Plastic: Middle-Class Family Takes a Harsh Cure for Credit-Card Abuse," *Wall Street Journal*, January 8, 1991, p. A1; Ellen E. Schultz, "Credit Card Crooks Devise New Scams," *Wall Street Journal*, July 17, 1992, pp. C1, C11; Richard B. Schmitt, "Visa, MasterCard Sue Telemarketers, Alleging Card Scam," *Wall Street Journal*, April 16, 1991, pp. B2, B7; "Credit Card Users Misled by Banks, Study Charges," *Wall Street Journal*, June 18, 1992, p. A5; Michael W. Miller, "Citicorp Creates Controversy With Plan to Sell Data on Credit-Card Purchases," *Wall Street Journal*, August 21, 1991, p. B7. Reprinted by permission of *Wall Street Journal*, © 1991, 1992, 1994, Dow Jones & Company, Inc. All Rights Reserved Worldwide.

Faulkner & Gray for Linda Punch, "The Jackpot in New Markets," *Credit Card Management*, April 1991; "How Cobranding Changed the Card Associations," *Credit Card News*, July 15, 1993; "The Pressure Builds to Make Convenience Users Pay," *Credit Card News*, May 15, 1993; "A Criminal Element Begins to Siphon Off Credit Card Gasoline Purchases," *Credit Card News*, October 1, 1992; *Credit Card News*, Vol. 4, No. 19, January 15, 1992; "Card Launderers Stay One Step Ahead of the Law," *Credit Card News*, October 1, 1993; "A New Merchant Fraud Fighter: Neural Networks," *Credit Card News*, September 11, 1993; *Credit Card News*, November 1, 1993; "Associations Explore International Waters for Cardholders," *Credit Card News*, November 29, 1993; Paul S. Nadler, "Politicians Create Credit Card Furor," *Bankers Monthly*, February 1992. Permission granted by Faulkner & Gray, 11 Penn Plaza, NY, NY 10001.

Financial World Magazine for Sharen Kindel, "The Esperanto of Documents," *Financial World*, July 7, 1992. p. 64.

Forbes for Bill Saporito, "Melting Point in the Plastic War," *Forbes*, May 20, 1991, p. 72. Reprinted by Permission of *Forbes* Magazine © Forbes Inc., 1991.

Institutional Investor for Saul Hansell, "Getting to Know You," *Institutional Investor*, June 1991, p. 73.

Lebhar-Friedman, Inc., for "Evaluating the Payments: More Is Better," *Chain Store Executive*, September 1992, p. 28; "A History of Debit and Credit: How Plastic Cards Changed Our Lives," *Chain Store Executive*, September 1992, p. 22.

Los Angeles Times for Russell Ben-Ali, "Urge to Spend Money Can Lead to Ruin, Therapy," May 6, 1991, p. B5; George White, "More Americans Turning to Their Credit Cards to Purchase Groceries," August 8, 1992, p. D3; Jeannine Stein, "Is There Life After Credit," October 12, 1987, p. E5; Denise Gellene, "Consumers Taking Hard Look at Credit Cards," November 20, 1991, p. D4; Bill Sing, "Good Credit Counselor Can Be Godsend," September 24, 1988, p. D3; Juli Tamaki and Michael Connelly, "Computer Skills Aid '90's Credit Card Scam," August 23, 1992, p. B5; Chris Woodyard, "Firm's Claim of 'Credit Repair' Sparks State Suit," August 1, 1991, p. D7; Chris Woodyard, "Bill May Curb Credit Reporting Abuses," June 13, 1990, p. D6; James S. Granelli, "Keeping a Computer's

Secrets," December 5, 1988, p. D6; Sam Fulwood III, "Data Crunchers: Marketing Boon or Threat to Privacy?" May 19, 1991, p. D18; Chris Woodyard, "Losing Faith in Credit Files," July 22, 1991, p. A1, A16; Scott Kraft, "Giving Euro Disneyland a Whirl," January 18, 1994, p. H5, H1; Jube Shiver, Jr., "Scoring System for Loan Seekers Stirs Debate," October 30, 1988, p. D5; James Bates, "Banks in the '90's Appear Headed Back to Basics," April 17, 1991, p. A14; Bill Sing, "Protect Your Credit Cards from Retail Practices," April 18, 1990. Copyright 1987, 1988, 1990, 1991, 1992, 1994, Los Angeles Times. Reprinted by permission.

Network World for Burton Crockett, "Bankers Create Group to Promote Wider Use of EDT," *Network World*, February 1989, p. 6. Copyright 1989, by Network World, Inc. Framingham, MA 01701 - Reprinted from Network World.

New York Magazine for John Crudel. "Hey, Big Spenders: Living Beyond One's Means." *New York Magazine*, February 20, 1989, p. 19.

The New York Times for Saul Hansell, "Into Banking's Future, Electronically," March 31, 1994; Stephanie Strom, "Holiday Shoppers Are Whipping Out the Plastic," December 18, 1993; Michael Quint, "D'Agostino to Accept Debit Cards for Purchases," May 19, 1990; Don Terry, "Police Station Becomes a Cash Station," April 1, 1994; Adam Bryant, "It Pays to Stick to Basics in Credit Cards," October 31, 1992; Karen DeWitt, "Using Credit Cards, Students Learn Hard Lesson," August 26, 1991; Leonard Sloane, "Credit Reports: The Overhaul Rolls On," January 4, 1992; Kenneth N. Gilpin, "Three Credit-Data Concerns Settle Charges," August 19, 1992; Jeffrey Rothfeder, "What Happened to Privacy," April 13, 1993 (op-ed); Erik Lundegaard, "About Men/Card Sharks," May 22, 1994 (magazine); Saul Hansell, "Into Banking's Future, Electronically," March 31, 1994; Michael Quint, "Bank's Plea: Drop That Checkbook," March 7, 1992; Michael deCourcy Hinds, "The New-Fashioned Way to Steal Money: Fake Credit," December 31, 1988; Barry Meier, "Sharing of Credit Card Numbers by Merchants Brings New Fears of Fraud," March 28, 1992; Barry Meier, "$1.50 Worth of Help for $200, But No Credit," February 9, 1991; Isabel Wilkerson, "For Shoppers, A Fast Flight to Paradise," December 20, 1993; "Nationsbank Card Features Savings Plan," January 7, 1993; Jan M. Rosen, "Maxed Charge Cards and Other Red Flags," December 12, 1992; Daniel Goleman, "A Constant Urge to Buy: Battling a Compulsion," July 17, 1991; "Shopping Addiction: Abused Substance Is Money," June 16, 1986; Saul Hansell, "Consumers Finally Respond to High Credit Card Interest," March 29, 1993; Barry Meier, "Credit Cards on the Rise in High Schools," September 5, 1992. Copyright 1991, 1992, 1993, 1994 by The New York Times Company. Reprinted by permission.

The Orlando Sentinel for Gene Yasuda, "The Big Cards on Campus," *The Orlando Sentinel*, November 1, 1993, p. D1.

Phillips Publishing International for "Associations Explore International Waters for Cardholders," *Card News*, November 29, 1993, p. 6.

Reuters News Agency for "French 'Cast Members' Get Used to the Rules in a Magic Kingdom of Jobs," *Chicago Tribune*, June 31, 1992, p. 2.

Marjorie Robins for "Awfully American for Grown-Ups," *Los Angeles Times*, May 3, 1992, p. L1; "Stopping the Juggernaut," *Los Angeles Times*, December 3, 1987, p. E1.

(acknowledgments continued on page 240)

1

The Credit Card

Private Troubles and Public Issues

The credit card has become an American icon. It is treasured, even worshipped, in the United States and, increasingly, throughout the rest of the world. The title of this book, *Expressing America*, therefore has a double meaning: The credit card expresses something about the essence of modern American society and, like an express train, is speeding across the world's landscape delivering American (and more generally consumer) culture. My goal in this book is to explain what the credit card tells us, both good and (mainly) bad, about the essence of modern America as well as why and how the credit card is helping to transform much of the world.

The credit card is not the first symbol of American culture to play such a role, nor will it be the last. Other important contemporary American icons include Coca-Cola, Levi's, Marlboro, Disney, and McDonald's. What they have in common is that, like credit cards, they are products at the very heart of American society, and they are highly valued by, and have had a profound effect on, many other societies throughout the world. However, the credit card is distinctive because it is a means that can be used to obtain those other icons, as well as virtually anything else available in the world's marketplaces. It is because of this greater versatility that the credit card may prove to be the most important American icon of all. If nothing else, it is likely to continue to exist long after other icons have become footnotes in the history of American culture. When the United States has an entirely new set of icons, the credit card will remain an important means for obtaining them.

A Window on Society

The credit card, as well as the industry that stands behind it and aggressively pushes its growth and expansion, is also important in itself and as a window on modern society. The idea of analyzing the credit card in order to understand society is derived from the theories of one of the great thinkers in the history of sociology, Georg Simmel. Among his innumerable insights was the view that "any item of culture can be the starting point for sociological research into the nature of the totality."[1] Simmel was a "relationist," meaning that he saw each aspect of society as related to every other aspect.[2] In his view, the study of any element of society will, if carried far enough, lead us to every other societal component and ultimately to a better sense of the social world in its entirety.

In his day, Simmel chose the study of money as a way of gaining insight into society. In this book I am replacing money with the more contemporary credit card, but my goal is the same as Simmel's: to explore some fundamental characteristics of the social world. Why, if everything is related to everything else, should we use money and the credit card to study society? The advantage of both is that they are so centrally important in modern consumer society that they take us very quickly to the core of that world. Choosing something else would eventually accomplish the goal, but by a lengthier and more laborious route.

What you will discover about the social world through this analysis of credit cards is a set of social problems that goes far beyond credit cards, including rampant consumerism, escalating indebtedness, pervasive fraud and crime, invasions of privacy, dehumanization of our daily lives, and increasing homogenization of the world's cultures. These are problems of concern to all of us, but we get a new and different sense of those problems by approaching them from a unique direction and by viewing them in an atypical way.

Credit cards also illustrate other important social problems. For example, the credit card industry tends to favor men over women. Thus, full-time homemakers may have difficulty obtaining credit cards because they lack outside income. In addition, the credit card business operates to the advantage of the relatively well-to-do and to the disadvantage of those who are not so well off economically. Those who are well off may be able to get lower interest rates or have their annual fees waived. The degree to which our culture values materialism is well reflected in the widespread popularity of the credit card. The individualism at the core of our cultural system is manifest, among other places, in the tendency to blame individual consumers, not our consumer society, for their problems with excessive debt.

Beyond this litany of specific problems is one that many sociologists consider to be the essential problem in the modern world: the oppressive and deforming impact of large-scale social structures on individuals. In the words of a popular analyst of the credit card business, Terry Galanoy, that industry and its products have "invaded, saturated, and altered our lives forever."[3] Galanoy asks,

> Which is the real plastic—your Visa or MasterCard, or you?
> Like those cards, you are being formed, shaped, plied, impressed. You are also being deformed continuously and permanently to go in the direction the pressure of the moneymen wants you to go.[4]

Thus, the credit card industry and the larger consumer society are just as oppressive and distorting as the other large-scale social structures (for example, capitalism and bureaucracies) that have long come under the scrutiny of sociologists.

The Advantages of Credit Cards

Although this book focuses on the problems created by the credit card industry, the credit card clearly has also made a number of positive contributions to society. Once again we can take our lead from the ideas of Georg Simmel. Simmel was a highly complex thinker, which means, among other things, that he was attuned to both the negative and the positive aspects of social phenomena. Thus, for example, he argues that "when one laments the alienating and separating effect of money transactions, one should not forget . . . money creates an extremely strong bond among the members of an economic circle."[5] Similarly, we must not lose sight of the positive characteristics of the credit card society.

The most notable advantage of credit cards, at least at the societal level, is that they permit people to spend more than they have. Credit cards thereby allow the economy to function at a much higher (and faster) level than it might if it relied solely on cash and cash-based instruments.

Credit cards also have a number of specific advantages to consumers, especially in comparison to using cash for transactions:

- Credit cards increase our spending power, thereby allowing us to enjoy a more expansive, even luxurious lifestyle.

- Credit cards save us money by permitting us to take advantage of sales, something that might not be possible if we had to rely on cash on hand.

- Credit cards are convenient. They can be used 24 hours a day to charge expenditures by phone, mail, or home computer.* Thus, we need no longer be inconvenienced by the fact that most shops and malls close overnight. Those whose mobility is limited or who are housebound can also still shop.

- Credit cards can be used virtually anywhere in the world, whereas cash (and certainly checks) cannot so easily cross national borders. For example, we are able to travel from Paris to Rome on the spur of the moment in the middle of the night without worrying about whether we have, or will be able to obtain on arrival, Italian lira.

- Credit cards smooth out consumption by allowing us to make purchases even when our incomes are low. If we happen to be laid off, we can continue to live the same lifestyle, at least for a time, with the anticipation that we will pay off our credit card balances when we are called back to work. We can make emergency purchases (of medicine, for example) even though we may have no cash on hand.

- Credit cards allow us to do a better job of organizing our finances, because we are provided each month with a clear accounting of expenditures and of money due.

- Credit cards may yield itemized invoices of tax-deductible expenses, giving us systematic records at tax time.

- Credit cards allow us to refuse to pay a disputed bill while the credit card company investigates the transaction. Credit card receipts also help us in disputes with merchants.

- Credit cards give us the option of paying our bills all at once or of stretching payments out over a length of time.

*The latter will soon become more convenient with the development of a generally available method of charging purchases in cyberspace. See John Markoff. "A Credit Card for On-Line Sprees." *New York Times*, October 15, 1994, pp. 37, 39.

◆ Credit cards are safer to carry than cash is and thus help to reduce cash-based crime.[6]

Of course, credit cards also carry advantages to merchants. Merchants who accept credit cards are, for example, likely to gain a
great deal of business they would not otherwise get. And, unlike
cash in the till, credit card receipts are not magnets for thieves.

Then there are the comparative disadvantages associated with
cash and checks. For example, cash is far more transient than
credit cards and can therefore more easily be stolen, lost, destroyed, or simply worn out. It is also not as portable as credit
cards because it is bulky, especially in large amounts, and it is not
easily used in other countries. Finally, to run a cash economy—to
"print, mint, replace, circulate, protect" money—costs a great
deal.[7] In contrast, credit cards have no direct cost to the state. The
credit card companies foot the bills out of profits derived from
their credit card business.

Checks have even greater problems. They, too, can be stolen,
lost, destroyed, or (less likely) worn out. Forgery is an ever-present
problem with checks. Checks are also awkward to use. For example,
each check must be written out individually, many places do not
honor checks, and even those that do frequently require one or
more forms of identification.

Credit card use has boomed because of its advantages as well as
the disadvantages of its main competitors—cash and checks. However, cash and checks do have some advantages over credit cards.
For example, cash and often checks can be used at no cost to the
consumer, whereas credit cards often end up entailing substantial
expense. More important, cash and checks avoid many of the social
problems associated with credit cards.

A Key Problem with Credit Cards

In the course of the twentieth century, the United States has gone
from a nation that cherished savings to one that reveres spending,
even spending beyond one's means. As one European observer of
America noted,

> If Americans were now to stop spending what they have not got their
> whole economy would falter. It is only by mortgaging their futures

they avoid bankruptcy. Thrift, so highly regarded by an earlier generation of Americans, has become a dirty word. Not to live beyond
your immediate means is antisocial.[8]

At one time, debt was something to be avoided at all costs, but today people seem to be rushing into debt as quickly and as deeply as
possible. Instead of being measured by the amount of money we
have in the bank, we are likely to be evaluated on the basis of how
far we have plunged into debt. The status symbol of an ever-in-
creasing bank balance has been replaced by efforts to impress our
friends with the magnitude of our mortgage loans and home equity
lines of credit, as well as the number of credit cards we possess and
their upper limits.

At the level of the national government, our addiction to spending is manifest in a once-unimaginable level of national debt, the
enormous growth rate of that debt, and the widespread belief that
the national debt cannot be significantly reduced, let alone eliminated. As a percentage of gross national product (GNP),* the federal debt declined rather steadily after World War II, reaching
33.3% in 1981. However, it then rose dramatically, reaching almost
73% of GNP in 1992. In dollar terms, the federal debt was just under $1 trillion in 1981, but by September 1993, it had more than
quadrupled, to over $4.4 trillion.[9] There is widespread fear that a
huge and growing federal debt may bankrupt the nation and a near
consensus that it will adversely affect future generations.

Our addiction to spending is also apparent among the aggregate
of American citizens. Total personal savings was less in 1991 than in
1984, in spite of the fact that the population was much larger in
1991. Savings fell again in the early 1990s from about 5.2% of dis-
posable income in late 1992 to approximately 4% in early 1994.[10] A
far smaller percentage of families (43.5%) had savings accounts in
1989 than did in 1983 (61.7%).[11] And the citizens of many other nations have a far higher savings rate. At the same time, our indebtedness to banks, mortgage companies, credit card firms, and so on is
increasing far more dramatically than similar indebtedness in other
nations.

---

*While the term *GNP* is still used for historical purposes, it should be noted that the term
GDP (gross domestic product) is now preferred. See Gary E. Clayton and Martin Gerhard
Giesbrecht. *A Guide to Everyday Economic Statistics.* New York: McGraw-Hill, 1992.

Dwindling or nonexistent savings accounts are a big problem for individual Americans. Most people have little or no financial reserves to sustain them if they should find themselves unemployed and without steady income. In other words, most people are able to survive only from paycheck to paycheck. Many of those same people owe comparatively large sums of money to banks, mortgage companies, and credit card firms ($777.3 billion altogether in 1991, as compared to $350.3 billion in 1980).[12] With little or nothing in the way of savings, such people are likely to descend rapidly into delinquency and ultimately bankruptcy if they should lose their jobs. In fact, many have plunged so deeply into debt that they are in danger of being forced into bankruptcy even while they are employed.

Who Is to Blame?

The choking level of indebtedness that faces the federal government (as well as state and local governments), the aggregate of Americans, and many individual Americans is a significant problem. Who is to blame for this situation? The main suspects are the individual, the government, business, and banks and other financial institutions.

The Individual

In a society that is inclined to "psychologize" all problems, we are likely to blame individuals for not saving enough, for spending too much, and for not putting sufficient pressure on officials to restrain government expenditures. We also tend to "medicalize" these problems, blaming them on conditions that are thought to exist within the individual.[13] One clinical psychologist noted, "Just about everyone [I treat] who has an eating disorder—bulimia, bulimarexia or just plain overeating, or who has a drug problem—also has the spending disorder."[14] Although there are elements of truth to psychologistic and medicalistic perspectives, there is also a strong element of what sociologists term "blaming the victim." That is, although individuals bear some of the responsibility for not saving, for accumulating mounting debt, and for permitting their elected officials to spend far more than the government takes in, in the main individuals have been victimized by a social and financial system that discourages saving and encourages indebtedness.

Why are we so inclined to psychologize and medicalize problems like indebtedness? For one thing, American culture strongly emphasizes individualism. We tend to trace both success and failure to individual efforts, not larger social conditions. For another, large social and financial systems expend a great deal of time, energy, and money seeking, often successfully, to convince us that they are not responsible for society's problems. Individuals lack the ability and the resources to similarly "pass the buck." Of perhaps greatest importance, however, is the fact that individual, especially medical, problems appear to be amenable to treatment and even seem curable. In contrast, large-scale social problems (pollution, for example) seem far more intractable. It is for these, as well as many other reasons, that American society has a strong tendency to blame individuals for social problems.

The Government

Where does the responsibility for high levels of indebtedness lie if individuals are not the main culprits? We can begin with the federal government, which is seemingly unable and certainly unwilling to restrain its own spending. As a result, it is forced to tax at a high level and thereby to drain funds from individuals that otherwise could be used to increase personal savings and to draw down debt. Since the federal debt binge began in 1981, the government has also been responsible for creating a climate in which financial imprudence seems acceptable. After all, the public is led to feel, if it is acceptable for the government to live beyond its means, why can't individual citizens do the same? If the government can seemingly go on borrowing without facing the consequences of its debt, why can't individuals?

If the federal government truly wanted to address society's problems, it could clearly do far more both to encourage individual savings and to discourage individual debt. For example, the government could lower the taxes on income from savings accounts or even make such income tax-free. Or it could levy higher taxes on organizations and agencies that encourage individual indebtedness.

The government could also do more to control and restrain the debt-creating and debt-increasing activities of the credit card industry.

Business

Although some of the blame for society's debt and savings problem must be placed on the federal government, the bulk of the responsibility belongs with those organizations and agencies associated with our consumer society that do all they can to get people to spend not only all of their income but also to plunge into debt in as many ways, and as deeply, as possible. We can begin with American business.

Those in manufacturing, retailing, advertising, and marketing (among others) devote their working hours and a large portion of their energies to figuring out ways of getting people to buy things that they probably do not need and that many of them cannot afford. There is no need to reiterate here historic criticisms of these key elements of the capitalistic system, but it might be worth noting a few of the more recent developments. One example is the dramatic proliferation of seductive catalogs that are mailed to our homes. Another is the advent and remarkable growth in popularity of the television home shopping networks. What these two developments have in common is their ability to allow us to spend our money quickly and efficiently without ever leaving our homes. Because the credit card is the preferred way to pay for goods purchased through these outlets, catalogs and home shopping networks also help us increase our level of indebtedness.

Banks and Other Financial Institutions

The historical mission of banks was to encourage savings and discourage debt. Today, however, banks and other financial institutions lead us away from savings and in the direction of debt. Saving is discouraged by, most importantly, the low interest rates paid by banks. It seems foolish to people to put their money in the bank at an interest rate of, say, 2.5% and then to pay taxes on the interest, thereby lowering the real rate of return to 2% or even less. This practice seems especially asinine when the inflation rate is, for example, 3% or 4%. Under such conditions, the saver's money is declining in value with each passing year. It seems obvious to most people that they are better off spending the money before it has a chance to lose any more value.

While banks are discouraging savings, they are in various ways encouraging debt. One good example is the high level of competition among the banks (and other financial institutions) to offer home equity lines of credit to consumers. As the name suggests, such lines of credit allow people to borrow against the equity they have built up in their homes. If one owns a $200,000 home but owes the bank only $120,000 on the mortgage, then one has $80,000 of equity in the house. Banks eagerly lend people money against this equity. Leaving the equity in the house is a kind of savings that appreciates with the value of the real estate, but borrowing against it allows people to buy more goods and services. In the process, however, they acquire a large new debt. And the house itself could be lost if one is unable to pay either the original mortgage or the home equity loan.

The credit card is yet another invention of the banks and other financial institutions to get people to save less and spend more. In the past, only the relatively well-to-do were able to get credit, and getting credit was a very cumbersome process (involving letters of credit, for example). Credit cards democratized credit, making it possible for the masses to obtain at least a minimal amount. Credit cards are also far easier to use than predecessors like letters of credit. Credit cards may thus be seen as convenient mechanisms whereby banks and other financial institutions can lend large numbers of people what collectively amounts to an enormous amount of money.

Normally, no collateral is needed to apply for a credit card.[15] The money advanced by the credit card firms can be seen as borrowing against future earnings. However, because there is no collateral in the conventional sense, the credit card companies usually feel free to charge usurious interest rates.

Credit cards certainly allow the people who hold them to spend more than they otherwise would. Many cardholders pay their bills in full each month, but a substantial majority are in perpetual debt to the credit card companies. When a credit limit on one card is reached, another card may be obtained. Some people even make monthly payments on one credit card by taking cash advances from another card. Others, overwhelmed by credit card debt, take out home equity lines of credit to pay it off. Then, with a clean slate, at least in the eyes of the credit card companies, such people are ready to begin charging again on their credit cards. Very soon many of them find themselves deeply in debt both to the bank that holds the home equity loan and to the credit card companies.

A representative of the credit card industry might say that no one forces people to take out home equity lines of credit or to obtain credit cards; people do so of their own volition and therefore are responsible for their financial predicament. Although this is certainly true at one level, at another level it is possible to view people as the victims of a financial (and economic) system that depends on them to go deeply into debt and itself grows wealthy as a result of that indebtedness. The newspapers, magazines, and broadcast media are full of advertisements offering various inducements to apply for a particular credit card or home equity loan rather than the ones offered by competitors. Many people are bombarded with mail offering all sorts of attractive benefits to those who sign up for yet another card or loan. More generally, one is made to feel foolish, even out of step, if one refuses to be an active part of the debtor society. Furthermore, it has become increasingly difficult to function in our society without a credit card. For example, people who do not have a record of credit card debt and payment find it difficult to get other kinds of credit, like home equity loans, car loans, or even mortgage loans.

An Indictment of the Financial System

The major blame for our society's lack of savings and our increasing indebtedness must be placed on the doorstep of large institutions. This book focuses on one of those institutions—the financial system, which is responsible for making credit card debt so easy and attractive that many of us have become deeply and perpetually indebted to the credit card firms. In offering us credit cards and other financial instruments, like home equity loans, the banks and other financial institutions appear to be offering us the keys to freedom. Credit cards seem to be the means to wealth, happiness, and liberation from our otherwise humdrum lives. However, for many, credit cards become instruments of bondage locking people into a lifetime of indebtedness. More generally, credit cards play a major role in helping people become more firmly embedded in the consumer society. Finally, people are locked into a lifetime of work, frequently in unsatisfying occupations, just so they can be active consumers and perhaps so they can make more than the minimum monthly payments on their credit card bills.

This book will not stop with blaming financial institutions for our low level of savings and high level of debt but will indict these systems for playing a major role in creating other important social problems. For example, in Chapter 4 I discuss various types of fraud committed against the credit card business. Again, we usually blame the individual for fraudulent acts, but my view is that the credit card firms, and the consumer culture of which they are part, bear a substantial portion of the responsibility by creating expectations that some can meet only by engaging in fraud. Furthermore, you will see that the credit card industry itself is guilty of a variety of questionable and fraudulent behaviors.

One more example, described in Chapter 5, is the threat to privacy in our credit card society. The usual tendency is to blame a few "bad apples" for prying into our business. However, my view is that the credit card industry and its policies and procedures are the real threat to privacy. Furthermore, the credit card industry is busy developing the technologies that make unprecedented intrusions into our privacy not only more possible but also more likely.

In its focus on the role played by the credit card industry, not individuals, in a number of major social problems, this is a distinctly sociological work. I do not wish to absolve the individual of responsibility for these problems, but I do wish to move away from psychologizing (and medicalizing) these problems and to move toward "sociologizing" them by emphasizing the role of the credit card industry and the consumer society more generally.

Case in Point: Getting Them Hooked While They're Young

Before moving on to a more specific discussion of the sociological perspective on the problems associated with credit cards, one more example of the way the credit card industry has created problems for people would be useful: the increasing effort by credit card firms to lure students into possessing their own credit cards. The over

9 million college students (of which 5.6 million are in school on a full-time basis) represent a huge and lucrative market for credit card companies. According to one estimate, about 82% of full-time college students now have credit cards.[16] The number of undergraduates with credit cards increased by 37% between 1988 and 1990.[17] The credit card companies have been aggressively targeting this population not only because of the immediate increase in business it offers but also because of the long-term income possibilities as the students move on to full-time jobs after graduation. To recruit college students, credit card firms are advertising heavily on campus, using on-campus booths to make their case and even hiring students to lure their peers into the credit card world. In addition, students have been offered a variety of inducements. I have in front of me a flyer aimed at a college-age audience. It proclaims that the cards have no annual fee, offer a comparatively low interest rate, and offer "special student benefits," including a 20% discount at retailers like MusicLand and Gold's Gym and a 5% discount on travel.

The credit card firms claim that the cards help teach students to be responsible with money (one professor calls it a "training-wheels operation"[18]). The critics claim that the cards teach students to spend, often beyond their means, instead of saving:

> I've seen kids with $50,000 to $70,000 in debt. . . . They spend money on clothes, pizza, tuition, books, fun travel, presents for girlfriends, shoes, watches, engagement presents, proms, formals. Kids just go haywire.[19]

Some students are even using credit cards to pay their tuition. Said the president of a nonprofit credit counseling firm: "They haven't been educated about credit. They think it's funny money."[20] According to an expert on credit cards, "We are taking the opportunity away from them to start on a healthy foot, to be able to take care of themselves."[21] Years after they have graduated, college students may end up paying off credit card debts run up in college. Some universities have grown uncomfortable about these problems and more generally with the incursion of credit card companies and have greatly restricted the marketing of credit cards on campus.

Some students find that they cannot pay their bills while they are still in college. Although parents are not legally liable for such bills, it is not unusual for parents to pay them. One parent who helped her daughter with a consolidation loan said, "You could say I got burned . . . but at least she learned in the process, at least I hope she did. . . . College is a time to learn, to make the transition to adulthood."[22] The credit card firms are willing to target college (and high school) students, most of whom have little or no income of their own, because they know that parents will often bail out children who get into trouble with credit card debt.

In running up credit card debt, it can be argued, college students are learning to live a lie. They are living at a level that they cannot afford at the time or perhaps even in the future. They may establish a pattern of consistently living beyond their means. However, they are merely postponing the day when they have to pay their debts.

The credit card companies have clearly been affected by the critics. Inside one brochure aimed at students is a so-called "Owner's Guide to a Chase Credit Card." Three guidelines are offered:

1. If you want to play, you've got to pay.
2. If you cannot pay your entire balance, pay at least the minimum due.
3. If you cannot pay the minimum, do not play.

The guide closes with a "bottom line": "To avoid a bad credit history, you must pay the minimum payment due each month." Thus, the credit card companies are trying to inform students of the potential dangers. However, they are doing so in the context of an extremely active advertising campaign aimed at a dramatic expansion of the use of such cards among college students.

Not satisfied with the invasion of college campuses, credit card companies have been devoting increasing attention to high schools. One survey found that as of 1993, 32% of the country's high school students had their own credit cards and others had access to an adult's card. Strong efforts are underway to greatly increase that percentage. The president of a marketing firm noted, "It used to be that college was the big free-for-all for new customers. . . . But now, the big push is to get them between 16 and 18."[23] Although adult approval is required for a person under 18 years of age to obtain a credit card, card companies have been pushing more aggressively to gain greater acceptance in this age group.

Their efforts have included annual supplements sponsored by the Discover card in magazines published by Scholastic Inc. and aimed at high school students. One supplement was titled "Extra Credit," and on the back page was an advertisement depicting a classroom, a Discover card, and this headline: "Go Ahead, We're Behind You." Similarly, Visa has developed financial education programs for the high schools that do not identify Visa as the sponsor and, at least according to the company, have the broad objective of teaching students about personal finance. To many observers, the problem with these programs is that the schools may be ceding the responsibility for teaching financial management to organizations that have a vested interest, at least to some degree, in encouraging financial mismanagement. A spokesperson for the National Association of Secondary School Principals admitted the need for such school-sponsored programs but contended that "we have to balance all needs against how many minutes there are in the day."[24] If the schools do not have time to prepare programs in financial management, the credit card companies are all too willing to fill the void. However, the credit card firms are not simply trying to help out the schools; their goal is also to increase their business. As one spokesperson for a consumer advocacy group said, "[Students] need to know that credit card companies are not doing them a favor but are in the business to make money off them."[25]

The motivation behind all these programs is the industry view that about two-thirds of all people remain loyal to their first brand of card for 15 or more years. Thus the credit card companies are trying to get high school and college students accustomed to using their card instead of a competitor's. The larger fear is that the credit card companies are getting young people accustomed to buying on credit, thereby creating a whole new generation of debtors.

A Sociology of Credit Cards

Sociology in general, and sociological theory in particular, offers a number of ways of dealing with the credit card industry and the individuals affected by it. Throughout much of the 20th century, sociological theory has been divided between macro theories (such as structural functionalism and conflict theory) that would be most useful in analyzing the credit card industry itself and micro theories (such as symbolic interactionism and phenomenological sociology) that would be most helpful in analyzing individuals within our consumer society. However, sociological theory has generally been plagued by an inability to deal in a fully adequate manner with micro-macro relationships, such as the relationships between the credit card industry and individuals. Sociologists have grown increasingly dissatisfied with having to choose between large-scale, macroscopic theories and small-scale, microscopic theories. Thus, there has been a growing interest in theories that integrate micro and macro concerns. In Europe, expanding interest in what is known there as agency-structure integration parallels the increasing American preoccupation with micro-macro integration.[26]

Mills: Personal Troubles, Public Issues

This new theoretical approach has important implications for the study of sociological issues in general—and in particular for the kinds of social problems discussed in this book.[27] Micro-macro integration leads the sociological study of social problems[28] back to one of its roots in the work of the American social critic and theorist C. Wright Mills (1916–1962).

Mills is important to us here for two reasons. First, in 1953 Mills coauthored, with Hans Gerth, a now almost-forgotten theory of micro-macro integration: *Character and Social Structure*. As the title suggests, the authors were interested in the relationship between micro-level character and macro-level social structure. According to Gerth and Mills, one of their goals was "to link the private and the public, the innermost acts of the individual with the widest kinds of socio-historical phenomena."[29] Thus, their thinking is in line with the most recent developments in sociological theory.[30]

Of more direct importance here is the now-famous distinction made by Mills in his 1959 work, *The Sociological Imagination*, between micro-level personal troubles and macro-level public issues.[31] Personal troubles tend to be problems that affect an individual and those immediately around him or her. For example, a father who commits incest with his daughter is creating personal troubles for the daughter, other members of the family, and perhaps himself. However, that single father's actions are not going to create a public issue; that is, they are not likely to lead to a public outcry that society ought to abandon the family as a social institution. Public issues, in comparison, tend to be problems that affect large numbers of people and perhaps society as a whole. The disintegration of the nuclear family would be such a public issue.

What, then, is the relationship between these two sets of distinctions—personal troubles/public issues and character/social structure—derived from the work of C. Wright Mills? The character of an individual can certainly cause personal troubles. For example, a psychotic individual can cause problems for himself and those immediately around him. When many individuals have the same character disorder (psychosis, for example), they can cause problems for the larger social structure (overtax the mental health system), thereby creating a public issue. The structure of society can also cause personal troubles for the individual. An example might be a person's depression resulting from the disjunction between the culturally instilled desire for economic success and the scarcity of well-paying jobs. And the structure of society can create public issues, as exemplified by the tendency of the capitalist economy to generate periodic recessions and depressions. All these connections and, more generally, a wide array of macro-micro relationships are possible.[32] However, the focus of this book is the credit card industry as an element of social structure and the way it generates both personal troubles and public issues.

A useful parallel can be drawn between the credit card and cigarette industries. The practices of the cigarette industry create a variety of personal troubles, especially illness and early death. Furthermore, those practices have created a number of public issues (the cost to society of death and illness traceable to cigarette smoke), and thus many people have come to see cigarette industry practices themselves as public issues. Examples of industry practices that have become public issues are the aggressive marketing of cigarettes overseas, where restrictions on such marketing are limited or nonexistent, as well as the marketing of cigarettes to young people in this country (for example, through advertisements featuring the controversial "Joe Camel"). Similarly, the practices of the credit card industry help to create personal problems (such as indebtedness) and public issues (such as the relatively low national savings rate). Furthermore, some industry practices—such as the aggressive marketing of credit cards to teenagers—have themselves become public issues.

One of the premises of this book is that we need to begin adopting the same kind of critical outlook toward the credit card industry that we use in scrutinizing the cigarette industry. Interestingly,

Galanoy has suggested a warning label for credit cards, like the ones found on cigarette packs:*

> Caution. Financial experts have determined that continued bank card use can lead to debt, loss of property, bankruptcy, plus unhealthful effects on long-lived standards and virtues.[33]

Mills's ideas give us remarkably contemporary theoretical tools for undertaking a critical analysis of the credit card industry and the problems it generates. His conception of the relationship between personal troubles and public issues is the major (although not the only) theory undergirding this book.

Marx: Capitalist Exploitation

In addition to adopting Mills's general approach, I will draw on several other important theoretical sources to deal with more specific aspects of the relationship between people and the credit card industry. One is the work of the German social theorist Karl Marx (1818–1881), especially his ideas on the exploitation that he saw as endemic to capitalist society. To Marx, this exploitation takes place in the labor market and the workplace, where capitalistic firms exploit their workers by paying them far less in wages than the value of what they produce. In Mills's terms, Marx believed that capitalistic firms create personal troubles for workers by exploiting them so greatly, and the impoverished state of the workers eventually becomes such an important public issue that the workers are likely to rise up and overthrow the capitalist system and replace it with a communist system.

Mills was in fact one of the first major American sociologists to be drawn in the direction of Marxian theory. However, time has not been kind to Marxian theory, and many of Marx's predictions have not come to pass. There have been many changes in the capitalist system, and a variety of issues have come to the fore that did not exist in Marx's day. As a result, a variety of neo-Marxian theories have arisen to deal with these new capitalist realities. One that concerns us here is the increasing importance to capitalists of the market for

*Similarly, in *The McDonaldization of Society*, a book that critiques the fast-food industry, I suggest that the following warning label be affixed to fast-food restaurants: "Sociologists warn us that habitual use of McDonaldized systems is destructive to our physical and psychological well-being as well as to society as a whole."

goods and services.[34] According to neo-Marxians, exploitation of the worker continues in the labor market, but capitalists also devote increasing attention to getting consumers to buy more goods and services. Higher profits can come from both cutting costs and selling more products.

The credit card industry plays a role by encouraging consumers to spend more money, in many cases far beyond their available cash, on the capitalists' goods and services. In a sense, the credit card companies have helped the capitalists to exploit consumers. Indeed, one could argue that modern capitalism has come to depend on a high level of consumer indebtedness. Capitalism could have progressed only so far by extracting cash from the consumers. It had to find a way to go further.

Capitalists' reliance on widespread consumer credit parallels early capitalists' exploitation of the labor market. In an effort to increase profits, they sought to progressively lengthen the workday in order to exploit more of the laborer's time and effort. When they had pushed the workday to unconscionable lengths, the government was forced to intervene by restricting work hours. The capitalists then sought new ways to exploit workers, and they eventually did so with technological advances that allowed workers to produce more in less time. When the capitalists reached a point of diminishing returns in their efforts to squeeze more out of workers for less, they turned their attention to consumers. With the aid of the credit card industry, as well as the advertising and marketing industries, they eventually discovered new ways of acquiring more of the consumer's economic resources, even resources the consumers did not yet have.

Simmel: The Money Economy

A second German social theorist, Georg Simmel (1858–1918), can also help us understand the personal troubles created by credit cards. Writing more than 40 years before the invention of the credit card, Simmel focused (as mentioned earlier in this chapter) on money, but much of what he had to say about the money economy and the personal troubles it creates are of help to us in understanding the modern world of credit cards.[35] Simmel pointed to many problems associated with a money economy, but three are of special concern in this book:

- The first problem, similar to one discussed in Marxian theory, is the "temptation to imprudence" associated with a money economy. Simmel argued that money, in comparison to its predecessors, such as barter, tends to tempt people into spending more and going into debt. My view is that credit cards are even more likely than money to make people imprudent. People using credit cards are not only likely to spend more but are also more likely to go deeply into debt. Thus, Simmel's work, like Marx's, leads us to a concern with the way in which the credit card industry creates personal troubles of overspending and indebtedness.

- Second, Simmel believed that money makes possible many types of "mean machinations" that were not possible, or were more difficult, in earlier economies. For example, bribes for political influence or payments for assassinations are more easily made with money than with barter. Clearly, bribery and assassination are public issues, but they also cause personal troubles for large numbers of people. Although bribes or assassinations are generally less likely to be paid for with a credit card than with cash, other types of mean machinations become more likely with credit cards. For example, some organizations associated with the credit card industry engage in fraudulent or deceptive practices in order to maximize their income from credit card users. Again, such practices are clearly public issues (or at least they should be) that cause personal troubles for the many victims.

- The third problem with a money economy that concerned Simmel was the issue of secrecy, especially the fact that a money economy makes payments of bribes and other types of secret transactions more possible. However, our main concern in this book is the increasing lack of secrecy and the invasion of privacy associated with the growth of the credit card industry.* That industry, as well as other entities within society, have been able to

*I am using Simmel's ideas as "sensitizing concepts"; in this case, Simmel's ideas on secrecy sensitize us to the issue of privacy. Three principles lie behind the idea of sensitizing concepts. First, they are ideas that suggest to the analyst what to look for in the social world. Second, they suggest where to look for those things. Finally, the emphasis is on the social world and not on the concepts. Thus, sensitizing concepts allow the social world to speak for itself as much as possible. The concepts guide the social thinker but must not be allowed to distort the social world. Sensitizing concepts allow us to see that world more clearly. See Herbert Blumer. "What Is Wrong With Social Theory," in Herbert Blumer, *Symbolic Interaction: Perspective and Method*. Englewood Cliffs, NJ: Prentice-Hall, 1969, pp. 140–152.

collect vast amounts of very personal information on millions of citizens. The existence of that information, and the ability of various agents to access some or all of it, is a major public issue. The way that information has been used has also created personal troubles for many individuals.

Weber: Rationalization

The next issue of concern has to do with the "rationalization" of society and its relationship to credit cards. Although Simmel wrote on rationalization, the premier theorist on the rationalization process was the German sociologist and economist Max Weber (1864–1920).* Weber defined rationalization as the process by which the modern world has come to be increasingly dominated by structures devoted to efficiency, predictability, calculability, and technological control.[36] Those rational structures (for example, the capitalist marketplace and the bureaucracy) have had a progressively negative effect on individuals.[37] Weber described a process by which more and more of us would come to be locked in an "iron cage of rationalization." This public issue can be seen as creating a variety of personal troubles, especially the dehumanization of daily life. For example, Weber saw the bureaucrat as becoming little more than a faceless cog in a bureaucratic machine. The credit card industry has also been an integral part of the rationalization process. By rationalizing the process by which consumer loans are made, the credit card industry has contributed to our society's dehumanization.

Interestingly, one school of neo-Marxian theory, critical theory, has brought together ideas from both Marx and Weber that are relevant to this analysis of the credit card industry.[38] While building on Marx's concern with the economy, the critical school focuses on culture.[39] Mass culture is seen as pacifying and stupefying. It could be argued that the consumer culture that credit cards help foster has such effects on people by helping to keep them immersed in the endless and mindless pursuit of goods and services. The critical

---

*One theoretical analyst argues that "Weber's account of rationalisation in modern societies . . . is an elaboration and extension of Simmel's account of money." See Bryan S. Turner, "Simmel, Rationalisation and the Sociology of Money." *Sociological Review* 34 (1986):105. Weber's work is also linked with C. Wright Mills's coauthor, Hans Gerth, who was a Weberian, and one of the goals of Gerth and Mills, *Character and Social Structure* (New York; Harcourt, Brace, and World, 1953), was to link Weber's ideas on the rationalization of macro structures to more microscopic phenomena.

school also disparages the rationalization process—especially the tendency to engage in technocratic thinking, in which the focus is merely the discovery of the optimum means to ends that are defined by those in control of the larger society. The credit card can be seen as a product of such thinking. Because it works so well as a means, people are discouraged from reflecting on the value of the ends (the goods and services of a consumer society), critically analyzing those ends, and finding alternatives to them.

Globalization and Americanization

A sociology of credit cards requires a look at the relationship among the credit card industry, personal troubles, and public issues on a global scale. It is not just the United States, but also much of the rest of the world, that is being affected by the credit card industry and the social problems it helps create. To some degree, this development is a result of globalization, a process that is at least partially autonomous of any single nation and that involves the reciprocal impact of many economies.[40] In the main, however, American credit card companies dominate the global market. Thus, in this book I will deal with the spread of the credit card industry around the world under the heading of Americanization rather than globalization. For this issue, instead of drawing on the ideas of long-dead thinkers like Mills, Marx, Simmel, and Weber, I will rely on more contemporary work.[41]

The central point is that, in many countries around the world, Americanization is a public issue that is causing personal troubles for their citizens. This book addresses the role played by the credit card industry in this process of Americanization and in the homogenization of life around the world, with the attendant loss of cultural and individual differences.

Micro-Macro Relationships

The various theoretical resources underpinning this book are all brought to bear on a central issue in the sociological study of a particular social problem: personal troubles, public issues, and the burgeoning credit card industry. Along the way, I will have a number of things to say about responses to these problems—which brings us back to the theory of micro-macro relationships. Although the book's focus is the way the macro-level credit card industry creates a variety of public issues and personal troubles, it is important to realize that people, at the micro level, create and re-create that industry by their actions. Not only did people create the industry historically, but they help to re-create it daily by acting in accord with its demands and expectations. However, people also have the capacity to refuse to conform to the demands of the credit card industry. If they were to do so on a reasonably large scale, the industry would be forced to alter the way it operates. People can also be more proactive in their efforts to change the credit card industry.

However, there are limits to what individuals, even when acting in concert, can do about macro-level problems. In many cases, macro-level problems require macro-level solutions. Thus, I will also deal with actions that the credit card industry, as well as the government, can take to deal with the public issues and personal troubles discussed throughout this book. The theoretical approach underlying this analysis allows us to understand both the adverse effects of the credit card industry and the steps that people and larger social structures can take to ameliorate or eliminate them.

Other Reasons for Devoting a Book to Credit Cards

Although problems associated with the credit card society are the major focus of this book, there are several other reasons credit cards are worthy of such extensive treatment. First, credit cards represent something new in the history of money. In fact, as I will discuss below, they might not even be subsumable under the heading of money. Second, since they burst on the American scene in mid-century, credit cards have experienced enormous growth, both in this country and around the world. Anything that has grown so rapidly and has become so ubiquitous demands attention. Third, credit cards are not only of monumental material significance but are also of great cultural, or symbolic, importance. As a well-known motivational researcher put it, "a credit card is a symbol of this age."[42]

Something New in the History of Money

Money in all its forms, especially (given the interests of this book) in its cash form, is part of a historical process.[43] It may seem hard to believe from today's vantage point, but at one time there was no money. Furthermore, some predict that there will come a time in which money, at least in the form of currency, will become less important if not disappear altogether, with the emergence of a "cashless society."[44]

Looking back, we can see a historical progression from the barter of material goods, to the use of valuable symbols like jewelry, to money made of precious metals (for example, gold coins), to money made of semiprecious metals, to paper money backed by precious metals (for example, the gold standard), to money backed solely and symbolically by the state's promise to honor it and to recognize it as having a specified value. Then there was the development of checks, which replaced currency to some extent. Checks imply that they are backed by the bank—given sufficient funds in the check writer's account. If currency is a symbol, then a check is a symbol of a symbol.

More important for our purposes, money in the form of currency is being increasingly supplanted by the credit card. Instead of plunking down cash or even writing a check, more of us are saying "Charge it!" This apparently modest act is, in fact, a truly revolutionary development in the history of money. Furthermore, it is having a revolutionary impact on the nature of consumption, the economy, and the social world more generally. In fact, rather than simply being yet another step in the development of money, I am inclined to agree with the contention that credit cards are "an entirely new idea in value exchange."[45] A variety of arguments can be marshaled in support of the idea that in credit cards we are seeing something entirely new in the history of economic exchange, especially relative to cash:

- Credit card companies are performing a function formerly limited to the federal government. That is, they create money (or what Joel Kurtzman calls "near money"); the Federal Reserve is no longer alone in this ability. The issuing of a new credit card with a $1,000 limit can be seen as creating $1,000.[46] Thus, the credit industry is creating many billions of dollars each year and, among other things, creating inflationary pressures in the process.

- Credit cards do not have a cash or currency form. In fact, they are not even backed by money until a charge is actually made.

- With cash we are restricted to the amount on hand or in the bank, but with credit cards our ceiling is less clear. We are restricted only by the ever-changing limits of each of our credit cards as well as by the aggregate of the limits of all those cards.

- Although we can use our cash anytime we wish, the use of our credit card requires the authorization of another party.

- Unlike cash, which allows for total anonymity, one's name is printed on the front of the credit card and written on the back; a credit card may even have one's picture on it. Furthermore, credit card companies have a great deal of computerized information on us that is drawn on to approve transactions.

- Although cash is simple to produce and to use over and over, credit cards require the backing of a complex, huge, and growing web of technologies.[47]

- There is no direct cost to the consumer for using cash, but fees and interest may well accrue with credit card use.

- Although everyone, at least theoretically, has access to cash, some groups (the poor, the homeless, the unemployed) may be denied access to credit cards. Such restrictions sometimes occur unethically or illegally through the "redlining" of certain types of consumers or geographic areas.

- Because of their accordionlike limits, credit cards are more likely than cash to lead to consumerism, overspending, and indebtedness.

In short, credit cards demand book-length treatment because in a variety of ways they represent something unique in the history of value exchange.

A Growing Industry

Another reason for focusing on credit cards is their astounding growth in recent years, which reflects their increasing importance in the social and economic worlds.* There are now more than a billion credit cards of all types in the United States.[48] Receivables for the industry as a whole in 1993 were up by almost 16% from the

---

*The major exception is Diners Club, which has experienced virtually no growth over the past several decades. See Charles Siler. "Easy To Leave Home Without It?" *Forbes*, September 4, 1989, p. 140. "Credit Card Issuer's Guide: 1995 Edition." *Credit Card News*, August 15, 1994, p. 3.

preceding year and by over 400% in a decade.[49] The staggering proliferation of credit cards is also reflected in other indicators of use in the United States:

- Sixty-one percent of Americans now have at least one credit card.
- The average cardholder carries nine different cards.
- In 1992, consumers used the cards to make 5 billion transactions, with a total value of $420 billion.[50]

There has been, among other things, growth in the number of people who have credit cards, the average number of credit cards held by each person, the amount of consumer debt attributable to credit card purchases, the number of facilities accepting credit cards, and the number of organizations issuing cards. For example, the number of major credit cards in use in the United States—Visa, MasterCard, Discover, and American Express*—increased by about 174 million (from 157 million to 331 million) between 1984 and 1993.[51] The average outstanding balance owed to Visa and Master-Card increased from less than $400 in the early 1980s to $970 in 1989 and to $1,096 in 1993.[52] The amount of high-interest credit card debt owed by American consumers rose from $2.7 billion in 1969 to $50 billion in 1980 and was approaching $300 billion in 1994.[53] Because the recession of the early 1990s prompted many people to limit the increases in their credit card debt, the total of such debt will probably not grow nearly as fast in the 1990s as it did in the 1980s, although it will still expand by a substantial amount.

The growth of credit cards has not been restricted to the United States but has spread throughout the world. Although the American market for credit cards might be approaching saturation, that is certainly not true of much of the rest of the world. According to one industry analyst, "outside of the U.S., the potential for growth is still quite phenomenal."[54] Thus, the international arena is likely to be a target for credit card companies in the coming years.

The growth in the use of credit cards has not been a function solely of consumer demand. Banks have been eager to issue more cards because their profits from those cards are far higher than the profits from other consumer loans.[55] Furthermore, the risk is spread

---

*The traditional American Express card is actually a charge card, not a credit card, because no credit is extended and the bills must be paid in full each month.

among many small accounts, which makes credit cards less hazardous than a few large business loans would be. Also fueling growth recently has been the entrance of many "nonbanks" (AT&T, General Motors, Shell) into the credit card industry. They want to get a share of the high profits of the credit card business and, perhaps more importantly, to help sell their own products. With so much competition, all organizations involved in the credit card business have been bombarding consumers with offers for cards with no annual fees, low interest rates, and rebates. So many organizations have become involved so actively in the credit card field that an American Express official described it as resembling a "shark feeding frenzy."[56]

A Symbol of American Values

A strong case can be made that the credit card is one of the leading symbols of 20th-century America or, as mentioned earlier, that the credit card is an American icon. Indeed, one observer calls the credit card "the twentieth century's symbol par excellence."[57] Among other things, the credit card is emblematic of affluence, mobility, and the capacity to overcome obstacles in the pursuit of one's goals. Thus, those hundreds of millions of people who carry credit cards are also carrying with them these important symbols. And when they use a credit card, they are turning the symbols into material reality.

Although credit cards are American in origin, only American Express retains the name of its country of origin. The other major credit card companies have deliberately adopted names that give the sense the cards are not confined to any nation. Although MasterCard, which was once known as Master Charge, has always sought to convey the image of "a card without a country," Visa was at one time called BankAmericard. American Express has created the Optima card with a name that disassociates it from the United States. Nevertheless, credit cards are clearly associated in the minds of most people around the world with America and its consumer culture.

Furthermore, even though they may be moving away from the use of the word *America*, the names of all of the major cards continue to reflect basic American values. The *Express* in American Express conjures up the image not only of someone or something on the move but also of great power and rapidity of movement. The name of the card conveys the sense that this thing is not going to stop anywhere or be stopped by anything; it has an inexorable quality. The holders of American Express cards are in possession of a bit of America. Therefore, such people are on the move, and everyone had better watch out.

MasterCard communicates the value Americans place on mastery, especially over others and over their environment. The possession of this credit card is supposed to allow holders to master their social and physical worlds. The name could also be interpreted in more imperialistic terms, as representing the power to handle any and all situations. There are many credit cards, but MasterCard wants us to believe that it is the master card, not only master of the world but dominant over all its competitors.

Visa gives its holders the sense that they are in possession of a pass that allows them to cross any border or of the master key that opens any lock. Again, the name of the card conveys a sense of power—the ability to go anywhere or to do anything one desires.

The names chosen for the cards are supported by the images on them. The American Express card has a picture of a helmeted warrior, whose powerful jaw and gaze fixed on the horizon support the idea of something that is moving forward and is unstoppable. The hologram on the Visa card is of a bird in flight, capable of going anywhere it pleases. And MasterCard offers a hologram of the globe, indicating that the entire world is its domain. Thus, the credit card in general has great symbolic importance, as does each specific brand of credit card.

Debunking Credit Card Myths

To most of us, credit cards appear to have near-magical powers, giving us greater access to a cornucopia of goods and services. They also seem to give us something for nothing. That is, without laying out any cash, we can leave the mall with an armload of purchases. Most of us like what we can acquire with credit cards, but some like credit cards so much that they accumulate as many as they can. Lots of credit cards, with higher and higher spending limits, are important symbols of success. That most people adopt a highly positive view of credit cards is borne out by the proliferation of the cards throughout the United States and the world.

To the dominant perspective on credit cards as marvels of the twentieth century must be added a more malignant viewpoint. Serious social problems are clearly associated with the widespread and frequent use of credit cards and this book is devoted to a discussion of those problems. The need for such a book is premised on the fact that, while the credit card companies spend billions of dollars bombarding us with propaganda on the advantages of credit cards, comparatively little time and energy is devoted to telling the other side of the story.

With its focus on the negative aspects of the credit card business, this book is strongly embedded in the idea that one of the essential tasks of sociology is the debunking of social myths. That is, good sociology is aimed at poking holes in, or (as Peter Berger puts it) "unmasking," such myths and revealing the truth that lies hidden beneath the surface. In the case of the credit card, one myth is that it is a benign and innocent means to whatever ends people choose. A far more dangerous myth is that the credit card is a wondrous "magic wand" that will allow people to fulfill their fondest wishes. The debunking analysis undertaken in this book will reveal that credit cards are often neither innocent nor magical. There is no wizardry in them, because whatever one may seemingly acquire almost by magic must ultimately be paid for. Furthermore, credit cards are far from innocent, because a wide variety of malignant effects are associated with them.

A debunking sociology is aimed at revealing the spuriousness of various ideologies. As Berger puts it, "In such analyses the ideas by which men explain their actions are unmasked as self-deception, sales talk, the kind of sincerity . . . of a man who habitually believes his own propaganda."[58] From this perspective, the credit card companies can be seen as purveyors of self-deceptive ideologies. They are, after all, in the business of selling their wares to the public, and they will say whatever is necessary to accomplish their goal. This book offers an alternative view to that of the credit card industry on the role of credit cards in society.

Given the significance of credit cards and the wide range of social problems associated with them, it seems remarkable that anyone could ever have contended that "credit cards remain in limbo, seemingly beyond the pale of fit subject matter for serious works of scholarship."[59] However, in recent years, credit cards have been attracting increasing attention from scholars. They have been analyzed most frequently, as one would expect, from economic and business points of view.[60] As a rule, such works offer many useful insights but fail to point up the negative effects of credit cards on individuals and society. Scholars representing other perspectives, especially sociology, have had comparatively little to say about credit cards.[61]

One of the main objectives in this book is to demonstrate that the social aspects and implications of credit cards are indeed worthy of much more serious sociological study and to demonstrate what sociology has to offer to our understanding of credit cards. Clearly, sociologists can no longer afford to ignore one of the most important creations of the United States and of the 20th century, especially a creation that is producing so many social problems. I will analyze those problems, but before I do, we need much more background on credit cards and related phenomena, background that is the subject of Chapter 2.

2

Socio-History of the Credit Card

We Probably Won't Recognize the Credit Card Field
by the End of the Century.[1]

The modern credit card emerged in the United States in the decade following World War II. It was this decade, give or take a few years, that was the launching pad for many other key elements of modern American "popular" culture as well.* Although all these developments had precursors, it was during this time that dramatic new forms exploded on the social scene: the first McDonald's franchise, which opened its doors in 1955; the opening of the first fully enclosed shopping mall (1956); the first mass-produced suburban housing in Levittown, New York (1947–1951); the founding of the Best Western (1946) and Holiday Inn (1952) motel chains; the beginning of mass production of television sets and the beginning of national television broadcasting (1946); and the opening of Disneyland (1955). Central to all these developments were massive expansion in the use of the automobile, the availability of cheap and abundant gasoline, the beginning of the dramatic growth of the American road and highway system, and the attendant growth of the service station chains.[2] The jet airplane arrived in 1952, and the first computer was constructed in 1946.

The historical link between credit cards and these other developments is primarily the affluence and the boom in mobility that occurred after World War II. People set free from the restraints and shortages imposed by the war started buying, and as a result, the economy began to boom in the postwar period. People bought,

---

*It is not fashionable in sociology (and postmodernism) to distinguish between "high" and "low" (or popular) culture (see Pierre Bourdieu. *Distinction: A Social Critique of the Judgment of Taste*. Cambridge, MA: Harvard University Press, 1984). Although I accept much of the contemporary view, the examples that follow would clearly be associated with what is generally considered popular culture.

among many other things, cars, and with gasoline plentiful and inexpensive, the road system began to expand to accommodate the increasing traffic. A few years later, with the coming of jet planes, airline travel boomed as well. The arrival of television helped open peoples' eyes to the world around them. With wider availability of cars and better roads to travel on, large numbers of people began moving to the suburbs. As more people moved to suburbia, they tired of traveling to the city to shop, which led to the development of shopping malls. Driving between home, work, schools, and shopping malls, they needed quick and accessible food and other goods and services—hence the rise of the fast-food restaurant and, later, myriad other chain stores. Vacations by car and plane became more common, leading to the growth of motel chains, amusement parks, and even places like Las Vegas.

Almost in anticipation of the coming need for it, the modern credit card came into existence in the late 1940s and early 1950s. It was to become an important means for people to achieve the ends of this affluent and mobile society. In a sense, the credit card was a kind of "grease" facilitating the development and expansion of many other things. As people became more mobile, they grew concerned about the dangers associated with carrying large sums of cash. Increasingly likely to be living in the suburbs and removed from their "urban villages," they were less likely to be known by bank tellers and shopkeepers, which made check cashing more difficult. Checks were even less likely to be accepted on vacation trips. Traveler's checks helped, but they required considerable planning and, more important, they required that the money be paid before one went on the trip. The credit card resolved all these problems: There was no need to carry large sums of cash, it was accepted by those who did not know the consumer, it did not require any advance planning (except to apply for the card), and it offered free credit if one paid the bill in full within the grace period. And even if payment was late, seemingly small amounts of interest were added to the bill.

The fact that the credit card is purely a means distinguishes it from the concurrent developments, which are best seen as ends. That is, people take as their objective eating at McDonald's, stopping at Holiday Inn, visiting Disneyland, gambling in Las Vegas, and shopping at the mall. It is its role as a means to virtually every aspect of contemporary society that makes the credit card both distinctive and crucially important.

The credit card eventually became a preferred mode of payment in suburban malls, service stations, motels, and amusement parks. As an example of the fit between the credit card and these other aspects of modern society, take the shopping mall—in particular, the Mall of America in Bloomington, Minnesota. This is the largest shopping mall in the United States. It has 400 shops and, among other amenities, a roller coaster. It has become so popular that Northwest Airlines began running special low-fare flights during the Christmas 1993 season to allow mall customers a one-day shopping binge. One such shopper took the bus from the airport to the mall "with her MasterCard at the ready." The true professionals among the group came with only the bare minimum to allow them to shop: "credit cards, driver's license and money."[3]

The credit card has only lately come to the fast-food restaurants, supermarkets, and movie theaters—but not because of any lack of fit between credit cards and these other modern developments. Rather, the average purchase in those settings has seemed too small for merchants, the issuers of credit cards, and credit card customers to bother with. However, as the credit card has grown more ubiquitous, people have increasingly wanted to use it to buy their Big Macs, loaves of bread, and tickets to the latest Arnold Schwarzenegger flick. The incursion of plastic into the fast-food industry has also been helped by the highly competitive nature of that business. Said one credit card industry executive, "The fast-food wars are so fierce and credit cards give them a competitive edge. If one has it, the other has to have it."[4]

A Brief History

Prior to World War I, credit cards were quite a rarity.[5] Furthermore, those that did exist were very different from what they have become today. The use of credit cards was restricted to a relatively few American hotels, department stores, and oil companies. American retailers did not begin using something akin to today's credit card until 1914, and by 1928 some department stores began issuing metal "charga-plates," which had some physical and functional resemblance to today's cards. In 1936, about a thousand Seattle retailers banded together to honor charges by their common customers, who then received a single monthly bill for their purchases in all those stores. Meanwhile, oil companies had begun offering what

were called "courtesy cards" in 1914. These were the forerunners of
modern credit cards, except that there was no revolving credit, and
the cards were made of cardboard and were reissued every three to
six months; however, the large-scale distribution of such cards did
not begin until just before the start of World War II. Metal credit
cards did not come to the oil industry until 1952. The first plastic
oil company cards arrived in the mid 1950s. American airlines began offering an early form of the credit card in 1931. Thus, precursors of the modern credit card had emerged in several sectors of the
American economy by mid-century.

Two keys to the modern credit card industry were pioneered by
retailers:

- The idea of revolving credit began to take root in the 1930s.
  Through this system, the customer could charge purchases (usually up to a predefined limit) and repay only part of the balance
  while paying interest on the remainder. Today, about two-thirds
  of credit card users are "revolvers" carrying balances from
  month to month and paying interest on the unpaid amount; one-
  third are "convenience users" who pay off their accounts in full
  each month.[6] Included in these two categories are "combination
  users," who some months revolve their accounts and other
  months pay them in full.

- The second innovation, the creation of an interest-free (grace or
  float) period, did not occur until the mid 1950s. Under such a
  system the charge customer pays no interest if the balance due is
  paid in full within a specified period of time, usually 25 days (although 50 days or more may actually elapse between purchase
  and payment).[7]

Revolving credit and an interest-free period remain cornerstones of
modern credit cards, although, as you will see, not all types of cards
offer revolving credit.

The Rise of the Universal Credit Card

The department store, oil, and airline cards—which are retail or
proprietary cards—are not the focus of this book. Rather, the focus
is the so-called universal cards, especially Visa, MasterCard, and
American Express. (The retail cards that will not concern us here
involve many cardholders and huge sums of money, but they pale in

economic and social significance compared with universal cards.) The universal card was the truly revolutionary development in the realm of consumer credit in the mid 20th century. It is now by far the dominant type of credit card. In 1980, only 41% of the total charged by Americans was charged on universal cards. However, by 1990, 78% of the total was charged on such cards.[8]

The universal credit card has several distinctive characteristics:

- It is not tied to a single vendor but can be used to make purchases from many different vendors—unlike, for example, a department store card that permits one to charge purchases at only, say, Nordstrom.

- It can be used to purchase a multitude of products rather than a single line of products—in contrast to, for example, Mobil's gasoline credit cards, which permit purchases of only gasoline and related products.

- It is not restricted geographically and can be used in many places throughout the United States and, increasingly, the rest of the world—unlike the 1930s retail credit card that could be used only in Seattle and unlike contemporary cards that can be used only in local or regional shops.

- The issuer of the card does so in order to make a profit from the credit card business itself*—unlike the issuers of earlier cards, who sought mainly to increase the sale of commodities like gasoline, airline tickets, or clothing.

Issuers of universal credit cards earn money in three major ways: through annual fees paid by those to whom the cards are issued, through interest paid by cardholders on unpaid balances, and through discounts paid by merchants on every credit card transaction.[9] It is not widely known, but in addition to the fees and interest paid by the consumer, the merchant also pays a percentage of each sale to the credit card companies that sponsor (for example, Visa) and that issue (for example, Citibank) the card.

Some credit cards charge higher annual fees than others, but in recent years we have witnessed the re-emergence of cards that carry no annual fee. (Prior to 1980 credit cards carried no annual

*See the discussion later in this chapter of the recent development of the rise of "co-branded" cards such as the GM card. While desirous of earning money from the credit card business, the issuers of these cards are something of a throwback to the early interest in using cards to hike the sales of products.

fee.) Interest rates also vary, and recently some cards have gained new business by lowering their interest rates. Finally, the discounts paid by merchants also vary (for example, 1% to 3% to Visa and MasterCard and 2.5% to 4.5% to American Express), although some merchants have been pressing for and getting lower discount rates, especially from American Express, whose charges are much higher than its competitors'.

A few precursors of the universal card were distributed in limited geographic areas in the late 1940s, but the first universal card to be marketed successfully on a large scale was Diners Club, which was formed in 1949 and began issuing cards in February 1950. Diners Club was the first of the "travel and entertainment" cards, which were to be used primarily for business-related travel and entertainment. In fact, travel and entertainment cards tend very strongly to be corporate cards.[10] In 1958 Diners Club was joined by Carte Blanche and American Express. American Express expanded into the card business from its base in traveler's checks, which had been invented in 1890.

Because they offer no credit and require that bills be paid in full each month, American Express and Diners Club can be said to issue "charge cards" rather than credit cards, which allow customers to maintain a running balance in their accounts. Charge cards are also distinguished from credit cards by the fact that they tend to charge higher annual fees and require a larger discount from merchants. Charge card profits come from these higher fees and discounts rather than from interest on customer balances. Furthermore, because balances must be paid in full each month, charge cards tend to attract a different clientele—especially the well-to-do and businesspeople whose expenses are reimbursed by the company. Businesses may even supply charge cards to their executives, who would therefore not be required to pay the annual fee.

In spite of these and other differences, for ease of analysis I will usually combine charge cards and credit cards in this discussion. However, in some cases the two types of cards should be kept distinct. For example, because they do not extend credit beyond the grace period, charge cards do not cause the problem of almost perpetual indebtedness associated with credit cards.

The other major type of credit card that came into existence during this period was the "bank card." Travel and entertainment cards were created by private companies (American Express, for example), but bank cards were produced by banks. Originally, bank cards were primarily intended to cover personal consumption, whereas travel and entertainment cards focused on business expenditures.

Bank cards were created in the late 1940s and early 1950s. Although accounts of the history vary, the first bank card is usually traced to 1951 and the Franklin National Bank of Long Island.[11] Franklin's first cards displayed both the cardholder's name and the amount of credit available. Local merchants signed agreements with the bank. When a card was presented, the merchant copied the information on the card onto a sales slip. For all purchases above a bank-determined limit, the merchant had to telephone the bank for approval. In return, the merchant's account at the bank was credited with the amount of the sale, less a discount. Cardholders were charged no annual fee or interest and had to repay their debt within a specified period.[12] Within two years, nearly 100 banks had followed Franklin into the bank card business. By 1959, 150 banks were in the business, and they had added revolving credit with finance charges on the unpaid balance.

The key developments in the expansion of the bank card were the founding of BankAmericard in 1958 and Master Charge in 1966. BankAmericard was created in California by the Bank of America. By 1966 that bank had signed licensing agreements with banks outside California permitting them to issue the cards.[13] Master Charge had similar roots in several large Chicago banks. These cards eventually adopted more generic names to reflect broadening services and an increasingly international market. The BankAmericard name was changed to Visa in 1977, and in 1979 Master Charge was renamed MasterCard.[14] Today Visa and MasterCard are consortiums, cooperative organizations made up largely of member banks and other financial institutions. The member banks actually issue the cards and advance credit to the cardholders.

Visa and MasterCard now dominate the bank card business, and American Express is the leading travel and entertainment card. In other words, Visa and MasterCard dominate the credit card business, and American Express is the leading purveyor of charge cards. However, although the distinction between a travel and entertainment card and a bank card made sense in the past, that is no longer the case. For one thing, large numbers of businesspeople use Visa and MasterCard, and they, like consumers in general, are likely to use them to pay for travel and entertainment expenses. It is easier to refer to all of them as universal credit cards.

The Entry of "Nonbanks"

What also makes the traditional labels less meaningful is the entry, beginning in the early 1980s, of "nonbanks" into the credit card business.[15] In 1986 Sears introduced its Discover card. It is a bank card because it is produced through Greenwood Trust; it is also a universal card designed to rival Visa and MasterCard. To compete with established cards, Discover charged no annual fee and offered a 1% rebate to consumers that could either be saved or used to buy Sears products. By the early 1990s, Sears had become the second largest single issuer of cards, with outstanding balances of almost $15 billion, about 8% of the total. It trailed only one bank—Citicorp, which had $34 billion in outstanding balances, 18% of the total owed to credit card companies.[16] However, the number of Visas and MasterCards attributable to all banks is far larger than the number of Sears Discover cards, and Visa and MasterCard are accepted by far more merchants. In 1993 Sears divested itself of its financial arm, Dean Witter, and so Dean Witter now controls the Discover card.[17]

In a move that has come to have a far more dramatic effect on the credit card business, AT&T entered the fray in March 1990. But instead of creating a new bank card, as Sears had done, AT&T offered Visa and MasterCard, with (at least at first) no annual fee for life. AT&T and other nonbanks could issue Visas and MasterCards only because, under nonbank pressure, first MasterCard and later Visa dropped their efforts to prevent nonbanks from issuing the cards. Given this development, it is very difficult to continue labeling Visa and MasterCard bank cards. It will also prove difficult for smaller banks to compete with these corporate giants, and some banks may eventually be forced out of the credit card business.[18] Although it is not likely, nonbanks could even come to dominate the "bank" card business.

Nonbank credit cards have grown rapidly. In 1987 there were only 7.5 million such cards in existence, but in five years that number had almost quadrupled. The number of outstanding cards issued by AT&T alone grew from 4.8 million in 1990 to 7.6 million in 1991, an increase of 63%. In the same period, cards issued by banks (and savings institutions and credit unions) increased by "only" 15%.[19]

Co-Branded Cards

AT&T was followed into the credit card business by many other companies, most notably General Electric, Ford, and General Motors. Their nonbank cards have come to be called co-branded cards because they carry two "brand names"—the name of the credit card company (Visa or MasterCard) and the name of the sponsoring company (General Motors, for example). The idea behind co-branded cards, from the point of view of the company sponsoring them, is both to earn profits from the credit cards and to increase the business done by the sponsoring company.[20] For this reason the cards are sometimes called "product benefit cards." Good examples are the first co-branded cards issued by airlines, such as the AAdvantage cards offered by Citibank and American Airlines. These cards offer a bonus of frequent-flier miles; the more money one charges on the card, the more miles one accrues. Typically, the consumer gets one free mile for every dollar charged. Similarly, those who use AT&T cards are offered a 10% discount on long-distance calls charged on the card. The General Motors card (as well as those of Ford, General Electric, and other companies) works in a similar way.

Co-branded cards have proliferated dramatically in just a few years, especially at MasterCard. Visa had been much more wary of co-branding, because the big banks that dominate the consortium were afraid of the incursion of large corporations into the credit card business. However, in early 1992 Visa, more fearful of being left behind by MasterCard than of working with the nonbanks, reversed its stand on co-branded cards. By 1993, 20% of MasterCard and Visa cards were co-branded, up from only 1% seven years earlier.[21] As to the future, Visa's executive vice president of marketing and sales has concluded, "There's no question that cobranding is going to continue to grow. . . . The big question is by how much and how fast."[22] American Express, which had lagged behind Visa and MasterCard in co-branded cards, announced in 1994 that it too would actively embrace such cards. According to a marketing consultant, "American Express arrogantly believed that it was invulnerable to co-branded cards. . . . But now the handwriting is on the wall: If they don't take advantage of strategic alliances of co-branding their business will dwindle to nothing."[23]

Following AT&T's lead, General Motors entered the credit card business in September 1992. (General Electric had come out with a similar card in the preceding week.) GM offered a MasterCard that charged no annual fee and set the interest rate at 10.4% above the prime interest rate. Given the then-current prime rate of 6%, GM was charging an interest rate of 16.4%, almost 2% below the national average at the time. In less than one month GM signed up a million credit card customers; by early 1994 GM had 6 million accounts and had issued 11 million cards in North America (although AT&T was still the leader, with 12 million accounts and 17 million cards).[24]

Why did General Motors enter the credit card business? It certainly hoped to make money from the cards, but its primary objective was to help GM's then-flagging automobile sales.[25] General Motors offers its card users rebates of up to 5% on the amount charged on its cards, to a maximum of $500 per year, which can be applied toward the purchase of most GM cars (or other products and services). The $500 rebate can accumulate for up to seven years, resulting in a maximum potential rebate of $3,500. (Ford's co-branded card works in much the same way.) GM clearly hopes that many of its card users will be lured by such rebates into purchasing GM automobiles. GM has taken credit card business away from other companies, especially the already beleaguered American Express.

Two other significant entrants into the market for co-branded cards are Shell and Apple. In 1993 Shell launched a vigorous campaign with its partner Citibank to market its co-branded card, which offers rebates on gasoline and related products. In 1994, Apple, also in partnership with Citibank, introduced a co-branded card offering a 5% rebate that can be applied to the purchase of Apple products, up to a maximum of $500 a year and $1,500 for three years. As with many of the other nonbanks, a major objective of Shell and Apple is to increase the sales of their products.

The entry of large corporations like General Motors, General Electric, Ford, AT&T, Shell, and Apple may lead to more diversity in the credit card industry in the short run, but in the long run it may well lead to domination of the industry by a few large corporations (such as General Motors) and banks (such as Citibank). Said one industry observer, "When you put all this together, it means you can't stay in this business unless you are big."[26]

Consumers may not be well served by the co-branded cards either. They may think that, with the rebates and other benefits, they are getting something for nothing. However, the fees and the interest they pay on outstanding balances may exceed the value of the benefits. Such customers would be better advised to seek cards with no membership fees and lower interest rates.

With the entry of so many nonbanks into the bank-card business, it is perhaps better to think of these cards as revolving credit cards rather than bank cards. We can also think of all bank credit cards, nonbank cards, co-branded cards, and charge cards as general-purpose cards—to distinguish them from the specific-purpose cards distributed by gasoline companies, department stores, and the like.

The Decline of the "Charge" Card

Among general-purpose cards, charge cards are a dwindling force. By the end of the 1980s, American Express had distributed cards to about 36 million people, and their charges on those cards were approximately $100 million per year. However, more than ten times as many bank cards were in use around the world. The credit card profits (approximately half a billion dollars) of just one of these banks rivaled the total profits reaped by American Express from its family of cards.[27] American Express, as well as many of the banks, was further hurt by the entry of AT&T and other nonbanks into the credit card business. Within a year, AT&T had become the fourth largest issuer of Visa and MasterCard. American Express was particularly vulnerable because its cards were among the most expensive in the industry—with an annual membership fee of $55 for its basic green card and higher fees for its higher-status Gold and Platinum cards. American Express was also made vulnerable by the fact that it charged merchants a higher discount fee than its main competitors did. As a result of the heightened competition, American Express's share of total U.S. charge volume dropped from 26% in 1984 to less than 19% in 1993.[28] Nevertheless, in spite of its losses and its relatively small number of cards, American Express does quite a bit of business. With less than a quarter of the number of cards that MasterCard issues, American Express does well over half as much business, because "on average, American Express customers charge \$4,266 per card per year, vs. \$1,577 among bankcard holders."[29]

Credit Bureaus

The major credit card companies are obviously central in today's credit card industry, but the credit bureaus (also known as credit reporting agencies) are important as well.[30] The credit bureaus collect information on the financial affairs of consumers, package it, and sell that information to the credit card companies (and to collection agencies, insurance companies, and so on). The three major credit bureaus in the United States are TRW, TransUnion, and Equifax. Thousands of local "affiliates" get their information from one of the major bureaus; the so-called "superbureaus" get their information from two or three bureaus. The credit bureaus are crucial to the credit card companies and to consumers. Their reports often determine whether one will receive a credit card. Furthermore, the errors that creep into credit bureau records often create great problems for consumers.

Industry Dynamics: Expand or Die

The credit card companies have been caught up in a hard law of capitalism: Either they must continually expand, or they will decline and perhaps even become extinct. Expansion is driven by economic considerations. Said one industry analyst, "In this business only two things count . . . the cost of money and economies of scale. The more cards you have out there, the lower the unit cost of processing each card."[31]

Expansion in the credit card business can take two basic forms. The first, which has already been discussed, is expansion in the sheer amount of business—number of cards issued, amount of money charged, profits earned from credit cards, and so on. The credit card industry enjoyed frenzied expansion in the 1980s, but in the 1990s growth has slowed to a more modest, but still appreciable, 8% to 10% a year (for bank cards). The slowdown causes some concern. However, there is still room to grow. For example, a smaller percentage of Americans than Canadians have bank cards, and on average Americans use their cards less frequently. Said one consultant, "There is ample evidence in a nearby marketplace [Canada] that suggests that there is room for card usage to grow. . . . The bank card remains the single most profitable product the banks have to offer."[32]

The second form of expansion increases the types or sources of business—either by offering fresh new credit card products or by luring new and different types of credit card users. Finding new credit card customers and developing new products are clearly related; the ultimate objective of both is the progressive expansion of the credit card business.

Finding New Business

The strenuous effort by credit card firms to interest high school and college students in obtaining credit cards and using them more frequently, described in Chapter 1, is but one example of how credit card firms are seeking to expand by reaching out to new groups of consumers.

Credit card companies have also tried to attract new customers through their highly publicized charities. For example, in 1984 American Express "pledged to donate one cent of every card transaction and one dollar for each new card" to the restoration of the Statue of Liberty.[33] As a result, $1.7 million was collected. The campaign worked: During the three months the pledge was in effect, American Express card usage increased 28%, and applications for new cards rose by 45%. The credit card companies have also engaged in various kinds of giveaways to attract new customers. For example, the Discover card ran a promotion in 1993 in which $5 million was to be given away in a drawing to people using the card before December 31. One person would win $1 million, and 4,000 others would be awarded $1,000 each. This may seem like a big outlay for the company, but at the time Discover had about $17 billion in serviced loans.[34]

Credit card companies have also sought ways to offer credit cards to people with poor credit ratings, including those who have gone bankrupt, those with no credit history (such as the recently widowed and recent immigrants), and those whose credit cards have previously been revoked—a potential customer base as high as 40 million people.[35] Credit card companies often offer these "poor risks" a secured credit card. Although a secured card might look like any other Visa or MasterCard, it requires that the cardholder maintain collateral with the issuing company. In 1993, between 600,000 and one million secured accounts were in existence.[36] Ordinarily, the amount that the cardholder deposits is 80% or more of the credit limit. Thus, both merchants and card issuers are insured to a high degree against default. Those who pay their bills on time over a set period are often then switched to unsecured cards. The secured cards are quite profitable. For one thing, those who use secured cards are far more likely than unsecured cardholders to revolve their accounts and thus pay interest to credit card firms. In addition, these cardholders are often so grateful to get a card that they willingly pay higher annual fees and interest rates, and they may even be willing to accept little or no interest on the money held as collateral.[37] The earnings from secured credit card accounts may thus be double, or more, the earnings from unsecured accounts. And because they are secured, the losses (or "chargeoffs") from secured accounts are actually less than those from unsecured accounts. Yet, secured cards can benefit consumers. For example, Oscar Hoyos had been unsuccessful in obtaining a regular credit card because he had no credit history. Responding to a television advertisement, he received a secured card with a $1,000 spending limit in exchange for a deposit of $1,000. He also paid an annual fee of $25, and over the next year and a half he paid interest (at a rate of 16.9%) of $168.21. With a record of paying his bills on time, Mr. Hoyos was able to apply for and receive a regular card. The bank returned his deposit plus $69.05 in accrued interest. Thus, the cost to Mr. Hoyos of doing what was necessary to receive a normal credit card was $124.16.[38]

Another tempting target for credit card companies is the traditional domain of American Express: the travel and entertainment, or corporate, business. American Express no longer has this segment of the industry largely to itself. Furthermore, all the companies involved in this portion of the industry have sought to go beyond executive travel and entertainment expenses and move into the potentially lucrative domain of corporate procurement. That is, they are seeking to get organizations to charge relatively small purchases of things like paper and pencils.[39] It is estimated that this business is worth $250 billion a year. The potential is so great that American Express was prompted in 1994 to bring out its first new card in seven years, the American Express Corporate Purchasing Card.[40]

Another recent area of expansion for credit card companies is small businesses (100 employees or fewer) using credit cards to pay for business expenses. Charging such expenses is particularly common in the first few years of business.[41] As the business grows, the owner may continue to rely heavily on credit cards because of their convenience and their built-in accounting features. The use of credit cards by government officials to make relatively small purchases has also grown. The federal government has already moved in this direction, and we can expect many state and local governments to follow.[42]

In another initiative, the credit card firms sought to reach whole new groups of customers in the mid 1980s with the creation of "affinity cards." Like co-branded cards, these carry two names: Visa or MasterCard, plus the name of another (usually nonprofit) entity. One type of affinity card is the "lifestyle" card, which is usually designed to attract members of a certain organization with which a substantial number of people are affiliated. Such organizations include charities (for example, the Caritas card, which is linked to the national Catholic Charities organization) and causes (Sierra Club or Sane/Freeze).[43] Professional organizations also offer affinity cards. For example, I have a credit card that bears the name of the American Sociological Association. When I was offered the card, I was told that not only would I receive benefits but so would my professional association. Such organizations do ordinarily get some small economic return from sponsoring such cards.

The second type of affinity card, the "personality" card, is designed to attract people who share interests and activities. For example, some personality cards carry the names of celebrities like Elvis Presley or of organizations like the New York Giants. Others allow people to express their own "personality" or "individuality" by displaying, say, their astrological sign. People acquire such cards presumably to identify with their favorite personality or organization or perhaps to demonstrate their own individuality, albeit in a highly conformist way.

Purveyors of credit cards introduced both types of affinity cards in order to reach new groups of people and to get new or additional cards into the hands of people who otherwise might not be interested in them. However, many banks have begun to lose interest in affinity cards because they do not attract enough new cardholders to make the effort profitable.[44] The number of affinity groups peaked in 1985 at 2,700 and declined to 2,100 by the beginning of 1993.[45]

One other significant source of new credit card users is other countries. The international use of credit cards has grown dramatically, but there is still plenty of room for expansion. For example, credit cards have just begun to make significant inroads in Japan, a nation notorious for its emphasis on thrift and saving and its aversion to debt.[46] Although the 124 million Japanese have about 200 million credit cards, less than 1% of all consumer purchases in Japan are charged to credit cards. One consultant noted, "They have them, they pay the membership fees, but they never use them."[47] That may be a bit of an overstatement, because the number of cards issued, the amount of debt carried, and individual bankruptcies are all growing at a far higher rate in Japan than in the United States. Of great importance to the future is the fact that it is the young Japanese who are particularly drawn to credit cards.

Similarly, Germany has long been hostile to credit cards. As a result, in the early 1990s, 61 million (West) Germans were using only about 5 million credit cards. About 85% of all consumer purchases were in cash; only 5% were made with cards. However, in 1991 German banks dropped their long-standing opposition to credit cards, and large numbers of Germans were expected to flock to them. Furthermore, given Germany's influence in Eastern Europe, it was anticipated that banks in these countries would also move rapidly into the credit card business.[48]

Although the use of general-purpose credit cards is growing in other parts of the world, it is important to remember that almost half of those cards are in the hands of Americans. Similarly, for Visa, MasterCard, and American Express, the total dollar volume of business in the United States in 1993 was $441.5 billion, of a worldwide total of $960 billion.[49] The closest competitors in Europe are France and the United Kingdom, but they lag far behind American use.

Increasing competition in the credit card industry led card issuers to come up with what have come to be called "value-added" cards, which offer a bewildering array of enhancements to attract users:

◆ No annual fee
◆ Rebates

◆ Discounts on products

◆ Free insurance (on airline tickets and rental cars)

◆ Extended warranties on products purchased with the card (introduced by American Express in 1987 to get people to use its cards for more than just travel and entertainment)[50]

◆ Exclusive access to tickets for special events

◆ Free worldwide emergency hotlines (for example, American Express's Global Assist)

◆ Price protection

From the card user's perspective, one problem with all these enhancements is that they are often difficult to take advantage of or that they turn out to offer very little. For example, Citibank's price-protection plan required that the consumer mail in a copy of the print ad containing the lower price, as well as copies of the sales and credit card receipts for the original purchase. Certain kinds of goods and services were excluded (food, tickets, coins). Some types of sales were also excluded (going-out-of-business sales, closeouts, and others). Refunds were limited to $250 per item and $1,000 annually. Such daunting rules are likely to keep many cardholders from ever filing a claim.[51] Similarly, one observer said of Citibank's "Citidollars" program, which offers the possibility of earning discount points to be applied to products offered in a mail-order catalog, "Trouble is, the product selection is generally limited and the discounts insignificant." That same observer goes on to make a point that applies to most "enhancements" offered by the credit card companies: "The idea of these enhancements is to create marketing value, not real value. The enhancements attract consumers, but most consumers don't use them."[52] The same kinds of criticisms apply to the effort by Shell Oil and Chemical Bank to market a co-branded card by offering discounts on gasoline and other Shell products. A credit card industry newsletter called it "the card that lacks octane," because the discounts were so meager and because so few people would gain any real benefits from the program.[53]

Burned by criticisms that credit cards help turn people into debtors, Nationsbank reached out to a new set of consumers: those who need to use credit cards but who are interested in building their savings. Each cardholder gets a tax-deferred annuity, and the bank contributes up to 1% of each purchase to the annuity. That sum may be supplemented by participating merchants, who can contribute as much as 6 percent of the total purchase. According to an official associated with the annuity program, "Until now, you've had only two choices with your money: You could either spend it or save it. . . . You could never do both at the same time."[54] This program is most likely to attract higher-income people, who pose less of a risk to the bank but who are also less likely to run up the huge credit card balances that lead to high interest payments. At base, of course, the Nationsbank program is just another enhancement. Given the small percentages involved, it too is vulnerable to the charge that it is little more than a marketing tool and is of little real value to the consumer.

The interest of credit card companies in most types of enhancement programs began to wane in the early 1990s. The editor of *Credit Card News* claimed, "The bells-and-whistles enhancements put on cards in the late 1980s have run their course."[55] For example, a number of banks dropped their travel accident insurance programs; others began experimenting with programs in which cardholders pay a fee for whatever enhancements they wish to have.[56] To many in the credit card industry, the gains of these enhancement programs seemed too low and the costs too high. For example, the costs of buyer-protection programs proved far higher than the card companies had anticipated. Thus, many shifted to offering lower interest rates and no annual fees, although some enhancements remain. It could also be argued that credit card enhancements have entered a new phase with the emergence of co-branded cards. Frequent-flyer miles and rebates on automobiles and other kinds of purchases are, in fact, enhancements offered by the co-branded cards. Consumers who charge a great deal and do not revolve their accounts can, indeed, get something for nearly nothing from these programs. However, consumers who revolve their accounts and charge relatively little are better off shopping for the card with the lowest annual fee and lowest interest rate.[57] Nevertheless, the rebate programs run by the co-branded cards have revived interest in credit card enhancements just as they seemed to have passed their prime.

The credit card companies are not only trying to expand their business by offering new promotions and enhancements; they are also extending the use of credit cards to new goods and services. For example, the number of supermarkets accepting credit cards increased sixfold between April 1991 and August 1992.[58] Giant, the largest chain of supermarkets in the Washington, D.C., area, decided in 1992 to begin allowing shoppers to use credit (and debit) cards throughout its system.[59] There have also been efforts to encourage more people to charge such things as magazine subscription renewals and vacations on cruise ships.[60]

The card companies have also targeted small, high-volume businesses, such as parking facilities (a $30 billion a year business), movie theaters, and fast-food restaurants like Pizza Hut and Arby's.[61] Given the total amount of business they do, the fast-food restaurants are particularly alluring, and the cards are being used for purchases as small as a soft drink. Said an executive of Master-Card: "Accepting credit cards in a fast-food environment is natural, since consumers look for both speed and convenience."[62] Even some New York City taxis have been testing high-tech meters that accept credit cards.[63]

Health and medical care is another attractive area for the credit card industry.[64] It is an enormous, rapidly growing segment of the American economy, and the card companies would like to see more clients charging their visits to physicians, dentists, and even hospitals.[65]

Credit card companies have also sought to expand into new markets in many other ways. For example, hurt by the success of credit cards, American Express undertook a long-term study that resulted in 1987 in the Optima card, offered to holders of American Express cards. This card is virtually identical to Visa and MasterCard, because it is aimed more at personal use than at business use and it is a true credit card, not a charge card. However, between 1990 and mid 1993, the Optima card lost nearly $2 billion.[66] According to the head of Optima operations, "If it was a stand-alone company, it would have gone bankrupt."[67] One explanation for these problems is that American Express cardholders, who pay off their bills each month, are inclined to be late and even delinquent in payments on their Optima cards. Furthermore, Optima has failed to attract many of the highly profitable "accidental revolvers," those who can afford to pay their bills but merely neglect to from time to time. Such revolvers are highly unlikely to become delinquent on their accounts.

American Express's Gold card was another attempt to offer something new, but the Gold card has ceased to be distinctive. The banks now also offer gold cards, and their membership fees for such cards are lower than those of American Express. In fact, a consultant recently concluded that "the gold card, in light of the widespread competition in the industry, is becoming commoditized. . . . Whereas once it was perceived as an upscale premium card, it's now becoming fuzzy."[68] American Express's response to commoditization of the gold card was its Platinum card, introduced in 1984. The fee for the card was set at $250 (although some in the company had argued for a $1,000 fee). The Platinum card was offered to American Express customers who were averaging at least $10,000 a year in charges. These customers were assumed to be among the most profitable.

In the end, in spite of all the efforts to differentiate themselves from one another, "charge cards, after all, have become 'commoditized,' like colas and toilet paper; there are no real differences among them."[69] The issue, then, is why we should discuss the differences among credit cards at all. The answer is that the original differences, as well as continuing efforts to manufacture a sense of difference, give us a great deal of insight into the nature of the credit card business.

The Competitive Environment in the 1990s

Credit card companies are likely to explore, perhaps at an accelerating rate, ways of finding new business. However, there is a pervasive sense in the credit card industry that its best, most profitable days may be behind it.[70] There are three reasons for this slowdown:

- ◆ The credit card industry has become far more crowded and much more competitive than it was a few years ago. Thus, credit card firms are making ever-escalating offers in an attempt to get competitors' customers to switch.[71] Today, our mailboxes are likely to be full of offers for cards with free membership (between 1991 and 1992, the number of no-fee cards doubled in distribution to 41% of everyone with a credit card), lower interest rates, rebates, enhancements, and so on. Established issuers of credit cards are going to have to match at least some of these offers or else find new ways to compete. Whatever actions they take are likely to cut into profit margins. This is all in stark contrast to the situation in the 1980s when, for example, credit card interest rates were not responsive to competition.[72]

- ◆ Consumers are becoming more conscious of the cost of credit, including annual fees and interest rates, in part as a result of the new entrants and their expensive advertising campaigns.[73] As a result, consumers are more likely to shop around for the lowest-cost credit cards and to put pressure on their credit card companies to lower interest rates and waive annual fees. It is also possible that more consumers will use their cards only for convenience charges, paying their bills within the grace period and thereby yielding no lucrative interest payments on revolving charges to the card companies. This change is crucial, because 90% of all bank card revenues come from those who use their cards on a revolving basis.

♦ In the long-running recession of the early 1990s, unemployment, bankruptcies, and the like all increased, leading to increases in unpaid credit card debt. Economic woes also led consumers to greater awareness of the problems of personal (and national) debt. Consumers seemed more inclined to pay down their credit card debt than to steadily increase it, as had been the case for years.[74]

In the new, more competitive environment, credit card companies are looking for ways to cut costs and increase profits. For example, because of the loss of annual fees and the lower interest rates, there is talk in the industry of eliminating the grace period on revolving credit cards and of cutting back on the enhancements offered to consumers.[75] Most striking, however, is talk of charging a fee for convenience users. This would serve to increase income, but as one bank official points out, there may be other reasons behind the fee: "The transaction fee would be used either to get convenience users to change their habits, or get them off our books. . . . I think a transaction fee for us in the next year or two is going to become a reality."[76]

In spite of the current problems and other short-run difficulties that might arise, however, the credit card business remains very attractive. It will be quite lucrative for those companies that survive the competitive shakeout.

Credit Legislation

Over the years, the federal government has passed a variety of laws to deal with both personal troubles and public issues associated with credit cards. Here I will briefly review the key aspects of those laws, but you should bear in mind that, given the social and personal problems related to credit cards that still exist, these laws have clearly been far from fully successful. Furthermore, recent efforts to regulate the credit card industry have failed to make their way through Congress. Most of the laws protecting consumers were passed before the credit card boom of the 1980s:

- *1968 Consumer Credit Protection Act (amended in 1980 and 1988).* Generally known as the Truth-in-Lending Act. Under this law, lenders must disclose such things as annual interest rates and other finance charges, fees, and costs. The law also prohibits credit card firms from mailing unsolicited credit cards. This law limits a customer's liability for a lost or stolen card to $50. It also limits the diversion of wages to pay credit card debts.

- *1971 Fair Credit Reporting Act.* Restricts the ability of credit agencies to disclose credit information. Consumers are also given "the right to know what is in their credit file and to correct inaccurate information."[77] Consumers are to be given the name and address of any source of a derogatory credit report that leads to the denial of credit.

- *1974 Fair Credit Billing Act.* Protects consumers against billing practices that are unfair or inaccurate. Consumers are to receive a statement of their rights before the first credit card transaction takes place. They have 60 days to dispute a charge, and the card issuer must either correct the error or provide the consumer with a written explanation of the disputed charge within 90 days. During the course of the dispute, the consumer cannot be charged interest on the contested portion of the account.

- *1974 Equal Credit Opportunity Act.* "Prohibits discrimination on the basis of credit applicant's sex, marital status, race, color, religion, national origin, age, or the fact that income is derived from any public assistance program."[78] Furthermore, this law prohibits discrimination against those who exercise their rights under the 1968 Consumer Credit Protection Act. The 1974 act includes other provisions, including several that relate to the rights of marriage partners. For example, if the partners qualify for a joint account, then each is entitled to a separate account.

- *1978 Financial Institutions Regulatory and Interest Rate Control Act.* Gives consumers protection in the event that the federal government requests their bank records.

- *1978 Electronic Funds Transfer Act.* Outlines the "rights, liabilities and responsibilities" of those who participate in electronic funds transfers. For example, the law outlines requirements for periodic statements as well as procedures for resolving errors.

- *1980 Truth-in-Lending Simplification and Reform Act.* Eased the requirements of the 1968 act. For example, the number of disclosures required was reduced, and advertising requirements were eased.

- *1988 Fair Credit and Charge Card Disclosure Act.* Required advertisements, solicitations, and application forms to disclose important terms. Among the required disclosures are the amount of the annual percentage rate and the way it is determined, annual fees (or other types of fees), minimum finance charges, the grace period, and the method used to calculate credit card balances.

It is important for credit card users to know their rights under these laws.[79] Among other things, consumers have the right to know why they have been turned down for credit, the right to know what is in their files, and the right to correct errors. A person who has been turned down for credit in the past 30 days can receive a free copy of her or his credit report. Consumers can get copies of those reports at any other time for a nominal fee.

Although these laws have reduced or eliminated some problems associated with credit cards, it will become progressively clear as this book unfolds that many problems remain. Better legislation is clearly needed, but government action alone cannot ameliorate all the personal troubles and public issues associated with credit cards.

Future: Increasingly Incredible CREDEBELS

Although the focus of this book is credit cards, they are only part of a broader domain that can be labeled CREDEBELS. CREDEBELS is an acronym that I have created for three interrelated phenomena: CREdit cards, DEBit cards, and ELectronic Funds TransferS. The latter two phenomena are briefly introduced here and mentioned, where appropriate, throughout the book; a more systematic treatment can be found in the Appendix.

Everyone is familiar with credit cards, but debit cards are just now becoming familiar to large numbers of Americans. Credit cards and debit cards resemble each other physically, may be issued by the same company or bank (Visa and MasterCard issue both credit and debit cards), and may be used for the same purposes. However, as the names suggest, credit cards offer access to a line of credit, but debit cards draw money directly from, or debit, a checking account (or other investment account).[80] The credit card is more oriented to being a replacement for cash; the debit card is more a replacement for checks. In other words, debit cards are a step toward not only a "cashless," but also a "checkless," society. In fact, Visa offers a debit card called Visa Check, and more generally, some call debit cards "plastic checks." Using a debit card is indeed far more convenient than writing a series of checks at different locations. As a result, there are those in the industry who believe that there may come a day when debit cards will make checks obsolete.[81]

At the moment, and for the foreseeable future, credit cards are of far greater importance than debit cards in the United States (but not in other parts of the world), because they have revolutionized the way we consume and, more generally, the way we live. Debit cards do not now come anywhere close to credit cards in extent of use or social impact, at least in the United States. But debit card use in the United States is projected to grow far faster than the use of credit cards in the coming years and will be a significant rival to credit cards by the middle of the 21st century.

A general debit card can be distinguished from another important element of the CREDEBEL society, the ATM (automatic teller machine) card. (The first full-fledged ATM became operational in 1970.[82]) An ATM card can be seen as a limited-purpose debit card. An ATM card generally allows one only to withdraw money from a bank account, but a debit card does that and permits the transfer of funds from one's checking account to a merchant's bank account at the point of sale (supermarket, pharmacy, and so on).[83] By 1994 there were more than 200 million ATM cards in the United States.[84] Between 1983 and 1993 the annual volume of ATM transactions increased from 2.4 billion to an estimated 8.0 billion.[85]

Today, in the United States, people generally use their ATM cards to withdraw money from their checking accounts, although the cards are being used increasingly for other kinds of debit transactions. In the future, people will be increasingly likely to replace their ATM cards with general debit cards that they use for both bank withdrawals and other purposes. As the president of the Electronic Funds Transfer Association said, "There's some that would say that in time debit transactions will dwarf ATM transactions. . . . But if you keep going at this rate, it's going to be a lot sooner than anybody thought."[86] At the present time, however, ATM cards account for 95% of all debit card activity in the United States.[87]

A development in the making is the multiple-application "smart card," a single card that can function as both a credit and a debit card as well as an ATM, phone, and frequent-flier card, among many other things. Smart cards have an embedded microchip that allows them to perform many functions simultaneously. Smart cards will free the consumer from the need to carry many different cards.[88]

Electronic funds transfers (EFTs) similarly permit the electronic transfer of funds (and, increasingly, data in the form of electronic data interchanges [EDIs]) from one account to another. EFTs frequently operate automatically and sometimes instantaneously. Credit card and debit card transactions ultimately involve electronic funds transfers, but there are other types of EFTs as well. For example, a consumer can use a "smart phone" or personal computer to pay bills via EFT. Similarly, recipients of welfare checks and food stamps may have benefits transferred by EFT directly from government accounts to their own accounts. Overall, annual EFT volume has risen from 2.4 billion transactions in 1983 to an estimated 8.6 billion in 1993.[89]

EFT technology is even more widely used in automated clearinghouses (ACHs),* which generally handle large money (and data) transactions between business and financial institutions. (Other EFTs usually handle smaller transactions involving consumers.) Like debit cards, ACHs are primarily oriented to the elimination of checks. The most visible ACH transaction, at least to the general public, is the direct deposit of payroll checks, in which funds are electronically transferred from the institution's bank to the banks of employees. (Other examples of ACH transactions are discussed in the Appendix.)

The expansion of the use of debit cards and other consumer-oriented EFT systems has been slowed in the United States, at least at present, by the fact that American consumers tend to prefer the

---

*There is a national association, the National Automated Clearing House Association (NACHA), with 40 member ACH associations.

short-term credit offered by credit cards to the more or less immediate debiting of their bank accounts that occurs in other EFT systems. But the desire of at least some credit card firms to eliminate "free" short-term credit (in particular, the grace period offered by credit cards), or the "float," is one of the main reasons that, at least in the long term, other EFT systems, especially debit cards, are likely to play an increasingly large role in the economy.[90]

There are other reasons as well for the greater popularity of credit cards. For example, debit card and ATM transactions tend to involve a fee for each use, but there is no such fee for each credit card use. More important, one does not build a credit record with debit and ATM transactions, and such a record is needed to qualify later for other types of credit. One can refuse to pay an erroneous bill with a credit card (or can stop payment on a check), but once a debit or ATM card has been used to pay a bill, the money is gone. Finally, consumer losses due to credit card fraud are greatly limited by law, but the fraudulent use of a debit card or ATM card may result in much greater losses.

In 1990 the dollar volume of cash and check transactions in the United States was approximately $2.8 trillion (82.9% of the total). The remaining transactions included $446.5 billion for credit cards (13.2%), $10.6 billion for debit cards (0.3%), and $121.8 billion for all other forms of payment (3.6%).[91] Thus we can understand why the vice president of marketing for MasterCard said, "Though people have for a long time talked about the cashless society, we are by no means all the way there."[92] However, by the year 2000 cash and check transactions are projected to amount to almost $4.5 trillion (down to 78.2% of the total), whereas credit transactions will grow to $875 billion (up strongly to 15.2%), debit card transactions are projected to increase to $142.8 billion (up even more strongly to 2.5%), and all other forms will also increase substantially to $234.5 billion (4.1%).[93] There is considerable feeling in the industry that these trends will continue, even accelerate, moving progressively closer, as we proceed through the 21st century, to parity between cash and checks on one side and credit and debit card transactions on the other.

In Chapter 1, I discussed some of the reasons credit cards represent something new in the history of money. Debit (and ATM) cards, as well as other elements of the CREDEBEL system, have many of those same characteristics. However, there are at least three crucial differences between credit cards and other CREDE-BELS. First, we must have a balance in our account (or overdraft protection) in order to use a debit card or an ATM card, but no such requirement generally exists for a credit card. Second, with debit cards and ATM cards, our spending is restricted to the sum available in our account. There is no money "available" in a credit card account, although it is possible to use the cards to obtain a cash advance. Third, and most important, while debit cards and ATM cards certainly make it easier to consume and to spend too much, they do not generally permit us, as do credit cards, to go deeply into debt and to become addicted to a lifestyle that requires debt. For these reasons and others, debit cards, ATM cards, and other CREDEBELS are not considered as revolutionary as credit cards.

In addition, credit cards more than other CREDEBELS pose some extraordinary dangers to individuals and to society. It is the credit card that is, at the moment, having the most profound effect on our lives, and it will continue to have an important impact. Nevertheless, where appropriate in the pages that follow, I will comment on the current use of debit cards and analyze the effect of their future growth. Other forms of EFTs will receive less attention, however, largely because the use of debit cards and credit cards involves EFTs and because the other forms of EFTs are, at least at the moment, of far less social significance. But a century or two from now, the situation may be reversed; then EFTs may be the focus of attention, and credit cards may be reduced to secondary status.

3

Credit Card Debt

Beware the Plastic Loan Shark[1]

W e generally have a very intimate relationship with money in the form of currency or even the sum at the bottom of our monthly bank statements. However, as Georg Simmel recognized, the advent of credit tended to distance us from money. Money that exists in the form of a line of credit (to take an example from Simmel's day) seems more distant from us than cash in our wallets or in our bank accounts. Because it is far more removed from us and far less tangible, credit, in Simmel's view, leads to a strong "temptation to imprudence."[2] In other words, when we have credit available to us, we are far more likely to spend to excess and to plunge into debt, sometimes deeply, than we are when we are restricted to cash on hand and in the bank.

However, it is not only the distance associated with credit that leads to imprudence. Credit also leads to a more rapid circulation of money than in a currency-based economy, for two main reasons. First, credit expands the amount of money available beyond cash on hand, thereby increasing the number of possible transactions. Second, with currency, transactions are usually limited to face-to-face dealings with others, but with credit they can more easily involve people and organizations that we do not interact with directly. Thus, credit serves not only to increase the amount of money available but also the size of the population with which we deal.

Each additional transaction made possible by credit leads to still other deals, with the result that both the number and the speed of economic transactions in general increase dramatically. With the increasing number and rapidity of transactions, any single deal and each dollar spent in that deal become progressively less important. As a result, it grows increasingly easy for us to part with money—

and so we part with more of it, more often. In Simmel's words, the "rapid circulation of money induces habits of spending and acquisition; it makes a specific quantity of money psychologically less significant and valuable."[3]

The Temptation to Imprudence

Simmel has provided us with a useful hypothesis about a CREDE-BEL society. That is, if credit leads to greater imprudence, then each additional advance in this realm should lead to still greater recklessness with money. Let us analyze this issue. If cash, credit cards, debit cards, and electronic funds transfers form a historical sequence, does each step forward lead to progressively more imprudence?

Credit Cards

In comparison to cash, credit cards do lead to greater imprudence. In Simmel's terms, there is a greater distance between people and money when a credit card intervenes in a cash economy. As a result, it is easier to part with money through a credit card, rather than a cash, transaction. Consider the introduction of credit cards into fast-food restaurants. The use of credit cards leads to more sales and to transactions that are 60% to 100% larger than cash transactions. According to a MasterCard vice president, "[Customers] often buy larger sizes of the more profitable items such as soft drinks and french fries."[4]

There is probably no greater distance between people and credit cards than there was between people and the credit instruments of Simmel's day. What is different about credit cards is that, in comparison to earlier forms of credit, they permit more and speedier transactions. We can use our credit cards far more often and far more quickly and easily than our predecessors could use letters of credit. Furthermore, far more people have access to modern credit cards than were able to obtain old-fashioned lines of credit. As a result, massive numbers of people who never before had the opportunity now can be imprudent.

With credit cards, money is so easy to part with that we can even spend money we do not have; we can go into debt. To some, the money involved in credit card transactions seems abstract and unreal. In fact, some people do not even seem to feel sure that they will eventually have to pay back their credit card debts. As one college student put it, "It just seemed like free money."[5] It is the unreality of credit card debt and the rapidity with which we can run up that debt that helps us understand the increasingly powerful tendency of credit card users to get into deep economic trouble.

It has come to be accepted as reality today that the use of credit cards stimulates spending. In fact, one journalist concluded sardonically, "If the card companies prove adept in meeting their goals, they may persuade Americans to loosen up on their wallets and give new meaning to the term cashless society."[6]

Not surprisingly, the American Bankers Association (ABA), speaking for the banks that issue a large number of our credit cards, takes just the opposite position:

> When used properly, bank cards can help consumers develop self-discipline in their spending habits. Consumers should recognize that the criteria used by banks for establishing individuals' credit lines represent expert judgment about the amount of additional debt the individual card holder can manage, and they should use credit accordingly. When the authorization mechanism tells consumers that they have reached their credit limit, this may be a signal that they have extended themselves about as far as they can without risking financial difficulty.
>
> Consumers who tend to overextend themselves by obtaining credit from a variety of sources can discipline themselves by using one credit card source—the bank card—that will let them know when they have reached their limit.[7]

Unfortunately, the bankers' position is hard to support. First, the ABA believes that banks can help consumers develop self-discipline, but it is the banks themselves (and other credit card companies) that are eroding that discipline by offering easy credit. Here is what a part-time bookstore warehouse worker (and writer) has to say about this:

> This is what accounts for the stench of hypocrisy in their offers. That aspect of me that they tirelessly praise (my tendency to pay my entire bill on time) is the very aspect they need to subvert if they hope to make any kind of money at all. It is akin to the man who likes virgins: his ultimate goal is to relieve them of what makes them so desirable in the first place.[8]

Second, it is the banks themselves that lack restraint. Who is going to help them develop the discipline needed to stop the indiscriminate offering of multiple credit cards to consumers and the frenzied effort to recruit new users, even among high school students? Third, there is something bizarre and very insulting about the idea that consumers need discipline and that it is the banks, themselves so promiscuous in the distribution of credit cards, that are going to provide them with it. This notion is similar to the idea that the brothel is going to help its prostitutes' customers develop self-restraint. Finally, using a single source of credit, the bank card, will not help, because many banks are going to great lengths to get us to use their cards by offering, for example, no annual fee or low introductory rates. The ABA would do far more good by making an effort to restrain banks than by giving condescending advice to cardholders. As it is, credit cards are a key factor in the temptation to economic imprudence in our society today, and the banks are a major contributor to the problem.

Debit Cards

Debit cards do not carry the same risk of imprudence and indebtedness that is associated with credit cards, let alone some additional risk related to their being an advance in the world of money. The simple reason is that, unless people have overdraft lines of credit associated with their debit cards (like overdraft protection associated with their checking accounts), they cannot spend more with their debit cards than the amount they have on deposit.

However, there is some danger of imprudence with debit cards, especially in comparison to cash or check transactions. Debit cards do increase the number and rapidity of economic transactions; it is far easier to use a debit card over and over than it is to continually replenish cash on hand. It is in this way that debit cards contribute to the growth of imprudence.

Furthermore, people are far more likely to spend freely when they are not actually handing cash to the merchant. Abstract numbers on some future bank statement are far less meaningful than out-of-pocket cash or a visibly diminishing checking account balance. In fact, in gas stations, where debit cards have been used for several years, people spend more money on gasoline when they use debit cards than when they use cash. Said a MasterCard representative, "If you drive into a gas station with $20 in your pocket, you put in $10 [worth of gasoline] and keep $10. With a debit card, you fill up."[9]

Similarly, with debit card transactions it is harder to know exactly how much one is spending and how much one has left in the bank—and hence easier to expend more than one would with a cash or check transaction. When debit cards are used, it is easier to lose track of how much is left in an account used for both debit card and check transactions, with the result that one is more likely to start bouncing checks and run up bounced-check fees.

Other fees are also associated with debit card use—currently, between 10¢ and $2 per transaction. Retailers may charge their own transaction fee of perhaps 10¢ to 20¢ per use. Taken together on a number of transactions per month, these fees may make debit card use quite costly.[10]

Thus, some imprudence, as well as other costs and dangers, is associated with debit cards. However, debit cards pose far fewer economic problems for consumers than do credit cards and are relatively innocent means to the attainment of our goals.

Electronic Funds Transfers

EFTs and debit cards have similar effects on the tendency to be reckless with money. (EFTs are involved in debit and credit card transactions, but let us focus here on the use of automated EFTs to pay bills via telephone or computer.) As is true of debit cards, the danger of imprudence and of increasing indebtedness through the use of automated EFTs is far less than with credit cards.[11] No credit is involved in such transactions; money is deducted directly from one's account.

That is not to say, however, that the users of automated EFTs do not face economic dangers. One hazard is that people need to be very organized to pay bills through an automated payment system. They must remember to enter those payments in their checkbooks, or they risk being overdrawn. One solution is to get an account with overdraft protection, although, that in itself will lead at least some people to spend more than they would if they were restricted to the balances in their checking accounts. Another danger, shared with the other CREDEBELS, is that automated payments provide no immediately visible or tangible reminder that one has spent money, as there is in a cash or even a check transaction. Without such visible reminders, people are more inclined to overextend themselves. Finally, EFTs permit the transfer of money, often huge sums of money, with a keystroke or a phone call, thereby potentially contributing to imprudence on a massive scale. EFTs also greatly increase the number and rapidity of economic transactions. Overall, however, EFTs pose fewer economic problems for consumers than do credit cards, because they do not lure people into debt.

Thus, it seems that Simmel was wrong, at least in part. Credit cards do, in comparison to cash, increase the temptation to imprudence, but further advances in the realm of money—debit cards and EFTs—are actually less risky than credit cards. Thus, in the remainder of this chapter the focus is on the main culprit in increasing financial imprudence—credit cards.

Consumer Debt as a Public Issue

The statistics indicate that credit cards have played a large and escalating role in helping Americans dig themselves deeper and deeper into debt. For example, in 1984, 22% of all credit was revolving credit, but by 1993 it had increased to 36%. Of the total amount of revolving credit, the percentage attributable to financial institutions has risen from 62% to 71%.[12] Interestingly, credit card debt has become the most common form of financial liability. A larger percentage of people now have credit card debts (39.9%) than have home mortgages (38.7%), car loans (35.1%), and other kinds of debts.[13]

However, credit card debt has leveled off, at least partly because of the 1986 change in the tax laws. The tax deduction for credit card interest was gradually eliminated over several years and ended entirely in 1991. It is interesting to note that until 1991 the government, through its tax laws, actually encouraged people to go into debt to the credit card companies by making paid interest tax deductible.

With the end of the tax deduction for interest paid to credit card companies, those who own homes have been encouraged to seek home equity lines of credit, on which interest remains tax deductible. Many people consolidated their credit card (and other) debts in such loans. Another factor leading people in the direction of home equity loans is the far lower interest rates associated with them in comparison to the rates on credit card debt. But one's house is at risk if one defaults on a home equity loan. Said one financial planner, "People who have a history of running up big credit card balances—I'm a little concerned about telling them to put their house on the line."[14]

The option of shifting from high-interest credit card debt to relatively low-interest home equity debt is available only to those who have substantial equity in their homes. In other words, home equity loans are available only to the more prosperous members of society. Those who are less well off are still restricted to credit card "loans," which carry higher interest rates and whose interest is not tax deductible. Thus, the "poor" are at a disadvantage vis-à-vis the well-to-do in the world of credit. However, it is worth noting that being able to put one's home at risk is at best a dubious honor.

As people began to pile up high-interest credit card debt in the 1980s and early 1990s, more and more of them had difficulty paying it off. As a result, they were more or less permanently in debt and paying extraordinarily high interest rates on the amount owed. Increasing numbers of people in the 1980s became delinquent, with accounts more than 30 days past due. According to the American Bankers Association, the delinquency rate was 27% higher in 1990 than in 1985.[15] The recession of the early 1990s then threw many people out of work, and some were forced into personal bankruptcy. Those in bankruptcy are deemed to be unable to pay, among other things, all of their credit card bills.

One by-product of the increase in delinquencies and bankruptcies was a boom in the collections business.[16] However, these agencies are able to collect less than 6% of the total past-due amount (down from 22% ten years ago).[17] Credit card debt is thus an issue for the credit card companies as well as for overextended consumers.

All the aggregate data reported in this section indicate that credit card debt is a major public issue, but what of the individuals and their personal troubles?

Consumer Debt as a Personal Trouble

Many horror stories have been told of people who have become deeply indebted to the credit card firms. The case of Peter and Pam Ward and their two children is as good (or bad) as any. On the basis of a combined family income of more than $60,000, Peter Ward was able to accumulate over the course of two years 25 credit cards and amass a credit card debt, at high interest, of $35,000. Mr. Ward utters a refrain quite common among those who find themselves deeply in debt to the credit card firms: "It never crossed my mind that I'd have to pay it all back."[18]

The Wards' problems began in 1987 when they bought a house with a mortgage in excess of $150,000. Because they were new homeowners, the credit card companies deluged them with offers for preapproved credit cards with high credit limits. Mr. Ward enjoyed collecting his credit cards: " 'It was like candy,' says Mr. Ward, who got a 'warm feeling' whenever a new card arrived." Mr. Ward managed to dig himself into a huge economic hole by, among other things, taking $200 every weekend in cash advances on his cards, spending $800 on Nintendo cartridges for his son, squandering $5,000 on a trip to Disneyland, renting a cottage each summer, purchasing a 1967 Mustang on impulse, buying his wife costly jewelry, flying first class, and staying at expensive hotels. To Mr. Ward, collecting credit cards and using them to buy these extras was linked to his self-esteem: "I figured I deserved these things—and if I had all these credit cards then I must be somebody."

Interestingly, Mr. Ward was a recovering alcoholic. When he began collecting credit cards and accumulating credit card debt, Mr. Ward explained, "I reverted to where I was 10 years ago. I switched addictions." Instead of being addicted to liquor, Mr. Ward became habituated to credit card consumption and debt. Whether or not Mr. Ward's use of credit cards is an addiction, he clearly developed the habit of using his credit cards to live beyond his means.

All this debt was accumulated unbeknown to Mrs. Ward, who only discovered her family's dire economic situation after her husband broke his leg sledding and she began opening the bills. She also discovered that half the debt was hers, because her husband had been taking out cards in her name as well. She contemplated leaving him but couldn't because she was responsible for half the debt. With the trips behind them and the clothes they had charged getting old, Mr. Ward finally concluded that not only had the credit binge ended but that they also did not "have anything to show for it."

The Wards ended up in a credit counseling program. Their counselor insisted, as such counselors often do, that the Wards cut up all their credit cards. He also advised Mr. Ward to enroll in

Debtors Anonymous, a 12-step program like Alcoholics Anonymous. The Wards started clipping coupons, taking brown-bag lunches to work, shopping in discount stores, and renting out part of their house. Within two years of the end of their credit card binge, they were able to repay $5,000 of their debt, but they remain on the edge of bankruptcy. They were forced to withdraw their money, at a penalty, from their Individual Retirement Account (IRA). They have no savings, and Mr. Ward, who had a heart attack a few years ago, has only $20,000 in life insurance. The Wards are a good example of a family brought to the brink of economic catastrophe by the imprudent use of credit cards.

Of course, the Wards are not alone. "Sally Bowman" (a pseudonym) is $20,000 in debt, a sum more than half her total yearly income. Here's how she explains her predicament:

> It all started when I graduated from college and took a low-paying job. . . . I didn't want to live like a student so I used credit cards to buy myself furniture and eat dinners out. I wasn't extravagant, I just didn't want to deprive myself. . . . When I got a new card with a $5,000 credit limit, it felt like someone just handed me $5,000. . . . The reality has been that I got in the hole financially.[19]

Then there is the case of a businessperson who had 41 credit cards with a total debt of $183,000. As a reward for being such a good customer, he was sent an unsolicited application for yet another card. Once the card was in hand, he immediately "maxed it out" by charging $500 worth of goods and taking a $4,500 cash advance. This proved to be the last straw financially, and he was forced to declare bankruptcy.[20]

A North Carolina couple exemplifies the extremes of credit card indebtedness. They collected 15 credit cards and over $10,000 in debt. When the creditors began to howl, the couple adopted what seems to be quite a logical solution to the problem. According to the wife, "We used a credit card to buy an answering machine to screen the creditors' calls."[21]

The importance to the economy of people like these was underscored in the midst of the long-running recession of the early 1990s. Merchants were worried about their Christmas 1992 business. However, despite high personal debt and the gloomy economy, many people like the Wards went out and tried to spend their way out of their personal doldrums. But they did so, apparently, by plunging themselves even more deeply into debt. Check cashing during the Christmas season was flat, but credit card spending was up an average of 20 percent. Said the president of the consumer group Bankcard Holders of America: "The bigger danger is that consumers will go deeper into debt than they're capable of managing and get carried away. . . . We'd like to see consumers handle that new debt somewhat more responsibly than they have in the past."[22]

Who Is Responsible for High Credit Card Debt?

The people whose stories I have just told are far from the only ones who have destroyed themselves financially because of their rampant consumerism and abuse of credit cards. According to one financial consultant, "Bankruptcies are up, and the size of credit card debt has gone up. . . . It used to be $30,000 or $40,000 was high. Now we are seeing people with $60,000—even $100,000 on 10, 20 even 30 credit cards from all levels of employment."[23] As I have already suggested, blame for this disastrous situation is shared by consumers and especially the credit card companies.

Consumers

Part of the responsibility certainly lies with consumers; unrestrained consumption is a huge factor. "People who say they are continually unable to control the urge to buy despite the overwhelming burden of debt" may be classified as compulsive consumers.[24] Some people, like Mr. Ward, are credit card "junkies" who use their cards to make themselves feel better. Said a woman habituated to consuming, "When I felt bad, I would shop. . . . I bought people gifts, never knowing that I was covering up, that I was trying to make my hurt feel better."[25] In Terry Galanoy's view, such people use their cards

> to get away from loveless, lonely households; to escape from nine-to-five tedium; to run away from dreary, cheerless lives—even for a little while. It felt good to be out among the spenders, to be able to walk right up to a counter and buy, to be accepted as 100% patriotic spend-for-the-economy's sake American. It was like drinking a double martini or absorbing the kind of coke that doesn't come in bottles.[26]

The analogies between debt and shopping addiction and addictions to alcohol and cocaine seem appropriate, especially in the case of Mr. Ward, who was a recovering alcoholic. One researcher contends that compulsive shopping "fits the addictive cycle, where you find that shopping relieves tension, so that the next time you feel anxious you go out and shop again. And because the shopping itself intensifies pressures, it feeds on itself."[27] Although compulsive spending existed before credit cards and exists among those who do not use credit cards, credit cards make the problem worse. According to one credit counselor, "We have a whole generation that has been brought up in a credit card society. They grew up with debt and use it freely."[28]

Individual consumers certainly bear some of the responsibility for their credit card indebtedness, but we can see the tendency to psychologize and medicalize the problem in popular analyses. According to this perspective, individuals get themselves into financial trouble because they are ill, because they suffer from such maladies as depression, compulsion, and addiction. However, although this perspective may explain the financial plight of some who spend their waking hours in the malls and, as a result, find themselves deeply in debt, it certainly does not explain a majority of the cases. What we need is a more sociological perspective on credit card debt.

Credit Card Companies

Sociologists tend to focus not on the consumer but on the role of organizations and institutions—namely, the credit card companies—in fostering rampant consumerism. (Although I will not deal with the issue here, some of the blame must also go to manufacturers and retailers for bombarding consumers with advertisements designed to entice them to purchase more than they need, as you saw in Chapter 1.) Credit card firms urge people to go deeply into debt, and they make it easy for people to do so. The companies make innumerable telephone calls and send out tons of mailings offering free cards, high credit limits, and low introductory interest rates. One man amassed 1,300 credit cards with a combined credit limit of $1.7 million to show how, once consumers get a card, they are inundated with offers for others.[29] The banks and other purveyors of credit cards are also constantly seeking new ways to lure people into increasing their indebtedness—for example, by charging their supermarket purchases. One consumer advocate said, "When the financially strapped start to use credit cards for essentials, it's a sign that they are about to go further into debt."[30]

Banks, in particular, have spent billions of dollars encouraging people to go deeply into debt on their credit cards. An industry expert said, "Banks are engaged in the indiscriminate issuance of credit cards. . . . It's the same as issuing money. . . . We have to have some control on them."[31] The banks are eager to distribute as many cards as possible because of the huge profits associated with the credit card business.

However, the reckless issuance of cards poses risks not only to consumers but also to the banks. In tough economic times, more consumers are forced to declare personal bankruptcy and default on their debts. Secured loans for houses and cars are likely to be paid, but unsecured credit card loans are the last and least likely debts to be paid. Between the first quarters of 1990 and 1991, credit card delinquency rates increased from 3.3% to 4.6%.[32]

Yet the credit card companies continue to market their wares aggressively. In the early 1990s, faced with declining applications for credit cards and slow growth in credit card spending, they urged their existing cardholders to use credit cards more often for cash advances. For that service, the banks generally charge a fee, and more important, interest usually begins accruing the day the money is withdrawn. During the early 1990s, for the first time in its history, MasterCard began running television advertisements to tout the simplicity and convenience of using its cards to get cash advances at ATM machines. To take credit card business away from competing banks, one San Francisco bank was paying a $50 "bonus" to anyone who took out $700 on a new card to settle other credit card debts. At the moment, cash advances represent only 1% of all credit card transactions, but in the 1990s they are projected to grow more than twice as fast as all other credit transactions.[33]

Characteristically, and despite the fact that they have been at least partly responsible for the growth in cash advances, the banks are worried about the dangers they themselves face. However, they show little concern about the dangers to consumers of high-interest cash advances. Readily available cash advances seem to encourage rash expenditures (for example, a day at the racetrack), which leave little or nothing to show for consumers' spending when the bills arrive. In an ordinary charge transaction, a consumer usually receives tangible goods or useful services in return.

Some people have routinely fallen into the trap of using cash advances to pay off debts on other credit cards. Said one user, who described herself as "living on plastic," "I would keep rotating them, making payments without income. It's a magical way of thinking you'll catch up."[34] But instead of catching up, this woman found herself $20,000 in debt.

There is great variation in the costs of a cash advance. In 1990, on a cash advance of $400, interest and fees could range between $3.96 and $24.96 a month.[35] At the high end, if not the low end as well, the consumer is paying a usurious interest rate. However, it should be said that people who have no alternative but to remain in debt to the credit card companies are better off taking a cash advance from the company with the lowest interest rate in order to pay off the others. Bankcard Holders of America says that switching from the highest-rate to the lowest-rate card, could save as much as $800 or $900 a year on the average credit card balance.[36] Unfortunately, some people no sooner switch than they begin again to run up debt on the higher-rate cards, especially if they have reached their credit limit on the low-interest card.

Particularly reprehensible are the efforts (discussed in Chapter 1) of credit card firms to get college and even high school students accustomed to buying with plastic. The editor of *Credit Card News* noted that the attention devoted by credit card companies to college students has "increased dramatically over the last five years. . . . They're hoping to establish students as customers, when the students are at a stage of forming brand loyalties."[37] More generally, the credit card companies are seeking to lure students into a lifetime of imprudence and indebtedness.

How to Overcome the Temptation to Imprudence

You have now read quite a bit about the tendency of the credit card industry to lead people into fiscal irresponsibility. People are not helpless victims, however. They have ways of coping with this problem.

Before they can take steps to deal with credit card abuse, people must accept the fact that their credit card debt is a personal trouble. They must overcome the common tendency to deny the existence of any difficulty; they must admit to themselves and to others that they are too deeply in debt to the credit card companies for their own good.

Be Aware of the Danger Signs

These are the danger signs that a person may be abusing credit cards:

- *Making only the minimum payments on credit card debt.* Such payments are unlikely to cut into the principal owed and may not even cover the monthly interest costs. By making only minimum payments, people virtually guarantee that their level of debt and interest payments will grow from month to month.

- *Getting cash advances on credit cards to pay off other liabilities.* This practice indicates that people are not able to handle their current level of debt on their present income. In addition, in spite of excessive debt, and perhaps because of it, they are taking on more debt.

- *Buying groceries on credit.* Most experts regard going into debt for everyday necessities like groceries as a sign that current income cannot support the person's lifestyle. Charging groceries might also encourage frivolous spending by freeing up cash that otherwise might have been used for everyday needs.

- *Having no money left after paying the month's bills, including credit card bills.* When people are living beyond their means they might be driven to get cash advances on their credit cards in order to survive until the next payday.

- *Going shopping—particularly on credit— because one is bored or depressed.* Going into debt to replace a worn-out pair of shoes is one thing, but going into debt to relieve boredom or depression is quite another.

- *Regularly requesting higher credit card limits.* This practice is a clear indication that one is too accustomed to debt and unable to make a dent in existing obligations, let alone the new higher level of debt.

- *Seeking a debt consolidation loan.* This is another clear indication of debt habituation. People often end up consolidating several credit card liabilities with such a loan and then proceed to begin again to accumulate credit card debt. They soon find themselves making payments on both the debt consolidation loan and on several credit card accounts.

♦ *If credit cards have been "maxed out," drawing repeatedly on a home equity line of credit.* People in this circumstance may also find themselves burdened with several different interest payments each month.

♦ *Not opening letters from credit card companies.* Such a person is not only in debt, but also hiding from that fact.

♦ *Having wages garnished.* When a person has gone far over his or her credit limit, the law steps in and develops a system to repay debts. Money is routinely drawn from the person's wages before what is left is passed on to the individual.[38]

Any of these danger signs indicates that the person should immediately take steps to curb the problem.

Stop Credit Card Abuse

Awareness of the danger signs is a necessary first step, but awareness is useless unless some action follows. One type of action involves not doing the things that lead to the danger signs. For example, pay as much as possible each month on credit card bills, never shop for groceries on credit, keep credit card limits low, and open and pay the bills. Above all, of course, do not run up credit card debts that cannot be repaid comfortably.

Here are some other practical steps that people can take to deal with credit card debt (and debt more generally):

♦ Try to avoid declaring personal bankruptcy as a solution to insurmountable credit card debt. People who do so tend to start accumulating new credit card debt almost immediately. Furthermore, bankruptcy carries a stigma that is likely to have an enduring adverse effect.

♦ Avoid trying to go "cold turkey" and swearing off credit card debt forever. Most of those accustomed to credit card debt are better advised to "take it one day at a time," doing their best to avoid any new debt, but accepting the occasional responsible use of a credit card.

♦ Recognize that it is impossible to get out of debt by borrowing more money, especially by taking cash advances on one card to pay debts on another.

- Recognize that many others have gotten out of debt and that you can do it too. You might even emulate those who have successfully extricated themselves from credit card debt.

- Create a spending record, and religiously make entries in it. Many people get themselves into trouble simply because they have little or no idea where their money goes.

- Cut up those credit cards and start over. This is the ultimate step.[39]

Although cutting up credit cards is an obvious solution for credit card abusers, even the severest critics recognize that few people are going to go so far. Too many powerful organizations earn too much money from credit cards and have too much invested in the associated technologies not to do all they can to prevent the mass destruction of plastic. More important, credit cards are simply too useful to be eliminated, too integral a part of our highly mobile society.

People who have been forced by adverse economic circumstances to give up their credit cards have reported all sorts of problems. One 41-year-old woman recounted feeling like a "nonperson" after giving up her cards. Among her other problems were these:

> I had to take my boss with me to the rental car office so that I could use her card. . . . Another time I tried to reserve a hotel room and ended up having to write them a letter and send a check for a one-night deposit, then wait 10 days to see if the check cleared. . . . I'd been doing business with this one small boutique for five years, and when I didn't have credit cards they refused to take my checks.[40]

However, some positive things did emerge from this experience: "It was rougher wondering if something was in my budget. If it wasn't, I just figured it wasn't meant to be." Once she got her cards back, she said, "I realize now it's a privilege."

Despite the kinds of problems this woman encountered, we can learn to live without credit cards; we do not need them in order to survive in the modern world. Jerrold Mundis argues that many of the specific reasons that people offer for needing credit cards turn out not to be true. For example, it is possible to use a driver's license rather than a credit card for identification. It is also possible to make telephone purchases on a COD (cash on delivery) basis, to rent a car without a credit card, and to handle business expenses with cash, check, or company credit card. About the fear of carrying cash as a reason for having credit cards, Mundis says, "How many times have you or any of your close friends been robbed? How many times have you lost your wallet?" As to the idea that we need credit cards for emergencies, Mundis says, "What emergencies? Nuclear attack? Riot and civil disorder?. . . . I've never had a single emergency in which a credit card could have done more for me than cash did, or a check or telephone call."[41]

The one exception to a cardless existence that Mundis is willing to permit, and that only cautiously, is the American Express card (and others like it)—which is, of course, a charge card, not a credit card. Nonetheless, it is possible to run up huge bills quite quickly with a charge card. Mundis suggests a five-step approach to surviving with an American Express card:

- Keep the card in your drawer and put it in your wallet only when you are going to use it.
- When you do put it in your wallet, know exactly what it is to be used for.
- Use the card only for that purpose.
- Put the card back in your drawer as soon as you return home.
- Write a check immediately for the amount of the purchase, and deduct it without delay from your balance.

Unfortunately, most suggestions for solving credit card problems put the burden on individual consumers. As Terry Galanoy says, "The bankers didn't do it. You and your friends did it. . . . You and your friends can undo it, too."[42] Thus, for example, he suggests that we restrict ourselves to one credit card of each type, that we accept sensible, practical limits on each card, and that we voluntarily restrict our use of credit cards. Doing so is, in a way, a blow against the exploitation of consumers:

> Vote against more debt, more invasion of privacy, more inflation, more dis-crediting of citizens, more theft and fraud, more unstable financial policies, more high interest, more bank profits, more rapid use of our scarce natural resources.[43]

In blaming the users of credit cards and suggesting various methods by which they ought to mend their ways, previous analysts have tended to let the credit card companies off the hook for their role in creating and sustaining high levels of credit card debt. In one particularly blatant example, a journalist says: "Credit cards don't cause the problem [overspending]; people who can't control overuse of them are the culprits."[44]

Reduce the Costs of Credit Card Debt

Those who are unable to restrict their credit card use or to stop using credit cards altogether can still take some steps to lower the costs associated with credit card use.[45] Here are some suggestions:

- Pay your credit card bill in full each month. Those who do not revolve their accounts are being given free credit by the card companies. They are being subsidized by those who do revolve their accounts and therefore pay exorbitant interest rates. It is better to receive such a subsidy than to do the subsidizing.

- If you revolve your account, pay your bill as soon after you receive it as possible to reduce the average daily balance which is used to calculate interest charges.

- If possible, pay more than the minimum due.

- Avoid exceeding your credit limit.

- Avoid being late with payments and having to pay the attendant late fees.

- Avoid cash advances. Because interest begins accruing from the moment the cash is taken, cash advances usually end up carrying stiffer interest charges than other types of credit card transactions.

- If it is not possible to pay the credit card bill in full each month, shop for the card with the lowest rates and fees. Said one cardholder who switched to a card with a lower rate, "If you have to pay interest, it makes sense to pay as little as possible."[46]

These steps may seem easy, but many people encounter difficulties in taking them. For example, cardholders who are deeply in debt would seem likely to switch to cards with lower interest rates; 55% of those sampled in a Gallup poll said they would indeed switch cards for a two-percentage-point cut in rates.[47] However, a 1991 survey found that only a fifth of those polled had taken the trouble to seek lower-rate cards in the preceding six months. A similar percentage switched when mailed an offer for a lower-rate card.[48] Said one credit card consultant, "Consumer sensitivity to interest rates was virtually nonexistent."[49]

Why did most people not switch cards when a lower rate was available? One explanation is that many people who revolve their accounts perceive themselves to be convenience users who pay off their balances each month. Because of this misperception, they do not feel the need to change cards. Second, some people continually plan to pay off their debt at the end of the month, only to fail to do so time after time. Third, some people do not plan to charge very much on their cards, although the evidence is that they regularly exceed their expectations. A fourth factor is that cardholders seem to prefer to have their cards with a well-known bank (say Citibank) and are willing to pay a higher rate in exchange for the "brand-name" credit card. Such "prestige" issuers are also likely to have more branches and to be more convenient to use. A fifth factor is that cardholders tend to be loyal to the issuer of their first card and do not switch even if a competitor offers a lower rate. Sixth, cardholders also are loyal to affinity cards, to cards that offer enhancements like buyer-protection plans, and to co-branded cards that offer rebates. Finally, although the situation seems to be improving, many people do not know the interest rates on their credit cards. In one Florida Gallup poll, 30% of respondents either did not know their interest rate or refused to say whether or not they knew it.[50]

However, in the past few years, more people seem to have become sensitive to high credit card rates. Many credit card companies are responding by lowering their rates, at least to their best customers. Thus, in 1990 almost 70% of credit card debt carried interest rates of 18% or higher, but by 1992 only 43% of that debt was at 18% or above; during the same period, the percentage of loans at rates of 16.5% or less had increased from 9% to 39%.[51] Unfortunately, with lower rates, banks grow more selective, and so many who apply for low-interest cards are likely to be rejected.[52] Of course, it is the poor who are most likely to be turned down for low-interest cards. Nevertheless, despite the banks' greater selectivity, the trend toward switching to cards with lower interest rates seems likely to continue, or even accelerate, in the near future.

Why the sudden awakening of long-slumbering consumers? First, the persistent recession of the early 1990s made people increasingly cost conscious. Second, escalating debate over high interest rates has increased public awareness of the issue. Third, the low interest rates available on other kinds of loans in the early 1990s (for example, mortgage and home equity loans) made credit card interest rates seem more outrageous than ever. The fourth factor is the competition banks are encountering from new entrants into the credit card business, such as General Motors and AT&T. Fifth, the credit card companies themselves have spurred competitive battles by trying to attract cardholders away from other companies with offers of lower interest rates.

Even with lower interest rates, sensible cardholders are using the credit card companies rather than being used by them. They are paying off their credit card debt each month and thus getting free credit—up to 25 days' worth or more—from their credit card companies. The card companies actually lose money on such consumers. However, many people are unable or unwilling to pay off their high-interest credit card debt each month; many can do little more than pay the interest, leaving the principal intact and accruing interest month after month. Some are beginning to understand the folly of such habits and are reducing or eliminating their credit card debt. For example, an Arlington, Virginia, couple cashed in a certificate of deposit, virtually wiping out their savings, in order to pay off their debts. Now in their mid 30s, the couple contrasted their present strategy to the one they practiced in the past: "When we were in our 20s we were more into just charge it . . . the credit-card mentality."[53]

Getting Outside Help

People who come to recognize that they have a problem with credit card debt may find that they cannot take adequate action on their own. They may conclude that they need help in coping with their problem, from, for example, one of the several hundred nonprofit consumer credit counseling centers throughout the United States. Credit counselors offer advice on budgeting and cost cutting. They may even see that the money left over after all necessities have been paid for is divided equitably among creditors. The office manager for one of these counseling services said,

> We tell [creditors] this is what is left, and they accept it. . . . The individual debtor has a difficult time getting that relationship with creditors. . . . The creditors like it. We are an excellent alternative to bankruptcy. . . . By cooperating with us, the creditors also have a better-educated potential customer again.[54]

Banks themselves are interested in counseling customers. Predictably, however, their interest is not in helping people avoid debt but rather in preventing customers from filing for bankruptcy and thereby making it difficult or impossible for the banks to collect their money. Of course, self-interested bankers claim that they are doing it all for the customer: "It's a crying shame, because they've ruined their whole future over something as small as that. We live in a society where credit is absolutely necessary."[55]

A more altruistic option for those who abuse credit cards are the self-help groups, such as local groups like SpenderMender in San Francisco and Shopaholics Anonymous in Brooklyn, New York, and national groups like Overspenders Anonymous and Debtors Anonymous (the largest).[56]

Overspenders Anonymous (O$A) was founded in 1979 by a self-confessed "spendaholic," Jeanne Fioretto. In fact, it is Fioretto who is quoted earlier in this chapter about her compulsion to shop. Realizing her spending problem and not willing or able to deal with it on her own, she decided to form an organization for overspenders modeled after Alcoholics Anonymous and Overeaters Anonymous. O$A groups meet periodically to discuss spending problems; sometimes guest speakers are invited. The key, however, is the network of people associated with each group. "Shopping buddies" and telephone teams help people avoid overspending. Members may bring nonessential purchases to meetings to be discussed and assessed by the group. O$A has developed twelve steps for the control of compulsive overspending:

1. Identify your problem.
2. Build a support network. Have friends, relatives or an O$A group help talk you out of unnecessary purchases and share your successes in resisting temptation.

3. Assess current debts and income and build a workable budget for paying off debts. (Do not continue to increase debts.)

4. Approach your creditors to negotiate payment plans you can fit into the budget you've built.

5. Use your support network to help you change your shopping/buying behavior.

6. Set up realistic financial goals and a timetable for meeting them.

7. Keep track of your progress: share your successes. Do what you can to stop backsliding, but don't dwell on it.

8. Pay off all outstanding credit card debts.

9. Set up new guidelines for responsible credit use.

10. Begin saving money for your financial goals.

11. Reward yourself for accomplishments (*not* by spending money).

12. Check your financial status on a regular basis and adjust any backsliding. Set new financial goals as you accomplish the old ones. And—now that you know the way—help someone else you know who is a chronic overspender.[57]

Debtors Anonymous was founded in 1976 and now has chapters throughout the United States and a number of foreign countries. Each chapter functions independently of the others; there are no dues or fees. Needed funds come from contributions by members. The goals of each member are to try to get out of debt, to stay out, and to help other members do the same. At each meeting one member is the principal speaker. For example, one participant began, "Hi, I'm Nora, a compulsive debtor and spender. . . . I just came back from the first vacation of my life that I didn't have to put on plastic."[58] The other participants support the main speaker and discuss their own experiences with debt and efforts to control it.

A different type of help is offered by the nonprofit National Foundation of Consumer Credit, which has 700 offices nationwide. It offers budget counseling and helps people consolidate credit card debts and create a plan to repay those debts. Its national referral telephone number is 1-800-388-2227.

These organizations do help, but the fundamental problem, especially with those modeled after Alcoholics Anonymous, is that they try to change the victim instead of the main source of the problem—the credit card industry. These organizations tend to psychologize and medicalize the problem of excessively high credit card debt. There may be some merit to considering alcoholism a disease, but it stretches credulity to consider indebtedness to credit card companies a disease.

What Government Can Do

On a more macroscopic level, the government can and must do more to stop many of the abuses in the credit card industry. For example, columnist Michael Schrage has an interesting suggestion: a "sin tax" of 2% on credit and charge card purchases. This tax would not only raise substantial revenue for the government but would also help restrict credit card expenditures and debt. A former undersecretary of the U.S. Treasury Department liked the idea: "It appeals to me on the basis that credit-card borrowing is really rather a free-for-all. . . . I come very reluctantly to the conclusion that government has a role to play when self-discipline doesn't work. This area needs some discipline." Even an industry analyst conceded that, "It's not a bad idea at all."[59] Unfortunately, should such a tax be enacted, it is consumers, not the credit card companies, who will be forced to pay it. This plan implicitly accepts the idea that the consumer bears most of the responsibility for the problem.

Yet the government can do various things to restrain credit card companies. For example, Galanoy suggests limitations on the profits from credit cards. Another possibility would be to restrict mail and telephone campaigns offering various inducements to accept new credit cards. There is an analogy here with smoking. The government finally banned certain types of cigarette advertisements to stop the tobacco companies from luring people into the smoking habit. Similarly, if the credit card companies cannot act responsibly, then the government should restrain their marketing efforts. Just as smoking harms people's physical health, excessive credit card debt harms their financial health.

What the Credit Card Industry Could Do

One of the contributions of a sociological perspective is to show us that large-scale institutions like the credit card industry are a major source of the problem of excessive credit card debt, and they must be reformed. The credit card companies need to put some restraints on themselves as well as on customers who abuse credit cards. However, it is unlikely that the credit card industry will take serious steps to deal with the problem. For one thing, consumers who accumulate credit card debt are by far the most profitable. For another, because of the highly competitive nature of the industry today, one credit card firm will exploit this group of consumers if another does not. Finally, the history of capitalism has few examples of industries exhibiting self-control when profits are at stake.

Nevertheless, the credit card industry could take several steps, if it were so inclined, to ameliorate the problem of consumer debt:

- Limit the number of any one type of card that an individual can hold. For example, Visa might consider a policy that no person may hold more than one of its credit cards.

- Coordinate offers and acceptances of new cards so people cannot easily acquire large numbers of cards.

- Coordinate credit limits on all cards in the possession of an individual so that it is impossible to run up a total debt far beyond the individual's ability to pay.

- Cease immediately the escalating efforts to recruit high school, and perhaps even college, students.

- Cease immediately the efforts to induce people to purchase essentials like food with their credit cards.

- Make it even clearer that all money borrowed and all interest accrued must eventually be paid.

Some in the industry have acknowledged their responsibility. Said one bank vice president: "I've seen customers who've had as many as 13 Visas and MasterCards. . . . Banks are guilty in that they make credit too easily available."[60] Although most observers seem to blame credit card users for excessive consumption and out-of-control credit card debt, at least one psychologist also blames larger forces: "My view overall is that the credit industry and the media and the advertising have gotten so out of control with more and more malls and credit cards . . . that it is harder for people to remain in control of their impulses."[61] Sociologists too place the bulk of the blame on the credit card industry and other key players in our consumption-oriented society.

4

Credit Card Fraud

Screw You, Mac—I Got Mine[1]

The point of departure for this chapter is Georg Simmel's argument that the money economy is a "fully compliant instrument for the meanest machinations."[2] Money in its currency form makes all sorts of unethical and criminal acts easier and more likely than they were with earlier forms of value exchange. Simmel noted, "Persons who are otherwise honest may participate in deceitful 'promotions,' and many people are likely to behave more unconscientiously and with more dubious ethics in money matters than elsewhere."[3] For example, bribes are easier and more secret in a cash form than they are in the form of, say, a herd of cattle. Slipping an assassin an envelope stuffed with cash is simpler and easier to hide than shipping a load of timber as payment for the dastardly deed. Cash payments leave no physical traces, but payments with cattle or timber are likely to be visible to many people and to leave physical signs that can be easily traced.

One issue implied in Simmel's position is that there is a historical progression in mean machinations corresponding to developments in the form of money. But are even meaner machinations more likely with credit cards than they are with currency? The answer is no. Because the use of credit cards leaves an electronic and paper trail, many of the meanest machinations are less likely to occur.[4] Drug deals, contract murders, and assassinations are more likely to be done on a cash basis than they are to be charged to Visa or MasterCard. In his study *Reducing Crime by Eliminating Cash*, David Warwick puts the issue this way:

> The lack of any type of recording and the unrestricted negotiability of cash makes it the most detection free medium of exchange criminals can use. It makes cash their most desired commodity, their prime

target, and the epicenter of most crime. One only needs to read the familiar sign fixed to many delivery trucks, "Driver carries no cash," to realize the worst feature of cash: Simply possessing it puts one at risk of being robbed, of being assaulted, or worse.

The most frequent crimes committed in America consist of thefts of cash itself or of property to sell for cash. . . .

Theft of cash often involves more than mere loss of property. Every minute, coast to coast, Americans are assaulted and/or murdered for the cash they possess, no matter how small the sum. . . .

There is the *indirect* relationship of cash to crime to consider as well. Murder-for-hire, arson, kidnapping and bribery are all commonly committed for payment in cash. Billions of dollars worth of stolen goods are fenced for cash each year. We also know . . . that the estimated $300 billion-a-year narcotics trade in the United States is conducted in cash.[5]

As a result, Warwick suggests credit cards (as well as the various forms of electronic money) as a *solution* to cash-based crime.

What of the other CREDEBELS? On the one hand, debit cards and electronic funds transfers (EFTs) are also less likely to be used for mean machinations, because they too leave paper and electronic trails. On the other hand, they allow the transfer of almost unimaginable sums of money. Thus, although drug barons might not use credit cards to pay for their deals, they might use other EFTs to move millions of dollars into unnumbered Swiss or Grand Cayman bank accounts. This sort of transaction, however, is likely to be restricted to the big players in the drug business. The street hustlers are likely to continue to do cash business.

Another question derived from Simmel's position is whether CREDEBELS have made new types of mean machinations, ones that did not exist in a purely cash economy, possible. The answer to this question is yes. A series of new mean machinations have come into existence with the advent of CREDEBELS. In the rest of this chapter I deal with fraud, sometimes involving criminal activities, associated with credit cards. (In the Appendix, I touch on fraud and its relationship to the other CREDEBELS.) In short, then, although Simmelian theory is wrong in implying that the meanest machinations are more likely to involve CREDEBELS than money, the theory is useful in sensitizing us to the new forms of criminal, unethical, and immoral activities associated with CREDEBELS.

Fraud Against the Card Companies and Users

As one might expect, fraud perpetrated against the credit card companies gets most of the attention, although it involves relatively small amounts of money. This bias reflects the dominant position of the credit card firms and their concern with their own interests. The industry is also concerned with the impact of fraud perpetrated against its customers; however, this concern has less to do with the welfare of those customers than with the industry's well-being because such fraud has a negative impact on the industry as a whole. The loss to a consumer due to fraud is limited by law to $50, so such fraud is actually perpetrated against the credit card industry. There is little interest, even awareness, of fraudulent activities perpetrated by the industry and the fact that such activities cause personal troubles for credit card users.

A variety of frauds are perpetrated against credit card companies.[6] The problem has been growing, although there is some indication that growth has leveled off, at least for the time being. In 1984 the cost of fraud to Visa and MasterCard was $150 million, but by 1993 that figure had grown to nearly $666 million.[7] And the cost may be much higher—one source reports that the cost of fraud for the credit card industry as a whole was almost $4 billion in 1993.[8] (Of course, to the cost of fraud must be added the undoubtedly higher cost of combating fraud.) In any case, what is most striking about these numbers is the relatively small amount of money involved in fraudulent activities. There were about 266 million Visa and MasterCard credit cards in use in the United States in 1993; the cost of fraud comes to a little more than $2 per card per year. A surcharge of $2 or $3 per card per year would have paid for the cost of fraud to those credit card companies. As one consultant pointed out, "While fraud is a big problem, it's still a small percentage of the bank's [or, more generally, the credit card industry's] profits."[9] Nevertheless, fraud offers the credit card industry a convenient excuse for high fees and interest rates.

Stolen Cards

The largest single source of losses due to credit card fraud is stolen cards. Individuals may have cards stolen from them directly, but the vast majority of credit card thefts involve the postal system in one way or another. Of these, the most common type results from infiltration of, and robbery within, the post office. Other types of credit card theft involving the postal system include the looting of mailboxes (primarily in apartment buildings), attacks on and thefts from mail carriers, and hijackings from the largest post offices by well-organized groups.[10] Those who steal from the postal system are lured by the fact that on any given day 500,000 credit cards are in the mail. Of thefts involving the postal system, a Secret Service spokesperson said, "It's a constant problem that is worsening. . . . It's not like stealing a welfare check or Social Security check in the mail. This is a new form of fraud that yields big gains."[11]

In a number of cities, organized gangs have engaged in credit card theft. For example, one gang in Los Angeles stole cards and gave them to prostitutes, who immediately used those cards to run up large purchases.[12] The purchases were then fenced to provide the gang with money.

A loosely organized gang in the Washington, D.C., area absconded with up to $10 million in 1993 as a result of thefts of credit cards, checkbooks, and information that could be used to fraudulently obtain money.[13] Forty people, including nine postal workers, were arrested for the crimes. Victims had as much as $300,000 charged against their credit card accounts by the criminals (although, of course, the credit card companies absorbed the losses).

An increase in the questionable use of credit cards at gasoline stations may be linked to credit card theft. With in-pump terminals, consumers can use credit cards without having any contact with clerks. The terminals seem to have an unusually high incidence of so-called "ghost transactions," in which authorization is given for a credit card transaction but none follows. It may be that many of these ghost transactions involve crooks testing out stolen cards on in-pump terminals before using them in places where the thieves may need to deal with clerks face to face. According to one corporate executive, "If you have a hot card and you know it's hot, the question is if it's been stopped or not. . . . So you go buy some gasoline, and if the card is O.K., you can go and buy something else."[14]

Stolen Credit Information

Even though a credit card remains safely in one's possession, fraud may still occur. For example, credit card numbers can be stolen by thieves rummaging through garbage for discarded credit card receipts; by dishonest store clerks, hotel receptionists, or airline employees who make duplicate imprints of a customer's card; and by people who telephone "marks" to say that they have won a trip and to ask for a credit card account number for "verification" purposes.[15] Another possibility is the submission by merchants of false or altered receipts to the credit card firms for payment. There have also been cases of computer hackers breaking into credit card files and either creating accounts or making charges on other people's accounts.[16]

The Washington, D.C., thieves mentioned earlier used information gleaned from stolen mail to call banks and fraudulently obtain personal identification numbers for ATM machines. In other instances, claiming to be bank employees, they called victims in an effort to verify information that could then be used to pilfer more funds. Said a U.S. postal inspector of such machinations:

> It is sophisticated in that they do not hit someone over the head, take the money and run. . . . They have to talk to banks and convince them that it is their account, and in other cases they call the victims and tell them they are the bank.[17]

The practice employed in many stores of writing credit card numbers on checks as protection against bad checks leaves people open to yet another kind of fraud. Those who are able to obtain a copy of that check will have a name, address, phone number and credit card number. With such information, a criminal could easily open a charge account at a department store in the name of the person who wrote the check. Several states now have legislation that prohibits the practice of asking those who pay by check for a credit card number. Interestingly, there is no justification for writing credit card numbers on checks, because Visa and MasterCard will not allow stores to charge credit card accounts for the cost of purchases made with checks that ultimately bounce.[18]

Another way to steal credit information involves computer theft from the database of a credit-reporting agency. In one case, in a few minutes a thief purloined a great deal of information about one individual, including "past addresses and employers, Social Security number, credit card numbers, mortgage information, bank accounts and all of the other personal data that appear on credit reports for . . . 160 million . . . Americans."[19] With that information, the credit thief was able to open nearly 30 different kinds of accounts and charge almost $100,000 in transactions. In this case, the thief

had virtually the same name as the victim and was able to access the
victim's account simply by using his address.

People who use phone cards, especially at public locations like
airports and train stations, are particularly vulnerable to fraud. Said
an MCI executive, "Most of the fraud is over-the-shoulder, with
people using video cameras and binoculars to see the card number
and how you punch it in."[20] Eavesdropping by so-called "shoulder
surfers," especially if the caller is using a rotary phone and is forced
to give card numbers verbally, is another source for credit card
thieves. One victim of a shoulder surfer at New York's Pennsylvania
Station had $533.94 illegally charged against her card number by
the next day. Illegal charges like these are usually forgiven by the
long-distance telephone companies, but consumers in general must
ultimately foot the bill in terms of higher fees and interest rates.
And it is a large bill. Fraud against the long-distance telephone
companies is much more costly ($1.2 billion a year) than fraud
against credit card companies.*

Counterfeit and Altered Cards

Counterfeiting generally involves the unauthorized manufacture of
credit cards. Hong Kong is believed to be the current center of
such counterfeiting.[21] Counterfeiters may also heat stolen cards to
flatten the names and account numbers and then re-emboss them.
Credit cards may also be altered by shaving off, rearranging, and
gluing numbers or letters back onto a card or by altering the signature strip.[22] Or counterfeiters may replicate the hologram, the
three-dimensional laser-created image that appears on the face of
many credit cards. Holograms were introduced in 1985 by Visa
and MasterCard to reduce fraud, and they had some initial success
in reducing the danger posed by counterfeiting. However, the
counterfeiters soon obtained their own lasers and began copying
the holograms.

A related type of fraud is "skimming," or alteration, of the strip
of magnetic tape on the back of the cards. The use of magnetic
tape is traceable to the late 1960s, but its utilization exploded in
the 1980s after it was adopted by the major American credit cards.
In skimming, encoded data are transferred from a genuine strip of

---

*Of course, the distinction between credit cards and calling cards is not clear-cut. For ex-
ample, AT&T's credit cards double as calling cards.

magnetic tape to a fraudulent one. In one case, a 19-year-old student used skills learned in a computer class to illegally encode cards. He linked a $600 encoder he had purchased at a local computer store to his computer by modem. The student used some of the fraudulent cards himself, and he sold others for as much as $400 each. Said a U.S. Secret Service agent, "This 19-year-old kid—it's a normal run-of-the-mill case. . . . There is no big deal about it. It just takes someone with a little bit of computer knowledge and you can re-encode anything you want."[23] One Los Angeles detective observed that some of his colleagues "believe that re-encoding credit cards is going to be the savings and loan debacle of the '90s."[24]

Merchants may sometimes act in collusion with those who produce altered cards. For example, merchants may knowingly accept an altered card before it appears on the merchant warning bulletin or "hot card" file. In one case, a merchant in collusion with those involved in card alteration cost a bank several million dollars.[25]

Fraudulent Credit Card Applications

Fraudulent applications occur when falsified information leads to the issuance of a credit card. For example, an applicant might use a false name, address, or income information to obtain a card. According to a Secret Service officer, "Fraudulent applications are the banking industry's biggest headache."[26]

In one example of application fraud, at least 44 people were defrauded out of a minimum of $285,000.[27] Fifteen salespeople at an auto dealership in New Jersey used the dealership's computer to examine a number of credit histories. To get this information, all they needed was a person's name, address, and ZIP code and the dealer's password. The salespeople then selected those most likely to be granted credit and applied for credit cards in their names. They requested that the cards be sent to false addresses. Once they had the cards, the salespeople took cash advances on the cards or used the blank checks that had been sent with the cards.

The Washington, D.C., crimes described earlier also involved fraudulent applications.[28] Over weeks or even months, the thieves repeatedly returned to targeted mailboxes in search of just-delivered credit cards or checkbooks. Sometimes they also stole "preapproved" credit card applications, which they filled out in the name of the victim. After mailing in an application, the thieves

would check the mailbox continually until the new card was delivered. A spending spree would follow with the stolen card. In some
cases, the thieves would even intercept the credit card bills as they
came in and pay them with checks that had also been stolen from
the victim's mailbox. In this way the crime could be carried on over
a period of months.

Abuses by Telemarketers

The credit card companies are particularly concerned about increasing fraud by telemarketing companies. Said a senior vice president of Visa, "Telemarketing fraud is a monster and it's growing."[29]
One example of such fraud involved a small publishing company
that hired a large number of telephone salespeople and paid them a
hefty commission as soon as a sale was completed. Many of these
salespeople fraudulently charged sales to credit card numbers they
had obtained from previous jobs. The result was thousands of dollars in fraudulent commissions. The salespeople left the publisher
before the customers received their bills. When the customers refused to pay for merchandise they had not ordered, the credit card
companies turned the bills into "chargebacks" (deductions of
money previously credited to a merchant's account) against the publishing company.[30] By the time the chargebacks were made, the
salespeople had long since departed.

In another example, a telemarketer ran commercials offering
low-cost credit cards. Those who telephoned a toll-free number
were bombarded with "high pressure, deceptive telephone sales
pitches."[31] Callers were told that they qualified automatically for a
low-cost card. However, the fee for each card ultimately ranged between $70 and $200; altogether, about $20 million was obtained in
this way. In return for their money, the consumers received nothing
more than either a credit card application or a list of banks offering
credit cards with low rates. Such lists can often be found in newspapers or obtained from consumer organizations for a few dollars.

In the most common form of telemarketing fraud, the telemarketers obtain the names and credit card numbers of cardholders.
They may then call the customers and interpret any expression of
interest during the telephone conversation as permission to charge
a purchase. In one case, representatives of a travel club called people
to offer them trial memberships. Those who did not hang up were
told that the club already had their credit card numbers and, for

"convenience," would simply charge the fees to their accounts. The slightest hint of interest led to charges. Said one consumer, "I was shocked because I had never heard of these people before. . . . They had my card number without my authorization, and that to me is like stealing."[32]

A variation of this type of fraudulent activity involves the "laundering" (or factoring) of drafts. For example, a legitimate credit card merchant submits illegitimate charge slips commingled with legitimate slips to the credit card firm on behalf of an illegitimate telemarketer. In return, the merchant gets a portion of the illegal gain—10% or more. This scam works because credit card companies are more likely to accept a charge when it does not come from a known illegitimate telemarketer. In this case, the credit card firms often end up absorbing the chargebacks when the telemarketers go out of business or simply disappear.[33]

In recent years, illegitimate telemarketers have grown increasingly sophisticated in their laundering techniques. One trend is to have the laundering done by foreign rather than domestic merchants. Foreign merchants are attractive because they are more likely to be naive about such scams and are out of the reach of American law. Also, consumers are at a disadvantage when unfamiliar charges from foreign merchants appear on their bills. According to the director of fraud for Visa U.S.A.,

> The distance involved and the language make it much more difficult for the consumer to understand why there is a $399 charge on his statement. . . . If you were able to call Oman and find that merchant, it would be very difficult to communicate.[34]

Another innovation is for telemarketers to use middlemen to approach merchants about laundering receipts, thereby making it more difficult to track down the culprits. In still another development, illegitimate telemarketers use a number of different merchants to launder charges, thereby making it harder for the sophisticated computer programs of the credit card companies to discover that anything out of the ordinary is occurring.

Fraudulent Credit "Repair"

Yet another kind of fraud is practiced by so-called "credit repair clinics," which offer, for fees ranging from $250 to $2,000, to obtain credit cards for people regardless of credit history. Similarly, so-called "credit doctors" are supposed to fix bad credit reports. The problem is that these "clinics" and "doctors" (note the medical imagery) cannot fix such problems, at least not legally.[35] Said a representative of one of the largest credit reporting bureaus, TRW,

> We feel [the credit-repair clinics] do a tremendous disservice to consumers. . . . They promise to clean up credit from a credit report, and that's against the law. No one can make that promise. Negative, accurate information cannot be taken off a report by anybody.[36]

Furthermore, credit repair clinics frequently charge exorbitant fees to do things consumers can easily do themselves—for example, merely obtaining a credit record or an application for a secured card.[37] Finally, such clinics often fail to deliver on promised services or go out of business and take the consumer's fees with them.[38]

Some credit repair clinics have urged their clients to engage in actions themselves that could easily be considered mean machinations. For example, clients are sometimes advised to dispute negative information on their records over and over, with the objective of overloading the system. Or clients may be told to acquire a completely new identity. Some credit doctors even steal the credit files of good risks and sell them to bad ones.

Mean Machinations by Card Companies

A number of the credit card industry's activities may be viewed, in Simmel's terms, as mean machinations—that is, fraudulent or questionable efforts designed to extract inordinate profits from the credit card business. Those extraordinary profits come from consumers' pockets, especially the pockets of the majority who revolve their accounts. As a result, some consumers suffer significant financial hardship. The fact that the credit card companies cause personal troubles for so many people means that their activities should be considered a public issue, in the same way that fraud against the industry is considered a public issue.

However, in spite of the comparatively small sums of money involved, the mass media have devoted much more attention to the various types of fraud perpetrated against the credit card companies than to the industry's questionable activities. This imbalance is to be expected for several reasons. First, the media are more likely to reflect the concerns of the credit card industry than those of the consumer, and the industry is very concerned about fraud that cuts into its profits or destroys its credibility. Second, the types of fraud perpetrated against the industry sometimes make interesting news. Third, the types of questionable activity engaged in by the credit card industry are rather dull as far as the general public is concerned.

With little or no media attention, the credit card firms have little motivation to reevaluate their activities. In fact, they are making huge profits from credit cards, which have long been considered "cash cows." Before the recent spate of reductions in some credit card interest rates, the returns on credit cards were five times higher than the benchmark in the banking industry for good profitability. Even now, with the credit card business more competitive and interest rates somewhat lower, profits from credit card operations are still triple those of other bank operations.[39]

Excessive Interest Rates and Fees

Why are the profits from credit cards so much higher than those from other types of banking activities? We can start with credit card interest rates. Although other interest rates plummeted during the 1980s, and fell even more dramatically in the early 1990s, credit card rates tended to defy the trend during that period. In fact, the average credit card rate was actually higher in 1991 than it was in 1981.[40] In September 1992 the federal funds rate, a good indicator of the rate banks pay to borrow money, was reduced to 3%, but the average credit card rate at that time was 18%. The banks knew they had an extraordinary situation. Said one bank analyst, "The card business is still a bonanza"; said another, "Nobody has done anything to kill the golden goose."[41]

In early 1994, with interest rates on savings accounts at historic lows, credit card rates remained extraordinarily high. Banks were able to borrow money at about 3%, and many still charged credit card customers 15% or 20%. U.S. Representative Frank Annunzio identified greed as the culprit: "Credit card rates are set at the ridiculous levels of 17, 18 and 19 percent by the cartel of credit card banks who care only about lining their own pockets."[42] Legislators tried to deal with the problem by proposing laws that would, for example, provide more rate information to consumers and cap interest rates. The Senate did pass a bill limiting credit card interest rates in late 1991, but it never became law.[43] Thus, most credit card firms continue to charge customers who revolve their accounts what many consider to be usurious interest rates.

Credit card fees are another factor in the industry's profits. Prior to 1980, credit cards did not carry an annual fee. Today, despite some highly publicized offers of credit cards without annual fees, most cards do charge them. The highly competitive nature of today's credit card business makes it possible for some, especially those with good credit ratings, to get those fees waived. Nonetheless, most people, even those who only occasionally use their cards, continue to pay annual fees. Consumer organizations are asking, "If the banks are charging an annual fee to cover their administrative costs, why are they also charging sky-high interest rates?"[44] It could be argued that in the case of those who revolve their accounts, the credit card firms are often guilty of "double dipping" and even "triple dipping"—earning money before the cards are ever used, with each payment of the annual fee, as well as whenever the cards are used, for as long as the consumer has the card.

Exploitive Billing Tactics

The credit card companies also engage in a variety of practices that in the end lead customers to pay a higher rate than the stated annual percentage rate (APR). In most cases, the credit card companies are not actively deceiving their customers; rather, as one advocate for credit card users said, "It's just that how these dollar figures are arrived at is the grand mystery of the credit card billing."[45] Describing a study of this matter, the director of Bankcard Holders of America said, "The complex maze of secret billing tactics and fees exposed in the study means that millions of consumers are paying effective [interest] rates of 30% or more."[46] Several extra fees and costs drive up actual interest rates:

- Late fees (usually $10 to $15) are imposed when consumers fail to make the minimum payment by the due date.
- Higher rates are imposed for cash advances, and grace periods are generally eliminated for cash advances.
- If interest is accruing on a balance and that balance is not paid in full, then in the next month interest is charged on the previous month's interest; in other words, interest is charged on interest

(compound interest). The net result is that a published rate of, say, 18 percent may turn out in reality to be 19.56 percent.[47]

There are substantial variations in the way credit card firms handle grace periods. For example, customers who pay their bills in full each month are usually granted a grace period (the interest-free period between purchase and payment), but those who revolve their accounts are routinely charged interest from the moment a new charge is made.* Variations in this practice are not readily apparent to consumers, but they can lead to enormous differences in the cost of credit.

Another mean machination engaged in by many credit card companies is the practice of declaring "payment holidays" and encouraging, even urging, "deserving" customers to skip one or two payments a year without penalty. Unwary consumers are led to feel that they are being offered something for nothing—an offer they cannot refuse. It is true that customers who take these holidays do not pay late charges and are not regarded as delinquent on their accounts, but they are likely to pay interest on the accruing principal and interest. Furthermore, they may not be granted the grace period on later charges because they have a continuing balance. As a result, interest will accrue on those charges from the moment they are posted to the account. On an account with a $200 balance and a $200 charge the following month, a payment holiday would lead to a real interest rate of 26.4% rather than the official rate of 18%.[48] A similar gambit—an offer by one's credit card company to lower the minimum payment—can also greatly increase the total amount of interest paid by extending the time that it takes to repay the debt.[49]

Credit card companies like their customers to make only the minimum payment. That minimum is usually set at 3% to 5% of the balance due, but a few firms are asking that as little as 2% of the total be paid each month. According to credit expert Gerri Detweiler, "A $2500 balance at 18.5 percent APR would take 30 years to pay off at a minimum payment of just 2 percent."[50] Clearly, minimum

*In late 1994 American Express came out with a new product, the Optima True Grace card, that gives those who revolve their accounts a grace period on new purchases. (See Jay Mathews. "American Express Unveils New Line of Credit Cards." *Washington Post*, September 7, 1994, pp. F1, F3.) In a full-page advertisement in the October 13, 1994, edition of the *New York Times*, American Express claimed that Visa's customers paid $1.5 billion in unnecessary interest in 1993 because Visa does not offer a true grace period.

payments put people in a position of what amounts to lifetime bondage to the credit card companies.

With credit card profit margins shrinking somewhat in the early 1990s (but still extraordinarily high in comparison to profits from similar types of business), there was a trend in the industry toward changing the way interest is charged in order to preserve profits. For example, those who revolve their accounts would be charged interest from the date of the transaction instead of, as is now the case, from the date the transaction is posted to one's account.[51] For the credit card company, this is an attractive way of raising revenue because it is largely invisible to most consumers, who pay little attention to such matters. More overt methods, such as raising interest rates are likely to prompt an outcry among cardholders, consumer groups, and some legislators. Charging from the date of the transaction is not only furtive but also questionable ethically, because merchants are not paid by the credit card company on the date the transaction takes place. Instead, payment is not likely to take place until many days later. It would seem fairer for credit card companies to charge interest from the day they reimburse the merchant, rather than from either the date of the transaction or the day of posting.

Yet another ploy practiced by some credit card firms is the use of "teaser rates" in mailings aimed at recruiting new customers. One credit card company boldly announced an annual interest rate of 5.9%, but the fine print whispered the truth: The rate would soon rise to the prime rate (6% at the time) plus 9.9%, or a total interest rate of 15.9%.[52] Many consumers do not read the fine print, however, so they often end up paying higher than expected interest rates.

One area in which the credit card companies are clearly earning inordinate sums is on secured credit cards. Taking advantage of customers who are desperate for credit, the card companies charge them higher interest rates, higher annual fees, and in some cases application fees—and the clients are paid little or no interest on the money that is being held as security against charges made on the card. Said one consultant, "Basically, you're lending someone back their own money and charging them a lot of money for it."[53] As we saw earlier, there have been some success stories with secured cards, but potential users must be wary of the potentially high costs involved. Such cards are especially likely to be a bad deal for those who are unable to use the secured cards as a springboard for the acquisition of regular cards.

Mean Machinations by Card Users

Are credit card users entirely innocent of mean machinations? No. Terry Galanoy points to rampant greed and selfishness among consumers:

> Our children are growing up, not with images of Benjamin Franklin's thrift, or Lincoln's walk to return extra change, but with memories of Mommy looting the department-store racks and Daddy buying enough ski gear to outfit the Austrian downhill team.
>
> Nobody, especially not the bankers, has suggested that maybe part of the tens of billions spent on luxuries every year should go into cleaning up our ghettos, cutting medical costs, purifying our air, developing mass transportation, and strengthening our educational system. . . .
>
> The unofficial but legendary Marine Corps motto has come true. Screw you, Mac. I got mine.[54]

Beyond general greed, some consumers have responded to the meanness of the credit card system with fraudulent activities of their own. For example, in a scam uncovered in California, debt-ridden people coped with their inability to legally obtain credit cards by taking phony identities. One credit clinic charged $1,500 to give a customer a new name, driver's license, and Social Security number.[55] With a new name and a new identity, a person pretending to be a first-time credit card applicant is once again able to qualify for a credit card. Another relatively common type of credit card fraud is to claim personal bankruptcy falsely in order to relieve oneself of burdensome credit card (and other) debt.

Individuals must take blame for their own greed and fraudulent activities, but we should not lose sight of the fact that the credit card industry has played a key role in creating the context for such actions. The credit card companies, along with other elements of the capitalist system, have fostered our consumer society and the sometimes insatiable desire for goods and services. And it is the credit card industry, along with the economy of which it is part, that has made it increasingly difficult for people to survive without credit cards. We should not be too surprised when desperate people go to desperate lengths.

Weapons Against Credit Card Fraud

Most of the existing weapons against fraud protect the credit card industry and the merchants that accept credit cards. However, there are many ways consumers can protect themselves, as well as ways government and the credit card industry can minimize abuses of card users.

Protecting Credit Card Firms and Merchants

Credit card firms and the invaluable merchants that accept their cards have several means of defense against fraud, among them the following:[56]

- *Possession of the card by the consumer.* It is highly unlikely that a person presenting a credit card is unauthorized to do so. Possession of the card offers more security than, say, the mere presentation of the correct credit card number.

- *A signed card.* The signature on the back of the card allows the merchant to match it with the signature on the charge form. However, it is relatively simple to forge a person's signature; about a tenth of all cards are unsigned; and merchants seldom match signatures, and, when they do, it is rarely in more than a cursory manner. In any case, merchants and their clerks are unlikely to be qualified to distinguish valid from invalid signatures. However, MasterCard has created a new system for preventing forgery of signatures. The new signature panels make forgery very difficult and will discolor if tampered with.[57]

- *Identification numbers.* Personal identification numbers (PINs) are assigned to individuals and are supposed to be known only to them. PINs are common with ATM and debit cards but have not been widely used with credit cards. Alarmed by the rise in credit card fraud, the industry seems poised to adopt them. However, PINs cannot be totally safe. PINs can always fall into the hands of those who are not supposed to have them. For example, in a sweepstakes promotion, New York Telephone (Nynex) mailed to its cardholders 3 million replicas of calling cards, which included the genuine PINs. Anyone who intercepted one of the letters would have then had access to a valid PIN.[58] Moreover, if credit card PINs become universal, merchants will be required to obtain yet another expensive technology—PIN pads. And consumers may resist adding another PIN to those they are already likely to have with ATMs and, perhaps, debit cards.[59] But if the costs of credit card fraud continue to mount, we can expect to see the card companies press hard to overcome this opposition. After all, it is the card users who will have to memorize yet another PIN, and the cost can be passed on to consumers in the form of higher fees or interest rates.

- *User's photograph on the face of the card.*[60] This is part of an effort to send merchants a computer image of a cardholder, so the merchant will be able to compare the computer image to the face across the counter. One bank hopes to have this system operating early in 2000.[61] However, there are several problems with the use of photographs and computer images for security purposes. First, such images quickly become dated. Second, merchants and their clerks may not bother to compare the photos with the customers. Third, even when they bother to check, the verification of the fact that the image matches the card user's face is highly subjective. Finally, and most importantly, even if the use of photos and computer images may help in reducing fraud, they pose a serious threat to privacy, thereby exacerbating another of the problems associated with credit cards (see Chapter 5). Again, however, this last problem is of little concern to the credit card industry.

- *Encrypted code.* Visa has developed a system to deal with the problem of altered magnetic strips. Visa card issuers encrypt a numeric code in each card's strip. When a transaction is made, that numeric code is transmitted to the issuing bank for verification. If the number is different from the number on file or is nonexistent, the transaction is denied.[62]

- *Encoded physical information.* Examples include fingerprints, a palm print, a voice print, eye prints, hand geometry, and so on. Although the encoding of biometric data is expensive, it is regarded by experts as the only sure way to deal with the problem of credit card fraud. Unfortunately, it also represents a greater threat to privacy than other technologies do.

♦ *"Smart" card.* All the biometric information mentioned above, as well as other information (for example, signature information), can be encoded on smart cards in their powerful computer chips. Smart cards offer several advantages. For example, it is almost impossible to counterfeit the computer chip, and smart cards keep people from exceeding their credit limits, because those limits are encoded on the cards and purchases are recorded instantaneously. Said a representative of MasterCard, "On the economics alone, in its ability to drastically reduce fraud and credit losses, the technology can be justified."[63] Of course, this representative is characteristically unconcerned about the threats to the privacy of consumers should these cards fall into the wrong hands. In spite of the perceived utility of smart cards, they are not as yet in wide use.

♦ *Issuers Clearinghouse Service.* This service matches the names, addresses, and Social Security numbers of credit card applicants with those in the vast databases to which it has access. Often, criminals use the "correct" name and Social Security number but use a different address, so that they, rather than the "applicant," will receive the card. The clearinghouse is set up to spot such discrepancies and prevent the attendant fraud.[64]

♦ *Computerized system for detecting fraud.* Visa has developed its Central Deposit Monitoring program to monitor merchants' accounts on a daily basis (most banks now monitor weekly or biweekly) and, on occasion, to catch a crooked merchant within 24 hours of depositing illegal sales slips. The Visa system detects laundering by checking not only for larger-than-usual transactions but also for accounts in which the same value appears repeatedly.[65] Another computerized system looks at merchants' accounts for suspicious transactions or an above-average number of transactions. For example, this system discovered that credit card transactions at a dental clinic had increased from 12 to 3,500 a month. An investigation found that fake sales drafts were being processed by the clinic.[66] Still other computerized programs have been developed to identify fraudulent credit card applications. They are useful in spotting such things as an unusual number of applications made under one name.[67] One new system soon to be deployed relies on "neural networks," so named because they operate like the human brain, learning to detect patterns in data that they can then apply to new information. Here is the way a neural network works:

> Neural nets rapidly sift through dozens of pieces of data to find patterns that often escape human observation. Card issuers feed into the network information about individual accounts and their entire card base so that the net learns to identify those variables that tend to indicate fraud, and assign weights to them. Using the data, the net calculates a score to show fraud risk, for instance, when a card usually used for small retail purchases suddenly starts getting frequent use at casinos.[68]

◆ *Card activation.* The credit card company pinpoints areas of the country in which cards are most likely to be lost or stolen. It then mails out "dead plastic"—that is, cards that are useless until they have been activated by the cardholder. To activate the card, the consumer must call the company and provide information known only to the cardholder (for example, the maiden name of the cardholder's mother). If the information provided meshes with the information on hand, the company activates the card. Banks find that this technique cuts losses dramatically for lost or stolen cards.

Other innovations are likely to emerge in the coming years. Keep in mind, however, that because overall losses due to fraud are low in comparison to the total number of cards in existence and the total dollar amount of credit card business, all these efforts are aimed mainly at protecting the integrity of the industry. They do little to protect consumers from personal losses due to fraud.

Protecting Consumers: Self-Preservation

As pointed out earlier, consumers do have one enormously important safeguard against credit card fraud. Under the terms of the Consumer Credit Protection Act, costs associated with the unauthorized use of consumers' credit cards are in almost all cases limited to $50 per year. In fact, credit card companies rarely assess a fraud victim for even that sum. The problem is that many people are unaware of this protection. They might needlessly pay hundreds or even thousands of dollars to settle fraudulent charges against their accounts.

Individuals can do a number of other things to reduce credit card fraud:

- Protect their cards so that they are not lost or stolen.
- Guard against the various ways in which the cards themselves, or their numbers, can be obtained illegally.
- Secure mailboxes as much as possible, and empty them as soon after mail delivery as is feasible.
- Destroy credit card receipts and personal information forms that include credit card numbers. To thwart those who steal credit card numbers by collecting carbon copies of receipts, rip up the carbons.[69]
- Guard against shoulder surfers when using credit cards or phone cards in public telephone booths.
- Refuse to allow clerks to write credit card numbers on checks or to write telephone numbers and addresses on credit card receipts.
- Be particularly wary of the chicanery practiced by telemarketers.

All these measures place the burden on consumers to be vigilant, but because of the $50 limit, consumers who take these steps are really helping to protect the credit card companies, not themselves.

However, card users can do a few things to truly protect themselves. For example, they should carefully peruse their credit card bills each month to look for fraudulent charges. Someone who is unaware that fraudulent charges have been made may unwittingly pay them as part of the larger bill. In addition, cardholders should periodically, perhaps twice a year, review their credit reports from all three major credit bureaus (information on one may not appear on the others). Any evidence of fraudulent activity should be reported to both the credit bureaus and the creditors. If fraud has clearly been perpetrated, then the authorities should also be notified.

Some consumers may be tempted to sign up with one of the insurance companies that have come into existence to protect cardholders from card loss, card theft, and the like. However, this type of insurance is best avoided. It typically costs $25 a year, but, as we have seen, federal law limits a person's liability to $50 a year and banks often waive even that liability. It is not unusual for financial analysts to advise against this type of protection.[70]

The credit card companies themselves engage in certain activities that border on the fraudulent, and consumers need to protect themselves from these as well. For example, consumers can search out cards with low interest rates or pressure a firm that charges high rates to reduce them by threatening to switch. Consumers also need to be alert to the various ways in which credit card companies increase actual interest rates and then either act to avoid these charges or switch to companies that do not impose them. In addition, it is generally a good idea to avoid secured credit cards as well as credit repair clinics and credit doctors—which cost a lot and offer little or nothing in return.

Protecting Consumers: Government Action

The federal government and state and local governments have taken steps to protect consumers, but far more could be done. One of the most important things the government could do is to put a cap on excessively high interest rates. However, most government efforts to control the industry and put lids on interest rates have been thwarted. For example, in 1991 the Senate voted to cap credit card interest rates at 4% above the rate the Internal Revenue Service charges on overdue taxes. This vote followed a speech in which President George Bush urged the credit card companies to cut their interest rates. But the stock market reacted to the Senate's action with a drop of 120 points in the Dow-Jones average. The American Bankers Association came out with full-page advertisements seeking to scare consumers by asking, "Will Congress deny millions of Americans the right to keep their credit cards?"[71] (The assumption is that lower rates would cause credit card firms to become more conservative and cancel some credit cards.) The Bush administration backtracked, and eventually the Senate motion was tabled.

A professor of finance argued at the time that competition in the credit card industry was preferable to government regulation as a method for keeping credit card rates down. He concluded, "Hopefully, we have heard the last of the efforts to cap credit card rates."[72] The chances are that, because the credit card firms will do everything they can to keep rates as high as possible, we have not heard the last of government efforts to cap credit card rates. Nonetheless, it appears that the professor of finance has been proved right in the short run. Thanks to the entry of major new competitors like AT&T and General Motors and greater consumer awareness about credit card rates, those rates do seem to have come down (as have annual fees). The astute shopper can find credit card rates that are 5% or even 10% lower than their current rates.[73] Further declines are certainly possible, although it is unlikely that the credit card firms will, of their own volition, slash interest rates dramatically.

Another congressional effort to deal with the troubling policies of the credit card firms is the yet-to-be-passed Credit and Charge Card Disclosure and Interest Rate Amendment. This amendment to the Truth-in-Lending Act requires the companies that issue credit cards to do the following things, among others:

+ Disclose on monthly statements a running total of all payments

+ Give a year-to-date breakdown of interest and fees

+ Calculate the number of months it will take to pay off the balance if only the minimum amount is paid each month[74]

The main objective of this bill is to educate consumers about the long-term implications of making only the minimum payment required by the card companies. However, it is in the interest of the credit card firms to encourage minimum payments, because a large proportion of their profits comes from interest on unpaid balances.

The credit card industry has succeeded thus far in preventing the passage of new protective legislation. Consumers clearly cannot rely on the industry to look out for their interests. Instead, they need to mobilize in order to protect themselves and to force legislators to pass laws that will better protect them.

Protecting Consumers: Proposals for Industry Action

The credit card firms could take a few steps to help their customers, although it is not likely that the industry will ever be as vigilant in protecting its customers as it is in protecting itself. Here are some possibilities:

+ Charge a reasonable interest rate. Home equity lines of credit are frequently pegged at something like 1% above the prime rate. Taking into account the lack of collateral associated with credit cards, credit card interest rates could reasonably be set 2% to 4% above the prime rate. A more generous possibility is to set credit card interest rates at 4% above the rate charged by the Internal Revenue Service on late tax payments, as in the aborted 1991 Senate effort to cap interest rates.

- Charge convenience users a reasonable fee so that the interest rate charged those who revolve their accounts can be lowered. Heretofore, convenience users have been subsidized by the high rates charged revolvers.

- Do a better job of explaining the added costs and dangers associated with cash advances.

- Encourage maximum rather than minimum payments each month. Explain the benefits of larger payments.

- Eliminate most or all of the unduly complex billing practices that are beyond the ken of most consumers and that lead to higher-than-necessary credit card charges and debts.

- Develop an industry policy whereby grace periods are handled in the same way for both revolvers and convenience users.

- Cease the practice of urging customers to take holidays from payments. If the industry wants to continue payment holidays, then waive the accrual of interest during those periods.

- Discourage furtive methods of raising rates, such as changing the date from which interest is charged. If rates are to be raised, do so in a way that is abundantly clear to consumers.

- Ban the use of teaser rates that entice unwary consumers into applying for a card without realizing that they soon will be paying a far higher rate.

- Reduce some of the extraordinary charges associated with secured cards.

- Do more as an industry to combat the clearly fraudulent credit repair clinics and credit doctors.

Most generally, the credit card industry, and banks in particular, need to stop treating credit card loans as something entirely different from other types of loans. Although credit card firms are entitled to a higher interest rate than on other loans because of the absence of collateral, they are not entitled to a usurious rate. Furthermore, although the credit card business may require some distinctive practices, the banks should not employ questionable practices where credit cards are concerned that they would not dream of using in the case of other types of loans.

Fraud, Private Troubles, and Public Issues

Although the theme of private troubles and public issues has been implicit throughout much of this discussion of credit card fraud, I would like to close this chapter by making the linkages a bit more explicit.

First, because of the $50 limit on consumers' liability for unauthorized use of their credit cards, most types of fraud perpetrated against the credit card companies cause few if any personal troubles for consumers. On the other hand, such fraud is clearly regarded as a public issue by the credit card industry. However, this view is highly questionable given the relatively small losses attributable to fraud. It appears as if the industry considers the real issue not the fraud itself but rather the threat it poses, especially if it increases dramatically, to the integrity of the industry as a whole. Thus, the war on fraud is really an effort by the credit card industry to protect its good name.

Second, the mean machinations perpetrated by the credit card companies are, in my view, the cause of personal troubles, and these machinations are, and should be considered, serious public issues. The wide range of questionable billing practices that are common in the industry saddle people with unnecessarily high fees, interest rates, and monthly payments. What is worse, the industry does what it can to keep these practices hidden from the public. Clearly, this way of doing business constitutes an issue of concern to society as a whole. The industry needs to alter many of its practices, or more likely, it should be forced to change by legislative initiative.

Finally, the questionable actions of consumers are a source of personal troubles. For example, the mad pursuit of consumer goods, with little regard for the well-being of others, clearly leads to severe questions about individual morality. Such actions are also related to the public issue of a rampant and ultimately unsatisfying consumerism, which is becoming increasingly pervasive throughout the United States and much of the rest of the world.

5

Secrecy, Privacy, and Credit Cards
Who Isn't in Their Files?

One of Georg Simmel's most provocative theses is that "money, more than any other form of value, makes possible secrecy, invisibility and silence of exchange."[1] Simmel is quite right about secrecy in a cash economy, but the ability to keep transactions secret is generally less possible with credit cards and the other CREDEBELS than it is with currency. A prominent member of the community would be foolish to use a credit card, a debit card, or an electronic funds transfer to pay a prostitute, for example. One's name is associated with a CREDEBEL transaction, whereas a cash transaction may well remain anonymous. Furthermore, there are no records of a secret cash transaction, but paper and electronic evidence exists of a CREDEBEL deal. Potentially, many people can have access to the records of a CREDEBEL transaction.

A specific example of the lack of secrecy and the resulting personal troubles associated with credit card transactions is the case of Craig Spence, a one-time Washington lobbyist. In February 1989 the Secret Service raided a Washington house that was allegedly the site of a homosexual prostitution ring and confiscated hundreds of credit card vouchers. A few months later, it was reported that Spence had been a major client of the ring. Spence's career was ruined, and a series of events was set in motion that helped lead to Spence's suicide in November 1989.[2]

Access to credit card records represents a problem not just for the criminal or one who deviates from society's norms, but for everyone. CREDEBEL records, in combination with records associated with other types of documents (for example, Social Security cards, driver's licenses, and bank statements), make up huge centralized banks of information on many millions of people.[3] The fact that a variety of people and organizations have access to this information is a profound threat to individual privacy and has caused personal troubles for many individuals. Furthermore, that private threat poses the danger of the public issue of totalitarianism and even greater incursions into, and control over, people's personal lives. As Galanoy put it,

> Ultimately, the danger here is not merely a loss of privacy, but of a *1984* scenario where "Big Banker" replaces "Big Brother" in becoming all-seeing, all-knowing, all-controlling, capable of destroying any resistance.[4]

Thus, the advent of CREDEBELS has turned Simmel's theory of the relationship between money and secrecy on its head. Although money in the form of currency affords more secrecy than its predecessors, CREDEBELS generally greatly reduce the possibility of secrecy. But it is not just that CREDEBELS make secrecy more difficult. They also heighten enormously others' ability to invade our privacy. According to the general counsel of Citicorp's bank card program, "There's no question privacy is quickly evolving into one of the most important issues of the 1990s."[5]

Exacerbating the threat posed by this invasion of privacy is the fact that inaccuracies often creep into the records of CREDEBEL (and other) transactions.[6] It is not unusual for people to get poor credit ratings because of erroneous information in their files. Invasions of privacy are an enormous danger in themselves, but the dangers are heightened when they are based on misinformation. As you will see, many individuals have encountered personal difficulties as a result of the existence of misinformation on their credit card records.

The invasion of privacy, either as a private trouble or a public issue, is not a matter that seems to trouble the credit card organizations very much. They are likely only to become mobilized when there is a public outcry over it or the government threatens to become involved because of pressure from the public. There is, however, a comparatively minor issue that does seem to trouble the credit card industry: merchants writing on charge slips the telephone numbers, or sometimes even the addresses, of those using credit cards. It is not the fact that merchants are invading the privacy of consumers or the potential for further invasion that troubles the industry but, as we have seen before, the fact that such inquiries undermine the legitimacy of credit cards. In the view of the industry, credit cards should be accepted on their own, without any additional information. A request for additional information is seen as casting doubt on the credit card as a legitimate instrument in its own right. As usual, the industry focuses on its self-interest and only becomes concerned with customers' well-being when its own interests are imperiled.

Secrecy Problems

As mentioned above, the ability to keep a transaction secret tends to decline with credit cards (and the other CREDEBELS) in comparison to cash. In this sense, credit cards pose less of a potential social problem than cash; a cashless society would have fewer secret transactions—including the criminal kind. However, credit cards have introduced some new kinds of secrecy problems.

Nondisclosure of Credit Terms

Until 1989, credit card companies were allowed to mail solicitations to people without indicating the costs involved; in other words, they were able to keep cost information a secret. Those who accepted the offer of a card did not find out about the costs until the card arrived or even until they began using it. But a 1989 Federal Reserve ruling required that henceforth such solicitations should reveal interest rates, fees, the grace period, and other relevant information.

It is fair to say that, although this information is now being revealed to consumers, it remains a mystery, a secret, to many of them. Many people find it difficult, if not impossible, to understand the terms of their credit card agreement. They are discouraged by the obscure and difficult wording, as well as the small print (or "mouse type") of these revelations. Even the industry acknowledges this problem. According to an industry executive, "The old days of putting mouse type at the bottom of the page have to end. There needs to be full disclosure."[7] The clear implication is that secrets remain.

Erroneous Credit Records

Perhaps the major secrecy issue relating to credit cards, and the greatest source of personal troubles, involves the consumer credit data collected and disseminated by credit bureaus and credit reporting agencies, often without consumers' knowledge. Credit reports include information not only on credit card use but also on payment of other loans and of bills in general; they also include personal and job information and data derived from other sources, including legal judgments. Negative information can remain on one's record for as long as 7 years (after which, by law, it must be removed) or, in the case of bankruptcies, as long as 10 years. All too often, however, the information is erroneous. In innumerable cases, people have been denied credit cards or other forms of credit because of the inaccurate information in their credit records.

The scope of the problem is troubling. For example, the Consumers Union examined 161 credit records and found that serious enough errors existed in 19% of those reports to cause denial of credit; according to *Consumer Reports*, one industry estimate is that 2 million people per year are affected by mistakes in credit card records.[8] Another measure of the problem is the fact that the Federal Trade Commission (FTC) receives more complaints about the credit reporting industry than any other—including the perennial target of such grievances, auto repair shops.[9] In 1991 the FTC received 10,000 complaints about credit bureaus and reporting agencies, more than three times the number it received in 1983.[10]

The problem has been exacerbated by the fact that credit records have been treated, at least until recently, as secret and not available to the general public. Because the records have been confidential, credit users have not been able to correct errors in these reports. Unbeknown to them, they may have been turned down time after time for various things because of erroneous data in their credit records.

Errors find their way into credit reports largely because the Big Three credit bureaus—TRW, Equifax, and Trans Union—are entering 2 billion bits of information per month into credit records and are issuing about half a billion reports a year; altogether, this industry includes well over 1,000 consumer credit bureaus with records on over 150 million people.[11] As a result, the odds of a slip-up now and again are quite high. Another major source of error is the organizations that report the information to the credit agencies in the first place, such as banks, car dealers, and employers. People themselves sometimes unintentionally enter erroneous information on applications and the like. Criminals may electronically switch the records of sullied and unsullied borrowers. One of the most common errors is one person's credit information finding its way into another's record (often with the same or a similar name, address, or Social Security number). Another common error is an account showing an outstanding balance that was actually paid but never credited. The problem in all these instances is that the credit agencies simply store whatever information is sent to them without checking to see whether the data are "outdated, incomplete or inaccurate."[12] Local and regional credit bureaus can plug into the computers of the three main firms, so the erroneous information may be disseminated widely.

The use of erroneous credit information is a significant public issue, but it also causes serious personal troubles. For example, a Maryland man, Robert Corbey, applied for a $2,000 loan to put vinyl siding on his house:

> To Corbey's amazement, his lender refused, citing unpaid mortgage bills on his two homes in Virginia and an Internal Revenue Service lien against him and his wife, Ann. Corbey was furious. He had paid off his 30-year mortgage, he had never lived in Virginia, and he had never been married to anyone named Ann.[13]

Corbey, of course, had been confused with another man with the same name.

In another case, the wife of a journalist had her credit card refused when she attempted to purchase a blouse. The clerk ran the card through the computer three times and finally confiscated it. When contacted, the bank issuing the card said, "Sorry, you have a derogatory credit statement." As the journalist pursued the matter, he was told,

> "This is one of the worst credit reports I've seen," . . . a repossessed car, about $70,000 in tax liens, a bankruptcy adjustment plan and scads of debts unpaid. "That can't be me," I [the journalist] protested, explaining that I was a paragon of fiscal responsibility. He was unpersuaded.[14]

There was, of course, an error in the journalist's record that had previously been unknown to him. Characteristically, it was up to him, the victim, to correct it. Luckily, the journalist recalled an incident several years before when the Internal Revenue Service had inquired about a person with exactly the same name as his and with a bad credit history. When he told the bank official about this incident, the official told the journalist about a 1981 "death alert" against the journalist's Social Security number. As the journalist put it, "So not only was my credit a disaster, I was also officially dead."[15] Then followed weeks of efforts to correct the error, culminating in the signing of an affidavit attesting to the fact that the journalist was, indeed, alive. The journalist had been the victim of cross-merged files, the mixing of the files of people with similar names or addresses.

In a classic understatement, an Equifax executive said, "We recognize that the accuracy level [of credit records] could be better."[16] In fact, however, the industry is less than eager to solve the problem. The president of the trade association representing the credit industry said, "As desirable as it may be to have no incomplete or inaccurate information, this utopian state cannot be achieved in today's marketplace."[17] Executives associated with the credit industry can afford to be blasé, but consumers cannot. The logical question is, if error-free records cannot be achieved in "today's marketplace," then why not change the marketplace? The credit industry created this market, and therefore it is certainly in a position to change it.

The marketplace being referred to permits, on average, a million people per day to obtain credit. A Trans Union representative contended that this number translates into "15,000 homes, 40,000 autos and 500,000 major appliances every day."[18] The obvious answer is to slow the process a bit and handle fewer cases, more carefully. Most people would gladly accept a slightly slower credit approval process in exchange for an error-free system and an elimination of the kinds of personal troubles discussed above.

Consumers must also be made aware that they have a right to see their credit records and to correct errors in them. Of course, the process requires great effort. A senator from, and former governor of, Nevada ran into errors in his credit report. He was able to have them corrected, but he said, "I'm not unmindful that John Q. Public would have more problems."[19] People should also know that, because the three major credit bureaus do not share information, it is up to consumers to correct the records at each bureau.

And what if errors are found? Because of the public outcry over cases like Corbey's, and in an effort to forestall stronger government legislation, the credit reporting agencies are now putting procedures in place for settling disputes over credit records. If, for example, the credit bureaus refuse to change an erroneous entry, they must indicate in their records that the entry is in dispute. Complainants may even have a statement of their position included in the record. Many credit reporting agencies have also begun allowing consumers to request free or low-cost copies of their credit reports. The formats for these reports are being revised so they can more easily be understood by the layperson.[20]

More serious changes in the way the credit bureaus operate have been debated in Congress for years. Characteristically, the bureaus have resisted such legislation. The president of a trade association of credit bureaus argued, "We do not believe that [it] is prudent to alter radically a law and a system that has served both consumers and the credit granting community on the basis of a few horror stories."[21] As a result of such opposition, at least in part, no new major legislation has been passed.

Nonetheless, the veil of secrecy associated with credit reports has been lifted, at least to some degree. Yet most people are unaware of their rights or unwilling to avail themselves of them. The result is that for most people, their credit records remain a mystery.

Nondisclosure of Affinity Card Terms

Another secrecy issue involves affinity cards (discussed in Chapter 2), especially those issued in the name of a charity or a professional association. Cardholders are told that a percentage of the value of all purchases made with the card is to go to charity, but they are generally not told what that percentage is. For example, the affinity card brochure of the National Audubon Society informs its readers that an unspecified percentage of the amount that they charge on the credit card will be donated to the society.[22] They are not told the percentage because the bank, MBNA, has a secrecy clause in its agreement with the National Audubon Society—and with many other such organizations.

One reason for the secrecy clause is undoubtedly to conceal the true amount of the contribution to the organization. This is a "mean machination," because consumers are using an affinity card, rather than other possibilities, out of a belief that the charity is profiting from its use, perhaps handsomely. Such a card also usually carries an annual fee, and some people will continue paying the fee instead of switching to no-fee cards or those with lower interest rates because they believe that large sums of money are flowing into the charities. Most people would be appalled to learn how small a percentage actually goes to the charities. The Better Business Bureau decries this secret practice because it (and the consumer) is unable to tell whether charities are getting only a pittance from the banks.[23]

Some charities are rebelling against this secrecy and are revealing, or threatening to reveal, their cut of the credit card business. The National Audubon Society, for example, has revealed that it gets only one-half of one percent of retail sales involving use of its affinity card. This is a "crumb," as the Better Business Bureau might put it, although it does earn the Society over $100,000 a year. The Society asked to be released from the secrecy clause, but it did not immediately get a positive response from MBNA. In the absence of such a response, the Society said it would begin to release the information on its own. Other charities have been able to negotiate for the release of such information.

Banks want to keep their arrangements with one charity secret from other charities in order to improve their bargaining position with each charity. The banks are in a better position to negotiate higher annual fees, higher interest rates, and lower rebates to a charity that is unaware of the norms in the area. When the Defenders of Wildlife (DOW) raised the secrecy issue with MBNA, it was told that its royalty rate was extraordinarily good. If the DOW's royalty was widely known, other (unspecified) organizations would want theirs changed to match it. The DOW was told it was the secrecy policy that allowed it to retain such a high rate.[24] The clear threat is that DOW could be affected adversely if the rates were to be divulged.

What we have here are banks using secrecy as a weapon to keep their rebates to charities (and other organizations) low and their annual fees and interest rates high. If all this information were public, all charities would demand the highest rebate available and the lowest fee and rate structure. For example, DOW's card costs its members $25 a year; Audubon's is $20 a year. With such information now public, DOW can demand the same annual fee as the Audubon Society.

Privacy Problems

The secrecy issues associated with credit cards (and the other CREDEBELS) are important, but the threat to privacy they represent is the far greater source of personal troubles and a much more important public issue. Credit card companies, credit bureaus, and innumerable other agencies throughout society collect all sorts of information about large numbers of people. When the security chief at TRW was asked, "Are there people you don't have information on, besides children and those who live in the woods?", his answer was "I'd say that would be about it."[25] Privacy is endangered, at least potentially, when information on so many people exists—especially when there is a lot of it, it is concentrated in relatively few places, and it is readily accessed. On an individual level, people can experience personal troubles when very private information about them falls into the hands of people who might misuse such information. These sorts of personal troubles become a public issue when large numbers of people have their privacy invaded and when the enhanced capacity for centralized control threatens individual freedom.

A good place to begin this discussion of the threat to privacy in a credit card society is with a 1990 plan, later aborted because of public uproar, by Equifax and Lotus Development Corporation to market a CD-ROM called Marketplace containing information gleaned from 40 different sources. The CD was to include the names, addresses, approximate income, personal buying habits, and other lifestyle, demographic, and income information on 80 million American households.[26] (Incidentally, TRW's database covers nearly every adult American, about 150 million in all. The size of the database and the amount of information is so great that TRW is able to subdivide that population into about 600 different categories.[27]) Such information had been available only to big retailers, banks, and other credit organizations that could afford the steep fees, but the Equifax-Lotus CD would have been made available to anyone with a computer. The possibilities for invasion of privacy would have escalated greatly with this development. Said the publisher of *Privacy Times*, "Once they have established this precedent, there is nothing to stop the next guy from selling anything he wants [for use on personal computer] from your Christmas purchases to your genetic history."[28]

A similar uproar occurred in 1991, when Citicorp announced a plan to give marketers access, at a price, to its records on 21 million credit card holders. Said a technical writer,

> They know a lot about me and my buying habits, and there's a lot of knowledge there I'd be extremely upset to have disclosed.... There's

a quantum leap between Citicorp using that information for Citicorp things and them offering it to people I've never had a relationship with—and, in all statistical likelihood, never will.[29]

These particular threats to privacy were avoided. However, several other privacy issues are associated with credit cards and other CREDEBELS. Most important, although massive databases are not yet available to just anyone, the credit industry does have access to a great deal of data about nearly all American adults. There is much at stake in how well the industry protects that data, who is allowed access to that data, and under what circumstances such access is permitted.

Excessive Data Collection

Credit bureaus obtain lots of information about people through credit histories and credit checks, a good portion of it involving credit card use and abuse. Much of this information on purchases, payments, and nonpayments is obtained from retailers, banks, and other businesses. Additional information is acquired from publicly available courthouse records on bankruptcies, tax liens, judgments, foreclosures, and so on. Credit bureaus also track who has requested credit information on a person over the past two years. One company, Equifax, even collects information on a person's driving record.[30] Ultimately, of course, credit applicants themselves provide much of the information, including their name and spouse's name, number of children, addresses (present and past), year of birth, Social Security number, name of employer, estimated income, and value of car and of home.

Not only do the credit bureaus have information about us, but so do the banks and other companies that issue credit cards. Among other things, they know applicants' payment history and current balances, how long they have had particular credit cards, their age, their estimated income, what they purchase with credit cards, and where they purchase it. The credit card companies also might have such personal information as number of children, value of car and home, and even knowledge of hobbies.[31]

Among the other big businesses that have information about us are banks and thrifts, insurance companies, magazine publishers, mail-order companies, mutual funds and brokerage houses, retail chains and department stores, supermarkets, and telephone companies.[32] Taken together, these businesses possess a tremendous storehouse of information about us. And that does not even include information in the hands of local, city, state, and national governments.

Much of the time, information is collected needlessly—that is, it is not always needed to complete a transaction. For example, Waldenbooks compiles lists of people and their preferences from records of credit card transactions.[33] Additional information—such as address and telephone number—is often solicited from credit card customers to increase the amount of information available to the merchant for other purposes, such as developing a mailing list. (By the way, customers are within their rights to refuse such requests.) The practice of writing a person's address or telephone number on a charge slip is sometimes defended as protection for the store if the clerk has not obtained a clear imprint of the card. However, said one advocate of the rights of credit card users. "We don't want our privacy invaded just because a clerk makes a mistake."[34] A similar problem is posed when, in cashing a check, a merchant insists on writing the driver's license number (in many states, it is the customer's Social Security number) and credit card number on the check.[35] Not only do clerks and the merchant then have access to this information, but so do many other people involved in the process of clearing a check through two or more banks.

Note that consumers play a major role in the collection of all this information. Said one mass marketer, "Never underestimate the willingness of the American public to tell you about itself."[36] We provide more information every time we respond to a mail or telephone survey, apply for a loan, subscribe to a magazine, or comply with any request for more than the essential facts.

Illegitimate Access to Credit Records

We cannot rely on the credit bureaus to make sure every request for credit information is legitimate, if history is a guide. For example, private investigators have been able to gain credit information even though they have no legitimate need for it. An editor of *Business Week*, in an effort to demonstrate the abuses that exist in the system, was able to gain the credit history of then–Vice President Dan Quayle. More recently, to show that the system had not been reformed—in spite of his previous, well-publicized successes—the same editor was able to obtain the credit records of CBS news anchor Dan Rather.[37]

Today, employers sometimes check a job applicant's credit records for signs of stability, but under the Fair Credit Reporting Act, they are not supposed to do so without the applicant's knowledge. Nevertheless, applicants have been turned down for jobs because of bad credit ratings without being told that their credit histories had been a factor in the decision. In 1991 the Federal Trade Commission (FTC) reached an agreement with four employers to get them to change their policies on this issue and to inform potential employees of the bases for their decisions.[38] In spite of this agreement, many employers may continue to make hiring decisions on the basis of credit histories, at least in part, without informing potential employees.

But perhaps change is on the way. Under pressure from the FTC, a few California bureaus recently agreed to tighten their procedures through audits and "occasional" personal interviews to "verify the identity of current and prospective clients and their type of business, that the clients have a permissible purpose for use of credit reports, and have procedures intended to prevent unauthorized access to those reports."[39]

However, a vast "information underground" exists, which, for the right price, has a multitude of ways of accessing information. The *Business Week* editor mentioned above was having trouble getting information on Dan Rather's American Express account because it appeared to be a CBS corporate card rather than a personal card. The editor paid $150 up front to a participant in this underground for the necessary information. Within a few days, the editor was able to turn on his computer and view Dan Rather's corporate American Express card record with details on amounts charged, as well as when and where the charges were made.[40]

Another threat to privacy stems from unauthorized break-ins by outsiders into the computer files of credit bureaus and other databases. At least some organizations rely on the growing "information broker" industry, in which insiders steal data from U.S. government computers and then sell that information to an array of customers. In the main, the data come from employees who have been bribed, some for as little as $50. Some data have been provided by employees at the FBI's National Criminal Information Center, which has information on over 15 million arrests. From Social Security Administration records, an information broker can get employment histories and year-by-year salary information. Said one computer security expert, "With sufficient access to a few databases these days, you can get pretty close to somebody's life history with nothing more than a Social Security number."[41] One information broker was selling illegally obtained employment histories for between $100 and $175 and criminal histories for $100. Although the information could be used for "legitimate" purposes (such as a hiring decision), it also could be used for such criminal purposes as blackmail.

The credit bureaus have instituted procedures to protect against break-ins. These procedures include the use of passwords, audit trails, and periodic checks of the files for unusual activity.[42] These efforts help, but they have not been entirely successful.

The "smart card" threatens to greatly increase invasions of privacy. Embedded within its powerful computer chip would be a wide range of personal information, as well as many details about consumption patterns.[43] This technology would enormously increase the amount of available information about consumers. Furthermore, should criminals get access to these cards and this information, the threats posed to our privacy would greatly increase as well.

Sale of Credit and Lifestyle Information

Credit bureaus are in business to provide information to a wide range of agencies, including lenders, financial institutions, utilities, financial service companies, marketers of various types, and life and health insurers. Privacy issues arise because credit bureaus and credit card companies have been known to sell information to others for an entirely different purpose than it was originally given and without the permission of the individuals involved. In a study conducted by the Consumers Union, 27% of those who responded found that third parties had been granted access to their credit records without their permission, and another 27% could not be sure whether or not that had occurred.[44] According to a professor at Georgetown University, "Credit bureaus know as much about us as anybody. . . . They get information about us monthly, and many of those firms have direct-marketing operations, and they sell mailing lists that are based in part on our credit reports."[45] Such lists are even available from the Postal Service, which provides direct-mail firms with lists of people who have changed addresses.[46]

Selling information on credit histories and lifestyles to direct marketers is a big business. The FTC frowns on this practice, but it continues. Some of this information is used to target cardholders for special credit offers or mail-order offers. Credit card firms may also rent lists to a wide variety of organizations interested in particular audiences. The lists can be broken down on the basis of variables such as age, sex, location, and type of purchase. A large portion of the junk mail and unsolicited telephone calls we receive is accounted for by these lists.

The president of a consulting firm in this industry defends the development of such detailed lists in the following way:

> The worst thing we're going to do is try to sell you a product you actually want. . . . Really, we're using a computer to take a giant step backwards to the earlier part of the century when the small-town banker knew all the customers by name and would communicate with them on the basis of understanding their needs.[47]

A very different point of view is expressed by a senior financial executive:

> I'm starting to feel a little violated. Every time you buy anything, there is the opportunity for someone to capture the information and sell a list. . . . Someone is not only tracking my preferences for one hotel brand over another; they're tracking my movements.[48]

One of the ways in which the wide distribution of all this information shows up is in our receipt of solicitations for preapproved credit cards with specified credit limits. The credit card companies come up with lists of names, either from organizations with which they have had prior dealings or from lists provided by one of several marketing companies; names may also be obtained from real estate records, car dealerships, travel agencies, or stockbrokers. However the lists are obtained, the credit card firms then send them to credit reporting firms for "prescreening." The credit agency looks for such things as bankruptcies and credit card delinquencies. The "clean" names receive an unsolicited offer from the credit card company for a preapproved credit card.[49] Of course, this whole process has occurred unbeknown to those being considered for the credit card. The unauthorized examination of our records, the receipt of such solicitations, to say nothing of the visibility of all this information about us to the many people involved in various stages of the process, may well be considered an invasion of privacy.

The sale of confidential information to direct marketers has been loudly criticized. Equifax was earning $12 million a year from such sales but shut them down in 1991 as a result of the public uproar; in 1992 it extended its voluntary prohibition.[50] However, the other two major credit reporting companies, TRW and Trans Union, had not agreed to such a self-imposed limitation as of that date and continued to sell such information to direct marketers. Nevertheless, Equifax has been joined by American Express, which decided in 1992 to inform cardholders that it tracks their buying habits, compiles marketing lists, and then sells that information to merchants. The company was also going to tell its 20 million or so cardholders that they had the ability to prevent American Express from divulging this information about them.[51] The goal of these internal reforms is undoubtedly to forestall legislation, but one representative of a public interest group called them "definitely too little, too late to stop legislation."[52] Legislation to toughen overall requirements on the credit bureaus has been working its way through Congress over the past few years.

Changes in the credit card industry have also brought new threats to privacy. For example, Household International handles the co-branded GM card, and General Motors executives are now interested in using information derived from credit card accounts to target automobile promotions.[53] A flier promoting the kind of car that a given type of cardholder would be most likely to buy could be included with a credit card bill. Presumably, higher-income people would receive fliers on Cadillacs, and lower-income people would get promotional material on Chevrolets. Although GM is being provided with aggregate, not individual, data, invasion of privacy is still a concern. For one thing, who is to say that, once aggregate data are provided, individualized data will not follow? Even if only aggregate data are sold, various people and agencies will still learn about the categories (potential Chevrolet buyer, for example) into which specific individuals can be placed. Those who have the GM card and who do not want such information to be known are clearly having their privacy violated. The co-branding of credit cards makes such invasions of privacy much easier.

Computerized Databases

Many of the privacy and secrecy issues associated with the credit industry are exacerbated by computer technology, especially the increasing linkages among computers and their databases.[54] Said the consumer affairs commissioner of New York State, "As computers get more sophisticated, some of our most intimate information is passed around to strangers more quickly and more widely and more cheaply than ever."[55] American Express, for example, was able to use its computer system to analyze the way customers used airlines, hotels, and rental cars. American Express then sold that information to relevant companies. Through computer analysis, American Express was also able to divide its customers into six broad categories, from the "least affluent, 'value-oriented' customers to the most affluent, which it calls 'Rodeo Drive Chic.' "[56] Joint marketing ventures based on these lists were then undertaken with companies like American Airlines and Marriott. Said the New York State attorney general, "A consumer who pays with a credit card is entitled to as much privacy as one who pays by cash or check. . . . Credit card holders should not unknowingly have their spending patterns and lifestyles analyzed and categorized for the use of merchants fishing for good prospects."[57]

In the future, computer technology will permit even more detailed analyses of consumers and even greater intrusions into their privacy—and in the process make this an increasingly important public issue. For example, direct marketers have so far been able to target only relatively large groups of people and relatively large geographic areas. Computer technology will allow them to target smaller and smaller groups and increasingly limited areas. An executive of an agency that collects and sells data to companies said, "We can envision direct marketing down to individual members of a household."[58] That ability will be based on unprecedented intrusions into our privacy, however, and will at the same time extend such intrusions.

The ultimate threat to privacy, and the broadest public issue, stems from more interrelated and more centralized databases.[59] As the former chairman of the U.S. Privacy Protection Commission said, "The danger is not that direct-marketing companies will clog your mailbox or call you during dinner to hawk commemorative coins. . . . The danger is that employers, banks and government agencies will use data bases to make decisions about our lives without our knowing about it."[60] Such possibilities make it even more necessary that individuals and legislators remain vigilant to the potential threats to privacy posed by these developments.

Lest you think that all these threats to privacy are trivial and of concern only to muckraking journalists and sociologists, note that

American Express refuses to supply credit bureaus with any information on the accounts of its cardholders. Its reason: Supplying such information would violate customers' right to privacy.[61]

In sum, the current setup of the credit card industry poses a considerable threat to individual privacy. Furthermore, that threat is likely to increase and become an even greater public issue in the future, with the development of more computerized and centralized databases on consumers and their credit histories. As Jeffrey Rothfeder puts it,

> Increasingly people are at the whim of . . . large organizations—direct marketers, the credit bureaus, the government, and the entire information economy—that view individuals as nothing but lifeless data floating like microscopic entities in vast electronic chambers, data that exists to be captured, examined, collated and sold, regardless of the individual's desire to choose what should be concealed and what should be made public.[62]

Ways of Coping with Secrecy Problems

As you have now seen, credit cards pose both secrecy problems and privacy problems. The major secrecy issue is that many people have been adversely affected when false information has found its way into their credit reports and they have been unaware of it. The burden has fallen on consumers to be sure that no such thing happens. The credit bureaus have made it abundantly clear that they will not take the initiative in rooting out errors. Once again, it is the victims who must bear the bulk of the responsibility and the brunt of the work. But the customers are not the ones responsible for the fact that false information exists in their credit records. Furthermore, for them it is difficult, if not impossible, to solve these problems. According to a lawyer for the American Civil Liberties Union, "It is very, very hard for someone to argue against a computer tape and it is very difficult to fight something you don't know is occurring."[63]

Nevertheless, it is advisable for consumers to get copies of their credit reports from the three major credit agencies: Equifax, Trans Union, and TRW. A California company, Credco, offers a report that combines the information collected by all three of these firms.[64] *Consumer Reports* recommends getting copies of such reports every few years as well as before applying for any major loan.

When you find an error, it is up to you to be sure that it is eliminated from your credit record.

Ultimately, the credit agencies must take more responsibility for preventing errors from creeping into records and for eliminating them once they are in the records. Certainly they can afford to: Credit report sales are highly profitable; for example, Equifax has an operating margin of 23% on credit report sales, compared to 15% overall.[65] Among other things, the credit agencies must do a better job of checking the accuracy of the information they receive. They can do a much better job of being certain that such information is not outdated, inaccurate, or incomplete. Said one victim of an error in his credit record, "They get information from these people [credit grantors] and they don't attempt to verify it all. Garbage in. Garbage out."[66]

The fact is, however, that one cannot expect the credit bureaus to take the lead in reforming themselves. Consumer groups and especially the government must play an important role in this process. The government can, for example, pass legislation putting the burden on the credit agencies to help reduce, if not eliminate, errors in credit records. The government can also play more of a watchdog role, ensuring that the credit bureaus limit both errors and their adverse impact on consumers. However, the latest attempt to amend the 1971 Fair Credit Reporting Act died in the House of Representatives in 1992.[67] The bill would have made it easier for individuals to fix errors in their reports, required greater disclosure of consumer rights, and offered more protection of individual privacy. The issue that killed the bill was whether the new federal law should preempt state laws supervising credit bureaus. The credit bureau industry opposed preemption, and it won. However, similar legislation is likely to be reintroduced.

Although its opposition to the amendment was successful, the credit bureau industry adopted a series of new policies; among the provisions are the following:

- The credit bureaus must mail a copy of a credit report to a consumer within three days of receiving a request.
- Unless there are unusual circumstances and the consumer is informed of them, the credit bureau must reinvestigate any disputed information on the credit report within 30 days.
- A copy of the results of the reinvestigation must be mailed within five business days of its completion.

◆ Those who have been turned down for credit may receive a free copy of their report; those whose credit has been approved may receive a copy for no more than $8.[68]

Ways of Protecting Privacy

Many of the actions that can be taken to prevent fraud (discussed in Chapter 4) are also useful in protecting personal privacy. For example, consumers should refuse requests by merchants to use their credit cards for identification and should not permit credit card numbers to be written on checks. Similarly, they should refuse requests for additional information, such as addresses and telephone numbers, to be put on their credit card slips. Consumers should know that it is the position of the credit card companies that the cards themselves are sufficient identification. Most generally, consumers should be extremely wary about giving out any information about themselves. Such information can be rapidly and widely disseminated to organizations that might exploit it.

Interestingly, if consumers tried to stop a credit bureau from providing information about them to others, the bureau would effectively cut off their access to credit. And there is no way that consumers can stop the credit card issuers from collecting credit-related information. Consumers can, however, write letters to the three major credit bureaus requesting that their names not be used for marketing purposes. Consumers can also request that the credit card issuers stop targeting them for sales pitches.[69]

The credit bureaus have developed elaborate procedures to prevent illegal access to personal information, and they actively seek to prosecute hackers who attempt to break into their computer systems.[70] Unfortunately, the credit bureaus themselves are a serious threat to privacy by selling lists of various types of cardholders, usually without the cardholders' knowledge or permission. The credit bureaus have to do a better job of policing themselves in this area, or else the government needs to develop more stringent restrictions on the use of such personal information.

One of the recent reforms undertaken by the credit bureaus is the requirement that they run advertisements once a year explaining how they handle the marketing of lists of names and the prescreening of applicants. Consumers are to be provided with information on how they can be excluded from both.[71]

There are, of course, many other things that the credit bureaus can do, including

♦ Preventing, rather than encouraging, the widespread dissemination of information on customers.

♦ Rigorously enforcing the rule that customers must be informed if third parties are to be given information about them. Better yet, they should end the questionable practice of selling information to direct marketers; credit bureaus are supposed to be in the business of collecting information and selling it to those who are interested in granting credit, not in selling goods and services.

♦ Paying customers who allow personal information to be sold to direct marketers. The credit bureaus are profiting from this information, and consumers deserve a share of the profits.

♦ Limiting the kinds of information collected. Why, for example, do credit bureaus need information on driving records? What does a driving record have to do with creditworthiness?

♦ Refraining from linking up their databases with those of banks, other credit card companies, businesses, and the government. Information should only be exchanged for limited, well-defined purposes.

♦ Instituting fail-safe procedures to prevent illegitimate access to the highly personal information in their possession.

♦ Instituting fail-safe procedures to prevent break-ins to computer files.

There are also some actions that should be taken by credit card firms:

♦ They should not seek, or be permitted to have, access to the databases of the credit bureaus for such things as compiling lists of people who qualify for prescreened credit cards. Access to those databases should be limited to situations when consumers actually apply for credit cards.

♦ Like the credit bureaus, they (and merchants) should use the information given to them only for the purposes for which it was given.

♦ If they (and merchants) want to use credit information for other purposes, they should let consumers decide whether or not to allow the information to be used for those purposes.

◆ If that information is used for other purposes, they should adequately compensate consumers.

◆ They must become aware of, and capable of dealing with, the greater threats to privacy posed by technological advances such as smart cards and more sophisticated computer systems.

In the end, there are limits to what we can expect of the credit card industry. For one thing, the drive for profits will always push at least some elements of the industry to violate people's privacy. For another, some of the dangers, such as the totalitarian implications of a centralized database, extend far beyond the credit card industry and cannot be dealt with by it alone. For these reasons, the government must become more active in protecting the privacy of its citizens.

Up to now, relatively few federal laws dealing with privacy have been passed, and those that exist are notoriously weak. The U.S. Congress has debated a number of new laws, but none has passed. In the meantime, incursions into our privacy continue and even accelerate. Thus, as one observer put it, "If we wait much longer to begin debating the limits of privacy, there may be nothing left to define."[72]

6

Credit Cards, Fast-Food Restaurants, and Rationalization

All You Need Is 42 Digits to Make One Long-Distance Phone Call

As you saw in Chapter 2, both the credit card and the fast-food restaurant were products of post–World War II changes in American society. Both have, in turn, greatly contributed to an accelerating rate of change in our society. The concern of this chapter is the similarities and differences between these two seemingly mundane but nonetheless enormously important social and economic developments. The main focus is the degree to which the two are part of the general process of the rationalization of society. I will pay special attention to the private troubles and the public issues that accompany the rationalization process in the credit card industry.

Similarities Between the Credit Card and Fast-Food Industries

There are, of course, many differences between the credit card and fast-food industries. For example, the fast-food restaurants are marketing particular end products, whereas the credit card firms are pushing means to many ends. Nevertheless, there are some notable similarities between the two industries. The three I will discuss here—innovation, reliance on advertising, and expansion—are not the only ones, but they are highly revealing of the similar social and economic roles played by the two industries.

Lack of Innovativeness

Both credit cards and fast-food restaurants are products and producers of revolutionary changes in American society. Yet, despite their revolutionary character, neither was highly innovative. Here is what Lewis Mandell has to say about the "invention" in 1949 of the first important universal credit card, the Diners Club card:

> The founders of Diners Club introduced no radically new ideas. Rather, they combined a number of well-known and widely used techniques for extending credit and changed the way credit service was delivered to the customer. The key to their success was their recognition of the need and untapped demand for a mobile credit device.[1]

This is what I have said previously about Ray Kroc's franchising of the first McDonald's in 1955, six years after the founding of Diners Club:

> Kroc invented little that was new. Basically, he took the specific products and techniques of the McDonald brothers and combined them with the principles of other franchises (including other food-service franchises), bureaucracies, scientific management, and the assembly line. Kroc's genius was in bringing all of these well-known ideas and techniques to bear on the fast-food business and adding his ambition to turn it, through franchising, into a national, and international, business. *McDonald's and McDonaldization, then, do not represent something new, but rather the culmination of a series of rationalization processes that had been occurring throughout the twentieth century.*[2]

It is striking that two of the most far-reaching social and economic developments of the twentieth century were so lacking in innovativeness.

More specifically, neither industry was innovative technologically. Mandell notes that "innovations in the credit card industry have developed slowly. . . . Existing technology has usually been adapted to fit the needs of the developing industry."[3] Similarly, McDonald's has not made many technological innovations, preferring to rely on traditional technologies and labor-intensive processes rather than labor-saving, advanced technologies.

The fast-food restaurant's lack of innovativeness has not been restricted to technology; it has not done much to develop new products either. Similarly, there have been relatively few innovative products in the modern credit card industry since its inception in 1949.

Reliance on Advertising

Still another similarity between credit cards and fast-food restaurants is their reliance on advertising—especially by the industry leaders (Visa, MasterCard, and American Express in credit cards and McDonald's, Wendy's, and Burger King in fast foods). Because their products are more or less indistinguishable from competitors' products, the dominant firms have sought to achieve preeminence in their industry through costly and elaborate advertising campaigns. The leaders spend many billions of dollars on advertisements designed to manufacture a sense of difference for their products. This practice is made even more necessary by the fact that the dominant companies in both industries, at least until recently, have not wanted to compete on the basis of price—more precisely, by cutting prices.

American Express, for example, began advertising in earnest on television in 1976 and over the years has created a number of memorable advertising campaigns.[4] The legendary "Do You Know Me?" commercials were aired in the late 1970s and early 1980s. They featured people who were relatively little known, at least visually, explaining the virtues of the card and ending with the person's name being spelled out on the card. An earlier campaign in the mid 1970s introduced a phrase that has come to be synonymous with American Express: "Don't leave home without it." Of course, American Express's competitors soon launched their own highly successful advertising campaigns. Of particular note have been Visa's ads arguing that Visa cards, but not American Express cards, are honored at certain events and locales (most notably, the Olympics). Although the fast-food chains have not, in the main, created such notable advertising campaigns (an exception might be Wendy's "Where's the Beef" campaign), they have used an enormous number of diverse advertisements targeted at a wide variety of segments of the fast-food market.

In recent years, both credit card and fast-food firms have been forced to forgo their near-exclusive reliance on competitive marketing and engage in price competition. The hamburger chains, for example, have faced severe competition not only from each other but also from chains purveying fried chicken, pizza, and tacos. To meet the threat, McDonald's and the other chains have been forced to do such things as create low-priced specials and "value meals." For their part, the major credit card companies and banks have been faced with severe competition from the entry of "nonbanks" like AT&T and General Motors and their co-branded cards into the credit card business. They have been forced to compete by slashing interest rates and reducing or eliminating annual fees.

The dominant companies in both industries would prefer not to engage in price competition because it cuts directly into profits. In contrast, the costs of marketing and advertising efforts can be passed on to consumers in the form of higher prices, fees, and interest rates. Thus, price competition has been more or less forced on the leading players in the fast-food and credit card industries.

Expansion

Both fast-food restaurants and credit card companies have devoted considerable attention to expanding on their original base. In the case of charge card companies like American Express, that base was businesspeople, especially those associated with large and successful companies. Later American Express sought to attract less affluent and less successful businesspeople. Because most American Express cards were held by men, the company turned its attention to attracting women to what has come to be known as "the Card." Low-key ads featuring young female executives and professionals led to the statement by feminist Gloria Steinem that American Express "now makes women feel welcomed and invited."[5] As a result of such efforts, by 1984 one-third of new cardholders were women. For their part, the fast-food chains have sought at various times to attract every conceivable group including very young children, grandparents, "thirtysomething" married couples, and so on.

Credit card firms and fast-food restaurants have sought to expand in other ways as well. For example, fast-food restaurants have moved onto college campuses and are even beginning to make inroads in the nation's high schools.[6] Similarly, as you saw in Chapter 1, credit card firms have sought to attract college and even high school students to credit card use. For their part, fast-food restaurants have devoted great energy to moving beyond their traditional foundation of teenage customers.

Another route for expansion for both the fast-food industry and credit cards has been overseas. The big growth area for the fast-food restaurants in the next few years will be in foreign markets. The same can be said of the credit card firms, because the American market is growing more competitive and there are enormous and virtually untapped markets in many parts of the world.

Both fast-food restaurants and credit card companies have also sought to expand into their competitors' domains. For example,

American Express introduced its Optima credit card in 1987 in order to compete more directly with Visa and MasterCard. Expansion also took place in the other direction. American Express's Gold card ceased to be distinctive because the banks expanded into the gold card market. For example, Visa began offering gold cards in 1988. An illustration of this phenomenon in the fast-food industry is the fact that most, if not all, hamburger chains now handle many of the products that were at the root of the success of the chicken franchises. Similarly, various chains are marketing food items like tacos and burritos, products that made the Mexican fast-food chains the fastest growing in the market.

Like McDonald's and its widely advertised Ronald McDonald House, credit card companies have sought to find new customers through heavily publicized charities. For example, in addition to its previously discussed 1984 campaign to raise money to help restore the Statue of Liberty, in 1993 American Express ran a similar campaign, "Charge Against Hunger," in which the objective was to raise $5 million by contributing 2¢ per card purchase to a nonprofit hunger-relief organization, Share Our Strength (SOS).[7] But the main objective of American Express in these campaigns, as for McDonald's, is really to increase its own business. Said a vice president at American Express, "I can't deny that our motivation is to promote card use."[8] After all, American Express gives $30 million a year to charities; it simply could have given SOS the $5 million. But the SOS campaign, like Ronald McDonald House, is an example of "cause-related marketing," in which the real objective is the selling of the corporate product.[9]

Rationalization

Although all three of these similarities are important, the major similarity between fast-food restaurants and credit cards is that both can be seen as part of the process of rationalization. The theory of rationalization is most commonly associated with Max Weber, although, as we have seen, Georg Simmel had a very similar perspective.[10] Weber's theory suggests five basic components of rationalization:[11]

♦ *Calculability.* Rationalization involves an emphasis on things that can be calculated, counted, or quantified. There is a tendency to use quantity as a surrogate measure for quality, which leads to a sense that quality is equated with large quantities of things.

◆ *Efficiency.* Rationalization involves the search for the best possible means to whatever end we have in mind. In a rationalized society, efficiency can become an end in itself.

◆ *Predictability.* A rationalized world involves as few surprises as possible. Thus, goods and services will be very similar, if not identical, from one time or place to another.

◆ *Substitution of nonhuman for human technology.* This component is self-explanatory, although it should be noted that often the ultimate objective of such a change is to enhance the amount of control exercised over human beings.

◆ *Irrationality of rationality.* Rational systems seem inevitably to spawn a series of irrationalities that serve to limit, ultimately compromise, and perhaps even undermine rationality. The major example of such an irrationality is the dehumanization often associated with highly rational systems. Dehumanization causes a series of personal troubles for people, most notably difficulty in finding meaning in their lives. More generally, rationalization leads to what Weber termed the "iron cage" of rationalization. That is, we are increasingly trapped in rationalized structures like bureaucracies and fast-food restaurants from which there is less and less possibility of escape.

Rationalization, then, can be defined as the process by which the five components outlined above come to characterize more sectors of the social world. The process is well underway in the United States and to an increasing degree around the world as well.

The credit card, like the fast-food restaurant, is not only a part of this process of rationalization but is also a significant force in the development and spread of rationalization. Just as McDonald's rationalized the delivery of prepared food, the credit card rationalized (or "McDonaldized") the consumer loan business.[12] Prior to credit cards, the process of obtaining loans was slow, cumbersome, and nonrationalized. But obtaining a modern credit card (which can be though of as a noncollateralized consumer loan) is now a very efficient process, often requiring little more than filling out a short questionnaire. With credit bureaus and computerization, credit records can be checked and applications approved (or disapproved) very rapidly. Furthermore, the unpredictability of loan approval has been greatly reduced and, in the case of preapproved credit cards, completely eliminated. The decision to offer a preapproved card, or to approve an application for a card, is increasingly left to a nonhuman technology—the computer. Computerized scoring systems exert control over credit card company employees by, for example, preventing them from approving an application if the score falls below the agreed-on standard. And these scoring systems are, by definition, calculable, relying on quantitative measures rather than qualitative judgments about things like the applicant's "character." Thus, credit card loans, like fast-food hamburgers, are now being served up in a highly rationalized, assembly-line fashion. As a result, a variety of irrationalities of rationality, especially dehumanization, have come to be associated with both.

It is worth noting that the rationalization of credit card loans has played a central role in fostering the rationalization of other types of loans, such as automobile and home equity loans. Automobile loan approvals used to take days, but now a loan can be approved, and one can drive off in a new car, in a matter of hours, if not minutes. Similarly, home equity loans can now be obtained much more quickly and easily than was the case in the past. Such loans rely on many of the same technologies and procedures, such as scoring systems, that are used in decision making involving credit cards.[13] Thus, just as the process of rationalization in society as a whole has been spearheaded by the fast-food industry, it is reverberating across the banking and loan business led by the credit card industry. We can anticipate that over time other types of loans, involving larger and larger sums of money (mortgages and business loans, for example), will be increasingly rationalized. Virtually every facet of banking and finance will be moving in that direction.

We can get a glimpse of the rationalized future of banking at one branch of Huntington Bancshares of Columbus, Ohio. The branch in question is the busiest of the bank's 350 outlets, processing as many home equity loans as 100 typical branches and handling as many new credit cards as 220 of those branches. It is distinguished by the fact that none of its business is done in person—it is all done by telephone. Of the fear of alienating customers because of the dehumanization associated with this type of banking, the chairman of Huntington Bancshares says, "I don't mind offending customers and losing them if it benefits the bank in the long run. . . . I'd rather have fewer customers and make an awful lot of money on them than have a lot of customers and lose our shirt."[14]

Whatever its impact on customers, the branch is certainly efficient. For example, it is able to approve a loan in 10 minutes, even if the request is made by telephone in the middle of the night. Here is the way the system works:

> As soon as a "telephone banker" types the first few identifying details of an application onto the computer, the machine automatically finds the records of the customer's previous activity with Huntington and simultaneously orders an electronic version of the applicant's credit bureau file. The phone banker then contacts by pager one of two seasoned loan officers who roam the maze of office cubicles in the telephone center.
>
> With printouts of the banking records, credit file and computer-analyzed loan application in hand, a loan officer can generally make a decision in less than a minute. The bank says its credit problems are no greater than for loans from its branches.[15]

Huntington Bancshare's so-called "telephone banker" appears to be the counterpart to the McDonald's counterperson or the worker at the drive-through window. Telephone bankers are clearly far less skilled than their predecessors. They are reduced to glorified computer operators, with the truly important and difficult work (analyses of credit records and loan decisions) being done by the computer and the loan officers. Thus, "McDonaldized" banking brings with it deskilling and the further rationalization of bank work. It is forecast that about 40% of the 100,000 bank branches in the United States are likely to be closed over the next decade. Some of these closures will be due to mergers, but many will be due to the replacement of the less efficient, conventional branches and traditional bankers with new, more efficient branches and telephone bankers.

In sum, credit cards and CREDEBELS in general, like the fast-food restaurant, can be seen as part of the rationalization process. The growth of the credit card industry (like the fast-food industry) is a reflection of the increasing rationalization of society, and the industry is in turn furthering the rationalization process. This is an extremely important point. That is, the credit card and CREDEBELS are not merely key elements of a rationalizing society. They are also crucial to the efficient operation and the continued expansion of the rationalized business world. Debit cards additionally help the banking industry to grow more efficient, and other types of electronic funds transfers (EFTs) hold out the promise of a far more rationalized and efficient system of, among many others, health and medicine. Thus, CREDEBELS are deeply implicated in the further rationalization of many aspects of society. It is in this sense that credit cards, and CREDEBELS more generally, are central not only to the future rationalization of society but also to the emergence of the problems and irrationalities that are such worrisome aspects of a rationalizing society.

Now let us turn to a discussion of each of the components of rationalization and the ways in which they apply to the credit card business.

Calculability: The All-Important Credit Report

Calculability is reflected in the fast-food restaurants by, for example, the names they give to their products. These names usually emphasize that the products are large. Examples include the Big Mac, the Whopper, the Whaler, and Biggie fries. The emphasis on things that can be quantified is also reflected in, among other things, products like the Quarter Pounder and publicity on how many billions of hamburgers are sold and how quickly pizzas can be delivered.

The credit card industry also emphasizes things that are quantified, although this more conservative industry generally shies away from the clever names employed in the fast-food industry. (However, one is led to wonder just how long it will be before we see something like the "Whopper Card.") Among the most visible of the quantified aspects of credit cards are their credit limits, interest rates, and annual fees (or lack thereof). Credit cards permit people to maximize the number of things they can buy and optimize the amount of money they can spend. By offering instant credit up to a predefined but expandable limit, credit cards allow people not only to spend all their available money but also to go into debt for, in many cases, thousands of dollars. Furthermore, in an effort to increase their level of debt, people often seek to maximize the credit limit on each of their cards and to accumulate as many cards as possible, each with as high a credit limit as possible. In fact, increasingly important status symbols in our society are the number of credit cards one has in one's wallet and the collective credit limit available on those cards. The modern status symbol is thus debt rather than savings. In sum, credit cards emphasize a whole series of things that can be quantified—number of cards, credit limits, amount of debt, number of goods and services that can purchased, and so on.

Calculability involves not only an emphasis on quantity but also a comparative lack of interest in quality. The fast-food industry is concerned with large portions (Big Mac) and low prices (value meals) but not with taste (there is no "Delicious Mac" for sale at your local McDonald's). Similarly, the emphasis on the quantity of credit card debt allowed tends to lessen people's interest in the quality of the things that they can acquire while running up that debt. With a finite amount of cash on hand or in the bank, consumers tend to be more careful, buying a relatively small number of high-quality goods that promise to have a long and useful life. But consumers who buy things on seemingly ever-expandable credit often have less interest in quality. The accent is on buying large numbers of things, with comparatively little concern that those things might deteriorate swiftly. After all, if things wear out quickly, they can be replaced—perhaps when one's credit card has an even higher credit limit.

Relatedly, the ready availability of virtually anything and everything on credit leads to a leveling in the value of products. This leveling of everything to a common denominator leads to the cynical attitude discussed by Simmel: that everything has its price, that anything can be bought or sold on the market. Because anything can be bought at any time, people develop a blasé attitude toward things. Simmel describes this as a view of "all things as being of an equally dull and grey hue, as not worth getting excited about."[16] In slightly different terms, the credit card (and before that money) is the absolute enemy of esthetics, reducing everything to formlessness, to a purely quantitative phenomenon.*

Qualitative issues aside, it could be argued from the point of view of calculability that high levels of credit card debt make sense, at least in periods of high inflation. For example, in the late 1970s and early 1980s, when inflation rates were 10% or more, it made little sense to put money in the bank at $5\frac{1}{4}$%, because at those rates one would lose $4\frac{3}{4}$% on savings each year.[17] Furthermore, in buy-

---

*For a dissenting view on this issue, at least as far as money is concerned, see Viviana A. Zelizer. *The Social Meaning of Money*. New York: Basic Books, 1994.

ing on credit in inflationary times, one ends up repaying debts at a later time with cheaper (that is, inflated) dollars. An added incentive is the fact that interest payments were fully tax deductible until 1986. It was these kinds of realities that led to the dramatic rise in credit card debt.

In very different economic times, calculability should lead people to cut back on credit card purchases. Indeed, during the recession of the early 1990s, consumers tried to reduce their credit card debt and banks became more restrictive about issuing new cards and canceled some existing cards.[18] To take another example, in the year following the Tax Reform Act of 1986, which over a five-year period reduced and ultimately eliminated deductions for interest on credit card debt, a record number of people (40%) paid off their balances in full, compared to 33% in 1986. When people did the calculations, they found that it made sense to pay off the debt.

Although people clearly try to be sensible about debt, the lure of all those things one can buy with a credit card seems to overcome them in the long run. The rush to pay off credit card debt after tax-law changes in 1986 began to wane quickly, and by 1988 only 35% of cardholders were paying off their debts in full.[19] Today, about the same percentage of people pay off their credit card debts in full as did in 1986, the last year that interest on credit card debt was fully tax deductible.

A particularly revealing example of quantification in the credit card industry is the use of "credit scoring" in determining whether an applicant should be issued a credit card (or receive other kinds of credit). Of course, in the end the majority of applicants are approved by one credit card firm or another, because the profits from the credit card business are extraordinarily high. Credit card firms can afford to have a small proportion of cardholders who are delinquent in paying their bills or even who default on them. Nonetheless, it is obviously in the interest of the card companies to weed out those who will not be able to pay their bills.

Credit scoring is usually a two-step process.[20] First, the application itself is scored by the credit card company. For example, a homeowner might get more points than a person who rents. If an application scores a sufficient number of points, the lender then buys a credit report on the applicant from a credit bureau. The score on the credit report is key to the decision to issue a card. Said a vice president of a company in the business of designing scoring models for lenders: "You can have an application that's good as gold, but if you've got a lousy credit report, you'll get turned down every time."[21] In other words, it is the numbers, not qualitative factors, that are ultimately decisive.

Scoring models vary from one locale to another and are updated to reflect changing conditions. Despite great variation from report to report, the following items usually receive the most weight:

- *Possession of a number of credit and charge cards* (30% or more of the total points). Having too many cards may cost points, but having no cards at all may be an even more serious liability.

- *Record of paying off accumulated charges* (25% or more of the points). Being delinquent on a Visa or MasterCard is likely to cost more points than being late on a payment to a department store. The credit card companies have found that when people are having economic difficulties, they try to stay current on their credit card payment but might let their department store bill slide. Thus being delinquent on credit card bills is a sign of serious financial difficulties. Delinquencies of 30 days might not cost an applicant many points, but delinquencies of 60 days or more might well scuttle one's chances of getting a card.

- *Suits, judgments, and bankruptcies involving the applicant.* Bankruptcies are likely to be particularly costly. The president of a credit scoring firm said, "Lenders aren't very forgiving about bankruptcy. . . . They figure a bankrupt ripped off a creditor and got away with it legally."[22]

- *Measures of stability.* These include applicants' tenure on the job and in their place of residence. Someone who has lived in the same place for three or more years might get twice as many points as someone who has recently moved.

- *Income.* The higher the income of the applicant, the greater the number of points on this dimension.

- *Occupation and employer.* The highest-rated occupations, executives and professionals, are likely to earn an applicant a large number of points. Similarly, being in the employ of a stable and profitable firm is likely to garner the applicant many points, whereas employment in a firm on the edge of bankruptcy is likely to be very costly.

- *Age.* Generally, the older the applicant, the greater the number of points.

◆ *Possession of savings and checking accounts.* Checking accounts, because they tend to require more ability to manage finances, generally get twice as many points as savings accounts.

◆ *Homeownership* (often 15% of the total points). An applicant who owns a home is more stable than one who rents, has a sizable asset to protect, and is responsible for regular payments.

Scoring systems clearly quantify the decision-making process. In doing so, they reduce human qualities to abstract quantities. That is, they reduce the individual quality of creditworthiness to a simple, single number that "decides" whether or not an applicant is, in fact, worthy of credit. The more human judgment of an official of a credit card firm is then considered unnecessary. One banking consultant claims that "the character of an individual is much more important than [a credit score]. You can't decide who to lend to by using a computer."[23] However, with a crush of applicants brought in large part by active recruiting efforts, credit card firms are increasingly relying on computerized scoring systems and paying more attention to quantifiable scores.

Scoring systems are not used just to weed out applicants but are also increasingly employed to evaluate existing credit card customers. Said the president of a company with 2 million credit card accounts:

> The software goes in and looks at attributes of a customer's account and how that account is being handled [by the customer]. And through a statistical methodology . . . [i]t looks at payment patterns, usage patterns. . . . We look at every account automatically and assign a behavior score. That score is, if you will, an odds quote, 100 to 1 or 1,000 to 1.
>
> It can't predict a specific account. . . . It can look at a lot of accounts and predict that out of that pool of, say, 10,000 accounts that one of them will go delinquent. So we can look at that pool and get a sense of risk from the profile.[24]

A scoring system is used on existing credit card users with a number of different purposes in mind. First, the scoring system helps the credit card firm decide whether to increase a current cardholder's credit limit. The computer evaluates whether an increase in the limit is likely to lead the cardholder into delinquencies. Second, the scoring system helps with decisions on authorizing transactions over a credit card's limit. The computer can make such an authorization on its own, or it can pass the decision to a human evaluator.[25] Third, a credit card company might develop scores based on its own records or on those of the credit bureaus that it can use to determine whether cardholders are likely to pay their bills. Fourth, a scoring system helps decide whether cardholders who have just become delinquent will eventually return to "current" status (that is, no longer be delinquent) or become more seriously delinquent. The firm can then decide whether action is needed and, if so, what type of action (for example, wait to see what happens, begin a collection effort, or cut off the account completely). Fifth, scoring is sometimes used to determine which cardholders are likely to become bankrupt. Finally, accounts are scored to assess which ones are likely to be most profitable. Those that offer little in the way of profits (especially the accounts of convenience users) are likely to be dropped or not renewed.[26]

Efficiency: The Faster the Better

The second component of rationality—efficiency—is manifest in the fast-food industry, among many other ways, in the drive-through window. For customers the drive-through is a far more efficient way of obtaining a meal than parking one's car, walking to the counter, ordering, paying, and returning to the car. (Walking into the restaurant, of course, is, in turn, a much more efficient method for obtaining a meal than cooking from scratch.) To take one other example, finger foods like Chicken McNuggets are far more efficient to eat than chicken parts like wings, legs, and breasts. Unlike chicken wings, Chicken McNuggets can be tossed into one's mouth as one drives to the next rationally and efficiently organized activity.

Similarly, the credit card is a highly efficient method for obtaining, granting, and expending loans. Applicants need do little more than fill out a brief application, and in the case of preapproved credit cards, even that requirement may be waived. In most cases, the customer is granted a line of credit, which is accessed and expended quickly and easily each time the card is used. Assuming a good credit record, as the credit limit is approached it will be increased automatically, thereby effortlessly increasing the potential total loan amount.

Furthermore, the credit card tends to greatly enhance the efficiency of virtually all kinds of shopping. Instead of carrying unwieldy amounts of cash, all one needs is a thin piece of plastic. There is no need to plan for purchases by going to the bank to obtain cash, no need to carry burdensome checkbooks and the identification needed to get checks approved. With their credit cards, consumers are no longer even required to know how to count out the needed amount of currency or to make sure the change is correct.

Credit (and debit) cards are also more efficient from the merchant's point of view. The average cash transaction at, for example, a supermarket is still fastest (16 to 30 seconds), but it is closely followed by card payment (20 to 30 seconds); a check transaction lags far behind (45 to 90 seconds). Although it might be a tad slower than cash at the checkout counter, a card transaction is ultimately far more efficient than a cash deal because it requires little from the merchant except the initial electronic transmission of the charge. Handling cash is, as one supermarket electronic banking services executive points out, "labor intensive. From the time it leaves the customer's hands to the time it hits the bank, cash may get handled six to eight different times, both at the store and at the bank level."[27] All these steps are eliminated in a charge (or debit) transaction.

Credit cards and debit cards are unquestionably more efficient than checks as far as the merchant is concerned. Debit cards, which can be thought of as "electronic checks," are more efficient because the amount of the bill is immediately deducted from the customer's account. Eliminated with both credit and debit cards are bounced checks and all the inefficiencies and costs associated with trying to collect on such checks. Furthermore, it is quicker to get a card transaction approved than it is for the customer to write a check and have it approved. Like other businesses, "grocery stores like the cards because they speed up the checkout line."[28] Other EFTs, such as paying bills by computer or telephone, promise even greater efficiencies because customers do not interact on a face-to-face basis with the merchant's staff.

Despite their greater efficiency in comparison to cash, credit and debit cards have rarely been accepted in that center of efficiency, the fast-food restaurant. The executive vice president of Visa describes the problem: "In the fast food arena, we have traditionally had next to no presence for one reason—speed. In a business where fast is beautiful, the card authorization and purchase process has been too slow to make cards attractive." However, some fast-food restaurants have tried to make credit charges more efficient, as the Visa executive explains:

> At the point of sale, the card is passed through a stripe reader and immediately checked against a hot-card file. If a card is good, the amount of the purchase is automatically credited to it. Then the authorization is flashed on a video screen in front of the checker.
>
> The entire process is instantaneous: no phone calls, no imprint and signature procedures. Consumers get more convenience and flexibility. And speed-minded merchants get a payment system that's even faster than cash.[29]

The highly rationalized Wal-Mart stores have also installed new technology that makes the process by which card transactions are approved almost instantaneous. According to a spokesperson for the company, "Not too long ago, customers hesitated to use their cards because it took so doggone long to get a transaction processed."[30] Such hesitation is clearly a thing of the past at Wal-Mart and increasingly at many other highly rationalized settings as well.

Predictability: Avoiding Those Painful Lulls

Predictability is manifest in the fast-food restaurant in the fact that the food, the physical structure, and the service are likely to be the same from one time or place to another. Even the demeanor and behavior of the employees is likely to be highly predictable. Predictable behavior is ensured by the fact that franchise owners and managers are socialized by institutions like McDonald's Hamburger University. The owners and managers in turn train employees to behave predictably, and they constantly monitor that behavior to be sure it conforms to the norms of the organization. Among other things, the employees often follow scripts that help ensure that they utter the lines expected of them.[31] For example, the Roy Rogers hamburger chain used to have its employees dress like cowboys and cowgirls. Following the corporate script, employees greeted customers with a friendly "Howdy, pardner," and bid them adieu after paying with a hearty "Happy trails."

The credit card has made the process of obtaining a loan quite predictable as well. Consumers have grown accustomed to routine steps (filling out the questionnaire, for example) that lead to the appearance of a new card in the mail. After all, many people have gone through these same steps many times. In the case of preapproved credit cards, the few remaining unpredictabilities have been eliminated, because offer and acceptance arrive in the very same letter.

Credit cards themselves are also highly predictable. Whatever company issues them, they are all likely to be made of the same materials, to feel the same, to be the same shape, to include similar information in similar places, and to do just about the same things. In fact, it is these similarities that prompt the credit card companies to attempt to distinguish their cards by, for example, their distinctive advertisements and array of enhancements. The fast-food restaurants do much the same thing (for example, giving away glasses or selling toys or videotapes of movies at bargain prices) because the hamburgers, fried chicken, french fries, and soft drinks of one are difficult to differentiate from those of competitors. The goal of both the credit card firms and the fast-food restaurants is to manufacture a sense of difference where none, in fact, exists.

Whenever human beings are involved in a transaction, unpredictability increases. Thus both fast-food restaurants and credit card companies seek to minimize interaction between their staff and customers. However, there is far less such human contact in the credit card industry than in the fast-food business. (And there is painfully little genuinely human contact in fast-food restaurants.) The limited contact that does exist in the credit card business is likely to take place over the telephone. It might take the form of unsolicited calls made in an effort to recruit new card users. More likely it involves calls by cardholders to the company to inquire about bills or by employees of the company to cardholders to find out why payments are late. However one comes into contact with employees of the credit card firms, much of the interaction is likely to be scripted. The telephone solicitors are clearly reciting scripts mindlessly. Even those responding to customer inquiries or complaints have been trained to select the appropriate scripts and subscripts depending on the nature of the inquiry or complaint and the direction taken by the conversation.

The credit card also serves to make consumption in general more predictable. Before credit cards, people had to spend more slowly, or even stop consuming altogether, when cash on hand or in the bank dipped too low. This unpredictability at the individual level was mirrored at the societal level by general slowdowns in consumption during recessionary periods. But the credit card frees consumers, at least to some degree, from the unpredictabilities associated with cash flow and the absence of cash on hand. It even frees them, at least for a time, from the limitations of depleted checking and savings accounts. Overall, the credit card has a smoothing effect on consumption. We are now better able to avoid "painful" lulls when we are unable to participate in the economy because of a lack of ready cash. Most generally, the credit card even allows people to consume, at least to some degree, during recessionary periods. For the purveyors of goods and services, the availability of credit cards makes the world more predictable by helping to ensure a steadier stream of customers during bad times as well as good ones.

Nonhuman for Human Technology: No Visitors, No Staff

A variety of nonhuman technologies are found in the fast-food restaurant: soft-drink machines that shut themselves off when the cups are full, french fry machines that buzz when the fries are done and automatically lift the baskets out of the oil—and soon robots rather than real human beings to serve customers. These technologies control employees, deskill jobs by transferring skills from people to machines, and ultimately replace people.

The credit card is itself a kind of nonhuman technology. More important, it has given birth to technologies that intervene between buyer and seller and serve to constrain both. Most notable is the vast computerized system that "decides" whether to authorize a new credit card and whether to authorize a given purchase. Shopkeeper and customer may both want to consummate a deal, but if the computer system says no (because, for example, the consumer's card is over its credit limit), then there is likely to be no sale. Similarly, an employee of a credit card firm may want to approve a sale but be loath, and perhaps forbidden, to do so if the computer indicates that the sale should be disapproved. The general trend within rationalized societies is to take decision-making power away from people (customers, shopkeepers, and credit card company employees alike) and give it to nonhuman technologies.

With the advent of smart cards, the card itself will "decide" whether a sale is to be consummated. Embedded in the card's computer chip will be such information as spending limits, so the card itself will be able to reject a purchase that is over the limit.

Not only do some aspects of our CREDEBEL society take decision making away from human beings, but other of its elements eliminate people altogether. Thus, widespread distribution of the smart card may eliminate many of the people who now operate the credit card companies' extensive computer systems. Today, ATMs have been increasingly replacing bank tellers. A bank vice president is quite explicit about the substitution of ATMs for human beings: "This might sound funny, but if we can keep people out of our branches, we don't have to hire staff to handle peak-time booms and the like. That drives down costs."[32] A similar point can be made about debit cards, which involve far less human labor than do the checks that they are designed to replace. The growth of debit cards has undoubtedly led to the loss of many bank positions involved in clearing checks. Similarly, because credit cards are designed to be used in place of cash, the increasing use of such cards has led to the loss of positions involved in a cash economy (for example, bank tellers needed to dole out cash).

The next steps in this historical process involve the further development of the so-called "information highway." Increasingly, people will not need to leave their homes in order to conduct financial transactions. They will be able to use their ATM, debit, and credit cards to transfers funds through their telephones, home computers and television screens.[33] The result will be even more nonhuman technology and even less contact with other human beings.

Various pressures have forced the credit card industry to pursue ever higher levels of rationalization through new nonhuman technologies. For example, both consumers and shopkeepers want quick authorizations of credit card sales, and so more sophisticated computers and computer programs have been developed The credit card companies also have a strong interest in seeing charges entered speedily into customer accounts so that the bills will be paid sooner or, better yet, so interest charges can begin accruing sooner on unpaid balances. The search for speedier billing has led to further technological advancement.

Consider Visa's computer system, Visanet, which serves as the intermediary among the merchant, the merchant's bank, and the card-issuing bank. Visanet is a huge network encompassing "9 million miles of fiber-optic cable . . . 20,000 banks and other financial institutions, and 10 million merchants in 247 countries and territories worldwide."[34] This system handles an average of 11,000 transactions per minute. Most of them go through two "super centers" in Virginia and England, as well as 1,400 smaller Visa computers. From swiping the card through the point-of-sale terminal to approving the transaction, the entire process ordinarily takes between 6 and 20 seconds. In this process, the system determines whether the card is stolen, whether the transaction exceeds the card's credit limit, and whether it is an unusual purchase that might not have been authorized by the cardholder.

On-line systems like Visa's Internet and MasterCard's Maestro also permit the instantaneous transfer of funds when a debit card is used. Transfers of funds using far less sophisticated off-line systems take a few days to complete (see the Appendix for more on this subject).

Another pressure toward further technological advancement and greater control is the need to quickly and correctly approve credit applications. As mentioned earlier, more of these decisions are being made by computerized credit scoring systems these days. The computer may even generate the acceptance or rejection letter, in which case the application might be handled without any human involvement whatsoever.

Perhaps the most visible example in the credit card business of taking control from humans and building it into the technology is the movement away from "country-club" billing to "descriptive billing." In country-club billing, customers receive with their monthly bills copies (or facsimiles) of the actual charge slips used for each purchase. American Express continues to provide this service but it is an expensive undertaking. In the main, credit card companies have adopted descriptive billing, in which cardholders merely get a list of the charges, dates, and amounts. The problem with descriptive billing is the loss of control by consumers. With copies of receipts, which include authorizing signatures, cardholders can clearly see whether or not they actually made each purchase. With only lists included in the bill, cardholders must rely on memory or on their own record keeping to verify purchases. People often get frustrated with the bother and assume the list of charges is correct, thereby surrendering control to the credit card companies and their computers.

By the way, the consumer's need to keep credit card records and to verify long lists of bills is indicative of another characteristic of a rationalizing society: making consumers do more of the work without being paid. In the fast-food restaurant, customers collect their own food and dispose of the remnants when they are done eating, thereby serving as their own servers and buspersons. In the credit card business, since most companies no longer provide us with copies of receipts, customers are required to keep the copies and check them against the list provided with their monthly bills. Consumers have also become responsible for detecting and correcting errors in their credit bureau records. As Gerri Detweiler puts it, *"The system is not user-friendly: you have to do all the work."*[35]

Irrationality of Rationality: Caught in the Heavy Machinery

The irrationality of rationality takes several forms. At one level, irrationality simply means that what is rational in planning does not work out that way in practice. For example, the drive-through window in the fast-food restaurant is supposed to be a very efficient way of obtaining a meal, but it often ends up being quite inefficient with long lines of cars inching toward the takeout window. Similarly, credit cards are supposed to offer greater efficiency but sometimes are quite inefficient. Take, for example, the Discover Card's program to allow its cardholders access to Sprint's long-distance service. To make a long-distance call with the card, "all you need do is dial Sprint's 11-digit access number. Then 0. Then a 10-digit phone number. Then the 16-digit account number from your Discover Card. Then a four-digit 'Personal Access Code.'"[36] A highly inefficient string of 42 digits must be entered just to make one long-distance telephone call. To take another example, the credit card companies are supposed to function highly predictably. Thus, for example, our bills should be error free. However, billing errors do find their way into monthly statements. For example, there may be charges that we did not make or the amount entered may be incorrect.

The most notable irrationality of rationality in the fast-food industry is the creation of a dehumanized and dehumanizing setting in which to eat or work. Such an inhuman, rationalized world is irrational from the point of view of those who must deal with it. Of course, the credit card world is also highly dehumanized, because people generally interact with nonhuman technologies, with such products as bills or overdue notices, or with people whose actions or decisions are constrained if not determined by nonhuman technologies. Horror stories abound of people caught in the "heavy machinery" of the credit card companies. Pity the poor consumers who get charged for things they did not buy or who are sent a series of computer letters with escalating threats because the computer erroneously considers them to be delinquent in their payments. Then there are the many complaints of people who get turned down for credit because erroneous information has crept into their credit reports. Trying to get satisfaction from the technologies, or from their often robotlike representatives, is perhaps the ultimate in the dehumanization associated with a rationalizing society.

More generally, the irrationality of rationality is a general label for the problems associated with rational systems. For example, credit card companies tend to discriminate against minorities and women. Women often are unable to get credit cards because they do not have a credit history (their credit cards have typically been issued in their husbands' names). Full-time homemakers often find it difficult to get credit cards on their own because they lack an independent income. Credit card companies also discriminate against those who in the past have resisted credit and paid in cash or by check for what they bought.

Various irrationalities are associated with rationalization of the process of granting credit card loans. Besides the dehumanization associated with the process, computerized credit approval is associated with a greater likelihood of delinquency and default (Huntington Bancshares is an exception) than when financial institutions employ more traditional methods. Credit card companies are willing to accept these risks because of the relatively small amounts involved in credit card loans and the fact that credit cards in general are so profitable. Such losses are hardly noticeable.

The largest set of problems is associated with actions taken by credit card companies to increase revenues and profits. For example, credit card companies have been known to alter their accounting methods so that customers end up paying more in interest than they expect to or should pay. Initially, General Motor's cobranded card featured a potentially costly "two-cycle billing method," which worked in the following way:

> A $500 purchase made Jan. 1 does not have to be paid off until late February under typical grace periods. If only a minimum payment is made, most cards calculate interest for the March billing period on the unpaid charges from the February bill. Under the two-cycle method, a card issuer will go back two cycles and calculate the interest from the time the purchase was made.

> This extra charge will be levied only once for people who carry balances from month to month. But for those who constantly switch from paying off to carrying a balance, this two-cycle method can be costly.[37]

It is interesting to note that GM was forced to drop its two-cycle billing method because of negative publicity and cardholder complaints.[38]

In spite of this successful effort, few customers are knowledgeable enough to understand the implications of such rational accounting procedures or even that they have been implemented. The problem, however, is more general: "A number of banks took advantage of consumer complaisance by changing annual fees, rates, grace periods, late charges, and other card restrictions without attracting a great deal of consumer attention."[39] Few consumers have the will or the ability to carefully oversee the activities of the credit card companies.

Perhaps the most persistent and reprehensible activities of the credit card companies, as you saw earlier, are their efforts to keep interest rates high even when interest rates in general are low or declining. Of course, many other irrationalities of the rationalized credit card industry have also been discussed throughout this book—the tendency of credit card companies to engage in practices that lead people to spend recklessly, the secrecy of many aspects of the credit card business, the invasion of the privacy of cardholders, and the fraudulent activities engaged in by various players in the credit card world.

Personal Troubles, Public Issues, and Rationalization

Let us look now more explicitly at the rationalization process as it applies to credit cards from the perspective of the twin themes that inform this book—personal troubles and public issues. Rationalization can be seen as a large-scale social process that manifests itself in the credit card industry (among many others) and is, in the process, creating personal troubles for individuals as well as public issues that are of concern to society as a whole.

Although my focus here is the problems that rationalization creates, it certainly carries with it a wide array of benefits.[40] In fact, most of the major components of rationalization may be seen as advantageous. Most of us regard the emphasis on things that can be counted (rather than qualitative judgments), efficient operations, predictable procedures and results, and the advances offered by nonhuman technologies as highly positive characteristics of a rational society.

Still, rationalization creates many personal troubles:

+ *Calculability.* Consumerism's emphasis on buying large numbers of easily replaced things leaves us surrounded by poor-quality goods that do not function well and that fall apart quickly. More important, when we can easily acquire, and reacquire, many of the things that we desire, we are left with a cynical and blasé attitude toward the world. In addition, the scoring systems relied on by credit card firms reduce all of us to a single number. Our fundamental character means little, and so society becomes a little more flat, dull, and characterless. Decision making is taken away from human officials and handed to the computers that calculate and assess creditworthiness. Consumers are left feeling that they are controlled by cold, inhuman systems. A perfect example of this control is the fact that, once the credit bureaus have a file on a person, it is impossible for that person to opt out of the system.

+ *Efficiency.* The greater efficiency of making purchases with credit cards in comparison to the alternatives, especially cash and checks, exacerbates our society's emphasis on speed. Lost in the process is a concern for the quality of the experience and the quality of the goods and services obtained. Overall, something important but indefinable is lost in a world that sometimes seems to value speed and efficiency above all else.

+ *Predictability.* A similar point can be made about the personal troubles associated with predictability. Something very important is lost when all the things that we consume and all the experiences that we have are highly predictable. Life becomes routine, dull, boring. The excitement associated with at least some unpredictability—a surprising discovery or an unexpected experience—is lost. When people had to rely on cash they were likely to experience self-denial at times. But when the cash supply was replenished, there was excitement in finally being able to afford some object or participate in some experience. The tendency to reduce or eliminate periods of self-denial eliminates, in the process, the excitement of obtaining something for which someone has had to wait.

♦ *Substitution of nonhuman for human technology.* A considerable amount of humanity is lost when people are in the thrall of large-scale computerized systems like those in the credit card industry. Instead of being in control, people are controlled by these systems. This phenomenon is well illustrated by the switch from country-club to descriptive billing in most of the credit card industry. Similarly, the technologies associated with credit cards tend to reduce or eliminate human interaction; tend to eliminate jobs, leaving many people without work and the income and meaning that work accords; and tend to bring with them greater speed and efficiency and thus other kinds of problems.

♦ *Irrationality of rationality.* Each of the major components of the rationalization of the credit card industry can be seen as causing personal troubles for individuals. Many of those troubles relate to the irrationality of those rational systems, especially their tendency toward dehumanization. In many ways our lives are less human because of the advances in the credit card industry and the rationalization process of which they are part.

What is the public issue associated with rationalization and credit cards? At one level, the aggregation of all these personal troubles can be seen as a public issue. At another level, the policies of the credit card industry that cause these problems can also be viewed as a public issue. However, the broadest public issue is the threat of totalitarianism posed by the credit card industry in concert with the other major elements of the rationalizing society. In his 1980 book, *Charge It,* Terry Galanoy called such a totalitarian system Lifebank, the logical derivative of the credit card society.[41] In the Lifebank system, he speculated, all of a person's assets will be combined into one account, which will be controlled by one or more banks or financial institutions and their computers. All of a person's credit cards will be replaced by a single Lifebank card. Virtually all consumption will be on credit. As the bills come due, they will be automatically deducted from each person's Lifebank account. However, each person will be granted an allowance for day-to-day expenses. There will, as a result, be little cash and little need for it. Checking accounts as we know them will have largely disappeared. Lifebank's computers will make virtually all economic decisions for individuals. Credit ratings will be continually updated. The Lifebank card will be the key to virtually everything, and those without such a card will not only not have any credit in a society that depends on credit but will literally have ceased to exist as far as Lifebank's computers are concerned. In sum,

> We will have lost control. Even the banks will have lost control. The Lifebank-type system will have its own reasoning, its own standards, its own momentum, its own energy, its own life; and operating without conscience, without soul, without social logic, it will also be out of control by all standards we should still live by today.[42]

Although such a system has yet to come into existence, many developments and technological advancements in the credit card industry have made something like Lifebank more possible today, and continued technological advances make it an even a greater possibility in the future.

Lifebank does resemble the "iron cage of rationality" that underlay Weber's concern with the rationalization process. Weber feared that the world was moving toward a seamless web of rational systems that would control more and more aspects of our lives. Furthermore, we would be less and less able to escape from the rational society. Eventually, all the escape routes would be closed off (or rationalized). We would be left with little more than the ability to choose among rational systems.

It is clear that the credit card industry has become highly rationalized and taken its place as a key element of our rational society. What is particularly disturbing about the role of the credit card is that it has become one of the preferred means to an increasingly wide array of rationalized ends and thus contributes to the further rationalization of all the ends to which it provides access. It should be pointed out that the credit card can also provide access to nonrationalized ends. In that sense, it can help to liberate people from rationalization, at least until the bills come due.[43] However, credit cards (and CREDEBELS more generally) are playing a distinctive and unusually powerful role in the emergence and solidification of the iron cage of rationalization. That is the central public issue as far as credit cards are concerned, and it subsumes the wide range of more specific issues discussed in this chapter that should also be of great public concern.

Ways of Coping with the Rationalized Credit Card Industry

How can we, as individuals, deal with the rationalized credit card society? The following are a few suggestions, most of them serious:

- Use cash whenever possible. Carry great wads of bills wherever you go.
- Write to the credit bureaus and have them block your name from prescreening.
- Instead of opening unsolicited offers from credit card companies, return them to sender.
- Alternatively, apply for every card that is offered to you but that you did not solicit. When the new cards arrive, cut them up immediately.
- When telephoning your credit card company for any reason, insist on speaking to a human being.
- Never buy anything with a credit card that you would not buy with cash.
- Even though credit cards allow you to do otherwise, buy erratically and deny yourself as many things as you possibly can.
- Always use human bank tellers rather than ATM machines or telephone or computer banking. Make a point of striking up personal relationships with as many bank tellers as possible.
- If your credit card company insists on descriptive billing, question at least one item on your bill each month.
- If you think an error has been made in your bill, contest it by putting your complaint in writing. The card issuer must investigate your complaint, and you can withhold payment during the investigation. Remember: "It is not your responsibility to prove there is an error."[44]

- If you are a woman or a minority group member, put continual pressure on the credit card industry to treat you the same as it treats men and majority-group members.
- Organize a group to routinely monitor and protest the questionable practices of the credit card firms.
- Start a business that accepts only cash, and offer customers a discount equal to what the cost of the credit card transaction would be.

These kinds of actions might help you cope with some of the personal troubles associated with the rationalized credit card society, but they are of little aid in dealing with the major public issue—the iron cage of rationalization to which credit cards are contributing so mightily. In fact, it is difficult to think of individual actions that would have much of an impact on that iron cage. It is for this reason that Weber, as well as those who look at the world from a Weberian point of view, are so pessimistic about the future.

7

An American Express

The Culture That Conquered the World[1]

The "American dream" is economic success and all the material trappings (BMWs, Hugo Boss suits, villas in the Caribbean) that go with such affluence. In other words, the American dream is to be an active participant in, and beneficiary of, the "consumer society."[2] This dream predated World War II, but it was given an enormous boost by the affluence and energy of the postwar period.

Despite the durability of the American dream, there have been periods in the not-too-distant past when that dream has been questioned in the United States. For example, in the 1960s radicals and hippies rejected economic success and material possessions. But times have changed, and although we may still find holdovers from the 1960s here and there, there is little organized resistance today to the American dream.

The American dream has also been questioned and criticized internationally, most notably by various communist theorists, parties, and nations. However, the communist alternative to the American emphasis on economic success, consumption, and material possessions has, like the hippie movement of the 1960s, largely been relegated to the dustbin of history. Russia and the other remnants of the old Soviet empire are desperately trying to survive in the hope that they too can someday adopt at least a modified version of the American dream. Even now, the most desirable commercial locations in cities like Moscow and St. Petersburg are being overrun with American chains and tony Western shops. After a brief hiatus following the Tianamen Square massacre, the Chinese too seem intent on achieving as much economic success and acquiring as many material goods as they can, even if they continue to pursue them under an increasingly meaningless "communist" banner.

Thus, the American dream is coming, increasingly, to be shared worldwide. Moreover, if the American dream is the desired end for more and more people throughout the world, then the means to that end for increasing numbers of people is the credit card. The advice offered by Francis Williams to fellow Britons three decades ago is even more true today: "If we want to buy like Americans we must first learn to borrow like Americans."[3] Having invented the objective, the "dream," the United States has not surprisingly also created a distinctive means, a seemingly "magical" tool, for the achievement of that dream. Furthermore, given the fact that the United States is the center of the process of rationalization, we should not be surprised that Americans have produced a highly rationalized method of acquiring the trappings of the dream.

The credit card can be seen, to play a bit with words (as in this book's title), as "an American express." The concept implies three separable ideas:

♦ The credit card is *an* American express, not *the* American express. That is, there have been and are today other phenomena (the fast-food restaurant, to take one example) that could qualify as American expresses.

♦ The credit card is an *American* express, meaning that its epicenter is the United States.

♦ The credit card is an American *express*, implying that it is racing across the landscape of not only the United States but of much of the rest of the world as well. This fact is reflected quite strikingly in the title of a song that hit the top of Taiwan's hit parade: "Do You Love Me More or Your Visa Card More?"[4]

The credit card is far from the first American express. In the past and to some extent to this day, Coca-Cola and Levi's, among other products, have been American expresses. That is, they came to define and dominate not only the American market for these products but also the world market. However, Coca-Cola and Levi's hearken to an earlier time in our history, perhaps even to the nineteenth century. Today, Coca-Cola and Levi's have been joined, perhaps supplanted, by more contemporary American expresses, including the fast-food restaurant (especially McDonald's), the motel chain (Holiday Inn, for example), the shopping mall (for example, Mall of America), the theme park (Disneyland in particular), and the credit card (especially American Express, Visa, and MasterCard). All are largely 20th-century American creations.

And all have come to be important physical presences throughout the United States and around the globe. Fast-food and motel chains are ubiquitous throughout the United States, and foreign nations represent key growth areas for them. Shopping malls dot the American landscape and are becoming increasingly common in other nations as well. Many theme parks have been built along the lines of the Disney model, and Disney itself has expanded into Japan and France. Credit cards, too, have followed this pattern. Signs indicating acceptance of one or more of the major credit cards are found on the doors and windows of more and more businesses in the United States and throughout the world.

However, the credit card, unlike all the others, is something that people carry with them. Thus, even though the other American expresses are ubiquitous, one can escape them. In contrast, the credit card is an almost inescapable physical presence. In this sense, and others, it is of greater material significance than its competitors for the position of *the* American express.

The Global Spread of Credit Cards

It is likely that in the coming years credit card use will increase far more dramatically outside the United States than within its borders. Although the American market is not completely saturated, there are far more inroads to be made in other parts of the world. Said the vice president of Visa International, "We're pursuing markets around the world. Our focus is global."[5] In 1983, for example, 67% of Visa's credit cards were in the United States; a decade later just under 50% of its cards were in this country. Similarly, in 1983, 62% of MasterCard's cards were in the United States, but by 1992 that percentage had declined to 53%.[6] To take a more specific example, General Motors began to expand into Great Britain with its co-branded card in January 1994, and it made significant inroads during the year. It seems unlikely that the expansion of the GM card will stop with Great Britain. Furthermore, other co-branded cards are likely to follow GM into the worldwide marketplace.

In 1993 the overseas charge volume for Visa, MasterCard, and American Express was $518.3 billion, an increase of 14% over the preceding year. The proportion of overseas volume to total volume was 58% for Visa and 57% for MasterCard. American Express remained largely an American company with only 28% of its volume overseas. The other major players in the world market are Diners Club* and JCB (Japan Credit Bureau). In 1993 general-purpose credit cards did more than $1 trillion in business worldwide.[7]

We get a better sense of the global penetration of credit cards when we look at a specific region of the world—Europe. In Europe's top ten card markets, there were about 150 million bank cards in existence in 1993, compared to about 137 million in 1992.[8] France was the leader with total credit card expenditures in excess of $93 billion, followed by the United Kingdom with just over $86 billion. Germany was third, but it lagged far behind the leaders with almost $23 billion.[9] However, the use of credit cards has been growing in Germany, a nation that until recently has not been receptive to general-purpose credit cards. In late 1993, Visa began a new card association, Visa Germany, to be better positioned to take advantage of this burgeoning market. Said the vice president of Visa International, "Our members felt the time was right to [form Visa Germany] because of the significant growth that credit payment systems have seen in Germany."[10] Germany is an economic powerhouse and, although it has a long way to go, could eventually become the leading user of cards in Europe. It is interesting to note that there has been a small amount of credit card business in the former communist nations of Europe, but it is growing dramatically. These nations, as long as they remain politically stable and economically viable, could clearly be big growth areas for credit card use in the future.

Credit card use in other parts of the world, most notably Asia (where Japan is, by far, the leader), is also growing substantially. Especially noteworthy is the enormous growth in credit card volume in China, a nation with a population of well over a billion people that is undergoing powerful economic expansion. China is likely to be a far bigger player in the world's credit card game in the coming years. In fact, given its huge population, China is likely to eventually supplant Japan as the largest user of general-purpose cards in Asia.

---

*The future of Diners Club was thrown into question, however, by the loss (to American Express) of its account with the U.S. federal government, which accounted for about 25% of its total domestic business. See "Diners Club Card Loses Biggest Account to AMEX," *Buffalo News*, October 2, 1993, p. 5.

It is not just American general-purpose cards that have global reach. For example, Visa issues cards in Great Britain that are used internationally. In the first half of 1993, holders of such Visa cards were involved in 32 million transactions overseas, valued at close to 2.5 billion pounds. Most of those transactions took place in America.[11] The BarclayCard is another British card that is accepted in other countries.

Japan's JCB card is another important entry. It is accepted in many parts of the world. JCB is owned by a group of Japanese financial institutions and has been in business since 1961. It is a charge card like American Express and Diners Club; that is, it does not permit revolving debt. What is notable is that JCB is turning the tables on the United States and establishing a presence in the American market, a first for a foreign credit card. The American JCB card was designed to be an upscale product, offering among other things a concierge service through which the "card holder can rely on the company to make travel arrangements, book restaurant reservations, fetch theater tickets or even do personal shopping."[12]

Other nations are also creating their own credit cards that emulate the American model. For example, a credit card based in Guangzhou, China, that deals in yuan, not dollars, is currently seeking to expand internationally. One local bank officer said, "Now many shops outside the mainland also accept payment in yuan. And more and more mainlanders go abroad frequently or are posted overseas. . . . Back in 1983, we had a job to persuade the White Swan Hotel to accept our cards. Now, karaoke bars rush to make a deal with us even before they are opened."[13] There are 70,000 of those Great Wall credit cards in circulation, most issued over the past two years. It is unlikely that we will see Great Wall cards in New York anytime soon, but the bank is trying to expand into Hong Kong and Macau. The bank has also issued about 500 foreign credit cards, but it believes that the local economy alone could use as many as 30,000 or 40,000 more of the cards. Currently only 1 in 1,000 Chinese citizens have credit cards of any type, so there is clearly an enormous untapped market within China for both indigenous and international credit card firms.

The American card companies also have international ambitions that extend beyond credit cards. Visa, for example, purchased the Plus ATM network, which encompasses 102,000 machines in 40 countries. Plus complements Visa's worldwide empire, which also includes credit cards and Visa Check, and Interlink debit cards. Said the new head of Plus, "Our long-term goal is to consolidate brands and position Visa as the primary brand globally."[14] Thus, Visa is seeking to emulate MasterCard, which has already made its brand name and logo common to a range of products: the conventional MasterCard, Cirrus ATM cards, and Maestro debit cards. The objective of the major card companies, to put it briefly, is to become ubiquitous.

Americanization and the Credit Card

While this discussion will revolve around the idea of Americanization, we need to address an increasingly popular alternative concept—globalization.[15] Unlike those who concentrate on Americanization, globalization theorists generally refuse to focus on any single nation, or even to use the nation as the unit of analysis. Rather, globalization implies a focus on worldwide processes that are, at least to some degree, independent of nations. Furthermore, there is a refusal to think of culture as flowing largely in one direction; rather, there is a focus on the resistance of other cultures and of their independent significance in shaping world culture. Although there is much merit in the concept of globalization, at this point in history the idea of Americanization is more helpful in understanding the worldwide impact of credit cards.* After all, the credit card is an American innovation. Credit cards emanating from the United States are encountering little serious resistance from foreign competitors, and the credit cards stemming from other parts of the world are having little impact on the American market. At some time in the future, the credit card world might better be described by the term globalization, but at the moment Americanization is a far more accurate description.

An idea derived from globalization theory that does seem to have some relevance to the credit card world at the moment is "third cultures," which can be thought of as partially autonomous

---

*Similarly, in describing the worldwide dominance of American lawyers and legal services, Dezalay says, "This globalization is for the most part an Americanization." See Yves Dezalay. "The *Big Bang* and the Law: The Internationalization and Restructuration of the Legal Field," in Mike Featherstone (ed.), *Global Culture: Nationalism, Globalization and Modernity.* London: Sage, 1990, p. 281.

cultures that transcend national boundaries and exist on a global basis.[16] Exchanges of information, knowledge, goods, and people take place within these third cultures. For example, the global "finanscape" is a third culture dealing with the "movement of megamonies through national turnstiles at blinding speed."[17] Clearly, the credit card industry—and even more, the CREDEBEL industry—is a crucial component of this finanscape. The credit card society can also be seen as part of the "ethnoscape," especially in terms of the movement of people through tourism, and the "technoscape," in that it employs technologies that girdle the world. To some degree, then, the credit card world is already part of these third cultures, and it is likely to grow progressively detached from its American roots and increasingly autonomous of any single nation. Yet at the moment it is dominated by the United States, and this is likely to be the case for the foreseeable future.

The concept of Americanization has a long intellectual tradition, most of the important work having been done by nonsociologists.[18] However, Georg Simmel was concerned with the growing "Americanism" of his day. To him, Americanism stood for the "enormous desire for happiness of modern man" and, more negatively, for "modern 'covetousness.' "[19] It is interesting to note that Simmel not only anticipated all the other major themes of this book but the motif of Americanization as well.

Americanization has been characterized in various terms, few of them flattering. For instance, in 1931 Georges Duhamel of France described America as "the devouring civilization":

> American civilization . . . is already mistress of the world. . . . There are on our continent . . . large regions that the spirit of old Europe has deserted. The American spirit colonizes [or taints] little by little such a province, such a city, such a house and such a soul.[20]

In the most famous work in this tradition, published in 1968, J.-J. Servan-Schreiber, also French, saw Americanization primarily in economic terms: "Fifteen years from now it is quite possible that the world's third greatest industrial power, just after the United States and Russia, will not be Europe, *but American industry in Europe*."[21] However, time has not borne out Servan-Schreiber's prediction, and today there is a far greater danger of industrial "Toyotaization" of Europe than of Americanization of that continent's industry.

Francis Williams in 1962's *The American Invasion* came closer to the mark from the vantage point of Great Britain:

> The American invasion is going on all over the world: American ideas, American methods, American customs, American habits of eating, drinking and dressing, American amusements, American social patterns, American capital.[22]

Although Williams regarded America's investment of capital in Europe as important, he considered the "impact of American ideas, . . . American social attitudes and ways of life . . . even more profound and all-pervasive."[23]

It is in the context of this literature that we examine Richard Kuisel's 1993 book, *Seducing the French: The Dilemma of Americanization*. Kuisel argues that "there is a kind of global imperative that goes by the name of Americanization."[24] He seems to have several different ideas in mind when he refers to Americanization, ideas that are all useful in helping us think about credit cards:

- By Americanization Kuisel means that the French, and more generally other nations, accept a wide range of American exports. That is, they "accept American economic aid and guidance; borrow American technology and economic practice; buy American products; imitate American social policy; even dress, speak and (perhaps worst of all) eat like Americans."[25]

- Kuisel clearly associates Americanization and rationalization: "*Americanisme*, defined as the quest for abundance through standardized mass production and consumption, evoked Henry Ford's assembly line, ubiquitous billboards, rows of simple wood houses, packaged foods, and tractors plying vast farms."[26] In the 1930s, the French referred to this process as becoming "Fordized."[27] Indeed, Fordism—especially its emphasis on mass, standardized production using assembly-line technology—can be seen as an excellent example of rationalization and as one of the precursors of a McDonaldized society.[28]

- Kuisel often seems to equate Americanization with modernity and modernization. For example, he describes his book as being concerned with how France "became modern or 'Americanized' and yet remained French"; later, he describes the "process of modernization that has swept across postwar France."[29]

- Kuisel disengages Americanization from America and sees it as the process by which more and more societies can be described as "consumer societies." As he puts it, "Although the phenomenon is still described as Americanization, it has become increasingly disconnected from America.* Perhaps it would be better described as the coming of the consumer society."[30]

The expansion of credit cards into France, Europe, and the rest of the world can be seen, to varying degrees, as an example of Americanization in the several senses of the term discussed by Kuisel. In the main, we can say that the credit card is an American export that is bringing with it other American goods and services, rationalization, modernism, and consumerism. Now let us further explore these four issues.

Acceptance of American Exports

How does Kuisel's first meaning of Americanization relate to credit cards? First, because credit cards were invented in America, they are in a sense exports. Interestingly, France is the leader in Europe in the use of credit cards, and its use of credit cards has increased substantially.

Credit cards can also be used to purchase, among other things, a wide range of American products. However, as Kuisel notes, American exports to France were not always the finest expressions of American industry and culture. Chewing gum, Hollywood films, and comics did not convey the noblest images of the United States.[31] Nevertheless, France and much of the rest of the world have eagerly become Americanized through the use of credit cards, at least in the sense that they have used the cards to buy an array of American products.

Rationalization

Not only does Kuisel see a general association between Americanization and rationalization in France, but he also sees linkages with more specific elements of rationalization. For example, there was concern in France over the American emphasis on calculability—the focus on quantity rather than quality. Kuisel singles out American films on this dimension: "American film making as an 'industry' that produced meters of banal celluloid escapism for profit [and]

---

*If, indeed, the consumer society has become disconnected from the United States, then it might be better thought of in terms of globalization.

subordinated quality to box office receipts."[32] More generally, American society was viewed as being "mechanized" (that is, dominated by nonhuman rather than human technologies) and "monotonous" (that is, predictable). Above all, Americanization was seen as producing the irrationality of rationality:

> Machines and factories degraded work and worker. The economy should be in the service of human beings, not the other way round . . . *dehumanized.* . . . America [exhibits] the "new barbarism" reducing human beings to animalistic needs, enslaving them to an economic monster, and defining them by their functions.[33]

The "functional anthill" of the United States was seen as threatening the nonrationalized, premodern world of traditional France, which was dominated by "the small pleasures of mischief, exuberance, uniqueness, and spontaneity as well as the sterner values of frugality, camaraderie, and heroism."[34]

More generally, as you saw in Chapter 6, credit cards are both a part of and a contributor to the process of rationalization. Although that process might not have had its origins in the United States, it has come to be closely associated with it.

At this point, it might be well to look at the related issue of Fordism, because the French closely linked Fordism with rationalization and Americanization.[35] Credit cards are Fordist in several senses. For one thing, credit cards are mass produced. Second, they are products of inflexible technologies, are themselves a kind of inflexible technology, and rely on inflexible computerized systems for the approval and processing of credit card transactions. Third, they are based on economies of scale in the sense that credit card companies are driven to maximize the number of credit cards in the hands of consumers; the greater the number of cards in use, the greater the profits. Finally, credit cards can be used to purchase mass-produced, homogenous products. They also help to foster a national, even an international, market for those products.

Yet at the same time, credit cards help in various ways to foster what can be called a post-Fordist society. With credit cards, consumers can purchase more of both mass-produced and customized products. Greater sales of customized and specialized products help to foster the development of smaller and more productive manufacturing systems. More is required from the workers in those systems, who thus need higher and more diverse levels of skill in order to handle the more sophisticated technologies. These more differentiated workers, in turn, lead more differentiated lifestyles than their predecessors working on the assembly line and in other Fordist production systems. People who live more differentiated lifestyles require, in turn, more diverse products and services.

Thus, credit cards contribute to the maintenance of elements of a Fordist society as well as to the development of at least some aspects of a post-Fordist society. This analysis of credit cards leads to the conclusion that the real world is far more complex than simple models and theories would have us believe.

This analysis also casts some doubt on the association between credit cards and the rationalization process in general. If credit cards can be linked to post-Fordist societies, then why can they not be associated with a "postrational" society as well? In some ways they can be, especially in terms of many of the irrationalities of rationality (see Chapter 6). Fundamentally, however, at this juncture credit cards have far more in common with rationalization and Fordism than they do with the theoretical alternatives. But someday, just as it might be more appropriate to think about credit cards in terms of globalization rather than Americanization, it might also be more appropriate to think of them in postrational or post-Fordist terms.

Modernism

Credit cards could also qualify as a modern phenomenon and thus, to the degree that we equate modernity with Americanization, as an example of Americanization in this sense of the term as well. The equation of modernity and Americanization is characteristic of what is called modernization theory, in which it is considered "self-evident that contemporary American society, its institutional structures, and its normative matrix [is] the society most advanced in modernity."[36] However, modernization theory has fallen into disrepute for a variety of reasons, not the least of which is its assumption that the United States is the model to be emulated by the rest of the world. But in associating modernity, the United States, and credit cards, I am not saying that any or all of them are unequivocally positive. Indeed, much of this book has dealt with problems associated with credit cards and therefore implicitly with problems with American society and modernity. The point here is that both the

United States and credit cards have a variety of modern characteristics and that credit cards have played a key role in bringing Americanization and modernity, for good and ill, to much of the rest of the world.

A related issue is the relationship between modernity and postmodernity. The credit card was certainly a product of the modern era; its creation and development predated the emergence of what has come to be called postmodern society.[37] Nevertheless, some would argue that the credit card might be better thought of as a postmodern phenomenon. There is considerable debate about whether we have, in fact, moved from a modern to a postmodern society, as well as disagreement over exactly what a postmodern society is and how it differs from a modern society. The following are some of the differences that have been suggested:

♦ A modern society is highly rational, whereas a postmodern society is far less rational, perhaps even nonrational or irrational.

♦ A modern world is rather inflexible, perhaps overly wedded to a rational model, whereas a postmodern world is far more flexible, as reflected in its openness to the nonrational and the irrational. Another way of putting it is that the modern world is a world of clear answers, whereas there are no such answers in a postmodern world. A related idea is that a modern society is one with powerful ideologies, whereas such ideologies are absent or weaker in a postmodern society. Yet another related difference is modernism's strong belief that society is progressing and the absence of such a belief in postmodernism.

♦ There is a tendency to draw clear boundary lines in a modern society, whereas boundaries are far more ambiguous in a postmodern society.

♦ There is a tendency to clearly differentiate "high" and "low" culture in the modern world, but no such clear dividing line can be drawn in the postmodern world.

♦ There is a common culture in a modern world, but the postmodern world is made up of a mélange of overlapping subcultures; it is a world of great cultural diversity.

♦ A postmodern world is more dominated by simulations than is a modern world.[38] Thus, instead of going to foreign lands, we go to simulations of them at amusement parks like Busch Gardens.

♦ In a modern society, people tend to believe that they are living in the "real" world, whereas in a postmodern society, they believe that they are living in "representations" of that world. In other words, postmodernists believe that there is no real world, merely a number of representations of it, and that we all live in one or another of those representations. The implication is that, because we all live in representations, one representation is no better than the others. Thus, the postmodern society tends toward relativism, whereas modern society tends to be more absolute.

Given this sense of postmodernism, are credit cards better thought of as being modern or postmodern? Let us consider one difference between these two types of society: rigidity (and rationality) versus flexibility (and nonrationality). Credit cards are associated more with the rigidity of a modern society than with the flexibility of a postmodern society. Among those rigidities are the fact that computerized systems handle all credit card transactions in the same way, most credit cards have fixed limits, and they lead everyone to consume in much the same way.

The paradox, however, is that the rigid, seemingly modern credit card permits all sorts of flexible, postmodern behaviors and realities. For example, instead of doing our shopping only during a store's business hours, we can order products any time of the day or night through catalogs or television shopping networks and charge our purchases to our credit cards. The cards can also be used to buy the most unusual and unique products; they need not be used to buy only standardized merchandise. The result is the development of all sorts of small market niches and a wider range of options for everyone.[39] Indeed, segmentation is one of the growing trends in the credit card industry. Furthermore, we are better able to go anywhere we want anytime we like with credit cards. We do not need to engage in lengthy planning and preparations; we can simply get up and go. Thus, credit cards are simultaneously inflexible instruments and ones that provide great flexibility; in other words, they have characteristics of both modern and postmodern society.

There are a number of other ways in which credit cards are part of both the modern and the postmodern worlds. Time and space compression are characteristic of both modern and postmodern societies,[40] and the credit card is a particularly good example of both types of compression. The credit card permits us to obtain things immediately rather than wait until we have accumulated enough cash, and in many cases, it eliminates the need to travel to distant locales to obtain unusual products. We can simply order them by telephone, pay for them with a credit card, and wait at our doorstep for our purchases to arrive from all corners of the globe. Given their capacity to compress time and space, credit cards would seem to be associated with both modern and postmodern society.

Both types of society are also characterized by simulations. In terms of the means of exchange, both currency (associated with modern society) and credit cards (associated here with postmodern society, although the association is not clear-cut) can be seen as simulations: At one time currency simulated gold, and today credit cards simulate currency. (Note that credit cards are thus a simulation of a simulation.) Furthermore, both currency and credit cards can be used to purchase either authentic or simulated experiences. Thus, we can use cash or a credit card to pay for a simulated Amazon River trip at an amusement park or for the real thing.

In sum, although credit cards are certainly a product of modern society, they are also consistent in many ways with postmodern society. Thus they help put the lie to the idea of a radical disjunction between modern and postmodern society. Yet, in the end, one must conclude that there is a stronger association between credit cards, as well as Americanization, and modernity than between credit cards and postmodernity. Although it has postmodern elements, the United States remains primarily a modern society (it is, for example, still better described as rational and inflexible) and the credit card is best viewed as an agent and an aspect of modernity.

Consumerism

The final meaning of Americanization suggested by Kuisel is perhaps most unambiguously associated with credit cards. With America's heavy industries in decline, the consumer culture and its products, and the means of consuming them (CREDEBELS), have become the nation's major export:

> It should come as no surprise that the global consumer culture—particularly in the realm of movies, music and food—has remained almost an American monopoly in a time when America's hegemony in

other industries, ranging from automobiles to consumer electronics, has been shattered irrevocably.[41]

America, the source and center of the consumer society, is equally the source and center of the credit card society.

More important, the credit card has given the consumer society an enormous boost. We can safely say that the consumer society has expanded greatly as a result of the advent and growth of the credit card. Consumption that otherwise would not take place now occurs because the credit card is available. People are able to spend all that they have, and then to go well beyond that level, with their credit cards. More generally, all the other CREDEBELS—debit cards, ATMs, and electronic funds transfers—also help to feed consumption-oriented society.

Anti-Americanism and the Credit Card

Although some would equate Americanization and anti-Americanism, the two are in fact different.[42] Whereas Americanization incorporates a range of attitudes, anti-Americanism is a negative state of mind—as Kuisel defines it, "sets of attitudes that are predominantly, if not systematically or permanently . . . critical" of America.[43] He makes it clear that a single critical comment does not qualify as anti-Americanism; it must be part of a larger complex. He also argues that "petty complaints" should not be considered as reflective of anti-Americanism: "Distaste for chewing gum or Hollywood does not qualify. Contempt for Americans or American foreign policy or consumer society as 'the American way of life' does."[44]

We cannot examine the Americanization of the credit card world without asking whether credit cards have inspired anti-Americanism. The first point to be made about the relationship between credit cards and anti-Americanism is that, except for American Express, nothing overt about the general-purpose cards indicates that they are associated with America. In fact, the names of the general-purpose cards—Visa, MasterCard, Discover, Optima, Diners Club, and Carte Blanche—are generic expressly to avoid simple identification with any nation. In addition, other nations are issuing at least some of these cards and producing their own cards, such as Japan's JCB, Great Britain's BarclayCard, and even the fledgling Great Wall card of China.

However, the most important point about credit cards and anti-Americanism is that, unlike most other American products, credit cards are means rather than ends. As a result, they can be used to purchase the goods and services of any nation and thus support any nation's economy. For this reason, credit cards are far less likely to spawn anti-Americanism than are other American products, which are likely to compete with and displace indigenous products. Of course, American credit cards do compete with and displace the cards of other nations. But far more commonly, Big Macs get eaten instead of Britain's fish and chips, people drive Fords instead of Sweden's Volvos, and people drink Coca-Cola in place of French wine. However, credit cards can just as easily be used to purchase fish and chips, Volvo parts (if not Volvos themselves), and French wine as they can be used to buy American substitutes.

This is a good place to take issue with Kuisel's point that "petty complaints" do not qualify as anti-Americanism. It seems to me that chewing gum, hamburgers, or even credit cards can easily be objects of anti-Americanism. Just because they are "petty products," part of "low culture" rather than "high culture," why shouldn't hostility to credit cards qualify as anti-Americanism?[45] In fact, that hostility can be a surrogate for broader hostility to "the American way of life." Indeed, hostility to the American Express card, or McDonald's, is in some ways a better indicator of anti-Americanism than opposition to American foreign policy. Comparatively few people have direct contact with American foreign policy, but virtually everyone comes into contact with America's seemingly "petty products." Furthermore, many of these seemingly minor objects are likely to be part of the American cultural express and, as such, are likely to evoke powerful reactions, both pro and con.

In many ways, it is possible to see the credit card as the most dangerous of America's exports to the world. Because it is a means, not an end like most other American exports, it seems either benign or a great boon to the consumers of every nation. Concealed beneath this surface appearance are the malignant effects of credit cards.

From the point of view of other societies, the most important malignant effect of credit cards and the most likely cause of anti-Americanism is the threat of homogenization. Homogenization can be both a cause of private troubles and a public issue. As the use of credit cards spreads, individuals are threatened with the destruction of long-cherished cultural practices and the elimination of many of the things that have made their lives meaningful. Similarly, societies are under threat because their distinctive features appear to be eroding, to be replaced by American culture. Even though credit cards can be used to support indigenous economies and cultures, they have also very effectively brought American products, processes, and values to most of the nations of the world. One journalist described "the general tidal pull toward homogenization at play everywhere in the world. . . . The general direction in the world is toward greater similarity, at least on the levels of material ambitions, architecture, food and ambient noise—a.k.a. music."[46]

Here is what Francis Williams had to say about the homogenization and Americanization of English culture:

> The impact of American ideas, and still more of American ways of life, is now so large, the drive of America to Americanize so great, that to ask how much of what is specifically English in our civilization will remain in a decade or two if the trend continues is by no means absurd. . . . An All-American world would be the last sad surrender to conformity. [What is endangered is] much that gives to English life its colour and zest and character.[47]

The fear of homogenization appeared in France in a flap over another American product, Coca-Cola, in the 1940s. There was fierce opposition to Coke, especially from the political left, and to the "coca-colonization" of France:

> The day when opposite Notre Dame there is a poster of 'The Pause That Refreshes' and on restaurant tables one sees as many Coke bottles as carafes of red wine, it will be not only the French, but also Americans, who will feel poorer.[48]

Such a fear continues in France to this day. For example, a French official was quoted in 1994 as saying that, if the American cultural invasion is not resisted, "there will soon develop a standardized world culture created according to American norms."[49]

By helping to make all societies similarly modern, credit cards thereby help to destroy many societies' characteristics. In fact, Kuisel describes French opposition to Americanization in the 1930s as "distinctly premodern."[50] Credit cards certainly play a key role in the consumer society that the French associated with the United States and feared so much. Credit cards can also help to make all societies similarly rationalized, thereby destroying their nonrational and irrational elements.

The French probably resist Americanization more than the people of most other nations. Perhaps they are so resistant because France shares with the United States an exalted view of itself and its role in the world. As Kuisel puts it, "France and the United States clash because they are the only two Western nations that harbor universal pretensions."[51] Nevertheless, many other far less pretentious nations have had their share of anti-Americanism.

Despite anti-Americanism in many places in the world, there have been few, if any, overt signs of national opposition to credit cards. Sometimes an American Express office is the object of protest or attack, but that company's obvious association with the United States, and not the credit card per se, is the likely irritant. Again, the credit card's status as a pure means, rather than an end, makes it a less likely target for anti-Americanism. Ironically, in many ways the credit card should be a prime target of anti-Americanism, because as a means it fosters many of the types of Americanization that elicit hostility in so many nations.

It is instructive in this regard to compare the French reactions to credit cards and to the Euro Disney theme park. As an end, Euro Disney became a lightning rod for hostility, as Coca-Cola had been earlier, but as a means the credit card has largely escaped criticism.

At a cost of $5 billion, Euro Disney opened with great fanfare in a suburb of Paris in April 1992. It ran into problems even before it opened. Labor unions were upset about the demand that male employees have short hair, be clean shaven (including no mustache), and wear only one ring per hand. Female employees were forbidden to wear showy jewelry, eye shadow, or false eyelashes and were instructed to wear "appropriate undergarments."[52]

After it opened, Euro Disney came under attack from all sides. One American journalist claimed that it reeks of "a kind of sterile Americana."[53] But the reaction of French journalists and intellectuals was far worse. Among many other things, Euro Disney was called "a terrifying giant step toward world homogenization," "a cultural Chernobyl," and a "conservatory of nothingness."[54]

As a result of such criticisms—as well as a number of other factors, such as poor weather, the high price of admission (higher than Disney's American parks), high hotel room rates ($345 per night at the premier park hotel) and food prices, and most important, a recession in Europe—Euro Disney has been a dismal failure financially.[55] It lost $920 million in its first full year of operation and was in danger of being shut down unless its finances were restructured.[56]

In fact, in 1994 the parent Disney Company did agree to spend about $750 million to bail out Euro Disney, and a Saudi Arabian prince agreed to chip in up to $439 million.[57] In spite of these financial woes, 18 million people visited Euro Disney between its opening and early 1994, "making it the single largest tourist attraction in France, far surpassing even the Eiffel Tower and the Louvre."[58]

Although the world has been Americanized to a great degree, the case of Euro Disney (at least from a financial point of view and to this point in time) demonstrates that Americanization has its limits. Francis Williams argued that it "is probably true that the complete Americanization of any country other than America itself is impossible."[59] A French culture will survive, even if Euro Disney does ultimately succeed. For reassurance, one has only to look to Japan, where Tokyo Disneyland has been a huge success but has elicited little hostility and has done little or nothing to change Japanese culture. (Of course, the orderly park does fit well with Japan's highly ordered society.)[60] As sociologist Todd Gitlin noted, American culture is likely to become "everyone's second culture."[61]

The credit card will increasingly become a part of and one of the preferred means in this second culture; the credit card will allow those in other cultures to use an Americanized means to attain a variety of Americanized ends. In this sense, it does pose a more profound threat than Euro Disney. Yet at the same time the credit card is unlikely to be more than a significant part of the second culture. Furthermore, as we have seen, the credit card can be used to purchase indigenous ends. The net result, paradoxically, is that the credit card represents both a threat to other cultures and a means by which those other cultures can be nurtured and sustained. Thus, although credit cards pose the danger of homogeneity, they can also foster heterogeneity.[62] It is perhaps for this reason, in addition to its comparative invisibility, that the credit card has escaped criticisms like those aimed at Euro Disney and other manifestations of the American express.

Summing Up

In concluding this book, I would like to return to its beginnings, to the view of Georg Simmel that one can gain insight into the totality as well as the essence of society by focusing on one of its key components. The issue is, What have we learned about society through this examination of credit cards? In fact, in C. Wright Mills's terms, the examination of credit cards has led us to many of the central public issues of our time:

- By every account, Americans are spending far more and plunging far more deeply into debt than they should. This problem is reflected, among other places, in the nation's perennial budget deficit, astronomical and burgeoning public debt, a relatively low rate of private savings, and a high rate of inflation (which may have abated for the moment but will undoubtedly return to haunt us). Credit cards and the companies that hawk them have helped to foster the consumerism that contributes to such problems, but merchants, manufacturers, retailers, banks (through such other credit mechanisms as home equity loans), and many others have also played a central role. Thus, the imprudence and indebtedness associated with credit cards provide a lens through which to view broader economic problems. It is not just as individuals, with credit cards in hand, that we are likely to behave in an imprudent manner, but the government and the nation as a whole behave imprudently in many different ways. It is not just that many of us endanger our financial well-being and our future each time we increase the credit limit on our cards, but society as a whole is similarly endangered each time Congress increases the nation's debt limit.

- America is a society characterized by an increasing array of "mean machinations." Again, although credit cards have helped spawn a number of fraudulent activities, many other aspects of society are also characterized by increasing fraudulent activity. More important, fraud is merely one of a nearly endless list of mean machinations in modern society. The fraudulent activities associated with credit cards are insignificant in comparison to the fraud associated with such things as the savings and loan scandal and the machinations in the 1980s of Wall Street tycoons like Michael Milken and Ivan Boesky. Then there are even meaner machinations like murder that make credit card fraud look almost benign. Still, credit card fraud is growing in magnitude and is becoming increasingly associated with meaner machinations. Examples include kidnappings, rapes, and murders linked to ATM-related crimes. In any case, it is no accident that the issue of mean machinations emerges as central in this analysis of credit cards—it is, after all, a growing concern in the larger society of which credit cards are an integral part.

- The threat to privacy is an increasingly important problem as our society grows more sophisticated technologically and as those technologies grow more tightly intertwined. I have discussed the various ways in which our privacy is threatened by the credit card industry, but it is only one of many entities that are collecting and storing information on us. That collective body of information, and the increasing possibility that it will be centralized, poses the greatest threat to our privacy. Again, given the fact that privacy is a growing problem within the larger society, it is not surprising that it emerges as a central issue as far as credit cards are concerned.

- We live in a society that is undergoing increasing rationalization. Credit cards are both an aspect of that process and are helping mightily to foster it. But virtually every sector of society is undergoing a process of rationalization. As a result, more sectors of society are moving progressively closer to the result most feared by Max Weber—the "iron cage of rationalization," a world in which there is no escape from rationalization. All we will be able to do in the not-too-distant future is to move from one rationalized system to another, and the credit card (along with other CREDEBELS) is the ideal tool to allow for smooth movement between such rationalized systems. Being in itself rationalized, the credit card is playing a crucial role in fostering the expansion of rationalization and, with it, the dehumanization of our lives.

- We live in a world characterized by Americanization. The credit card is, like many other goods and services, a quintessentially American product that is sweeping across the world. In the process, although it can help to sustain cultural differences, the credit card is helping to Americanize the world and erode national differences. This erosion of national differences, this homogenization of the world's cultures to at least some degree, is a great threat to us all. A world of increasing sameness is a world of decreasing interest.

In sum, the credit card is important not just in and of itself but also in its ability to shed light on other issues. Examining credit cards helps us understand the essence of the modern world, as well as some of the most pressing personal troubles and most fundamental public issues of our time.

Appendix

Those Other CREDEBELS

Debit Cards, Electronic Funds Transfers,
and Automated Clearinghouses

Although they have concerned us far less than credit cards throughout this book, more can be said about the other CREDEBELS than is to be found in the brief overview offered in Chapter 2. This Appendix is for those who want to learn more about the other CREDEBELS. The main goal is descriptive, but at the end I will analyze further the other CREDEBELS from the point of view of this book's twin themes: personal troubles and public issues.

Debit Cards

Practically everyone in the United States is quite familiar with and a frequent user of credit cards, but debit cards are another matter. Debit cards were introduced in the United States in the mid 1970s. However, it was not until well into the 1990s that debit card use began to take off, although debit cards continued to represent only a small percentage of the number of credit cards then in existence in the nation. In terms of annual dollar volume, debit cards compared even less favorably to credit cards.

In other parts of the world, debit cards are far more important. This is true in Europe and even more true in Asia where the vast majority of all cards in existence are debit cards. Not only are debit cards quite important worldwide, but they will be of increasing importance in the United States in the years to come. For example, Visa had about 15 million debit cards in 1994, but it expects to have 48 million debit cards by 1996.[1] More generally, in 1993 there were

27 million debit transactions per month, by 1996 there will be almost 100 million such transactions, and it is projected that by 2000 there will be 450 million debit transactions per month.[2]

Debit cards are distinguished from credit cards by the fact that the consumer's checking account is accessed when a transaction takes place. Access may be direct (or "on-line") or delayed (or "off-line"). In on-line systems, the merchant's point-of-sale system (POS), a computerized cash register, is directly linked to the customer's checking account via electronic funds transfer (EFT) networks. An immediate hold is put on the customer's account for the amount charged. A merchant knows immediately whether the customer has enough funds to cover a purchase. With off-line systems, however, clearing and settling a transaction may take up to several days. Thus off-line cards are likely to be issued only to a bank's best customers, whereas on-line cards can be issued to the vast majority of applicants. The main advantage of off-line systems is that they are considerably cheaper to operate than on-line systems.

Debit cards are generally issued by banks, increasingly in the United States under the Visa and MasterCard labels. Among the other types of organizations that are issuing debit cards are brokerage firms, so customers can automatically deduct money from their investment accounts. Such debit cards are expected to be a big growth area in the future.

Debit cards are very attractive to banks (and other financial institutions) because they eliminate the "float," the interest-free grace period between the time that consumers make a purchase and the time that they pay their credit card bill (assuming they do not "revolve" their account). Debit cards are also attractive to merchants, because they reduce paperwork, eliminate credit risks, and allow the immediate (or near-immediate) transfer of funds to merchant accounts. However, because customers pay no interest on unpaid debit card balances (there is no such thing) and because fees from merchants and customers are comparatively small and sometimes nonexistent (at least at the present time), debit cards do not offer the banks the kinds of profits that are derived from credit cards. Yet banks (and other firms) are eager to get into the debit card business because they believe it will become more profitable in the future. It also gives them advantages over competitors that do not offer debit cards (for example, offering debit cards can lure more checking account customers. As the vice president of one financial corporation said, "In the short term we're looking at [offering debit cards] as a competitive advantage. In the long term, it will become a competitive necessity."[3]

Debit card growth is likely to take off soon, because both Visa (through Interlink) and MasterCard (through Maestro) have developed nationwide systems (Maestro will also function internationally) of interconnected computers that will greatly facilitate on-line debit card transfers among consumers, merchants, and banks.* That growth is likely to be further fueled by the competition between Visa and MasterCard for this potentially highly lucrative market.[4] Banks can issue credit cards from both Visa and MasterCard, but as a result of a 1990 agreement by those two organizations,[5] banks must choose between Interlink and Maestro debit cards.

These national systems join a number of regional systems (such as NYCE and Mac) that issue debit cards and process debit card transactions. In fact, Interlink was a functioning regional system when it was purchased by Visa and transformed into a national system. For the foreseeable future, it is the regional networks that will continue to control the debit card business because it is dominated by close-to-home transactions like purchasing groceries and gasoline.[6]

Despite the projections for great growth, Americans have proved to be highly resistant to debit cards—for a number of reasons:

♦ A major reason, of course, is that many people prefer the free credit available during the grace period offered by credit cards. (However, at least some banks are moving toward shortening or even eliminating these grace periods, which may push more convenience users of credit cards toward debit cards.[7])

♦ The float on checks, or the few days that they take to clear the bank, is also surrendered when one switches to debit cards. In fact, it is claimed that many people hate debit cards because of the fact that money is deducted from their accounts almost instantaneously.[8]

---

*Both companies already had off-line debit cards, Visa Debit and Master Debit. In addition, Visa offers the debit card called Visa Check, which functions through its existing credit card system rather than the all-electronic Interlink system. The difference is that Visa Check transactions are not always checked electronically, and paper-based receipts may take several days to clear. See Saul Hansell. "Visa U.S.A.'s Head Hunts Markets." *New York Times*, October 7, 1993, p. D1.

◆ People are bothered by the fees (perhaps 25¢ to $1 per transaction) charged by banks to use a debit card.

◆ In contrast to paying by check, there is no stop-payment procedure available on debit cards.

◆ People using credit cards instead of debit cards have a greater ability to settle disputes over purchases, because they can withhold payment and contest a charge.

◆ The personal liability of a lost or stolen debit card is likely to be higher than the $50 limit on lost or stolen credit cards.

◆ Finally, people are generally resistant to new technologies.[9]

Nevertheless, debit cards offer several attractions to consumers.[10] For example, they enforce discipline, because consumers cannot spend more than is in their bank (or other) accounts (unless they have overdraft protection). Debit cards can also be used more easily than checks, especially where the consumer is not known to the merchant. They eliminate or reduce the number of checks one writes and the time involved in balancing checking account statements. The need to carry checks, or cash for that matter, is reduced. And debit cards are likely to be attractive to those who already pay off their credit card bills each month. In fact with a debit card, the need to pay that monthly bill is eliminated, because the funds are deducted on an ongoing basis.[11] Finally, because debit cards tend to be used for small-ticket items like gasoline, groceries, and fast food, which would ordinarily be paid for by cash or check, they often eliminate the problem of being short of cash.[12] For big-ticket items like airline tickets, people tend to prefer credit cards and their float.[13]

Not only have consumers in this country been slow to see the benefits of debit cards, but so have many retailers and banks. Retailers have been resistant because the technology, including a POS system and personal identification number (PIN) pads, is costly; because debit cards do not appear to generate new business; and because the fees paid to banks seem too high. For their part, the banks understand that debit cards will never be as profitable as credit cards because of the absence of interest on debt. The banks wonder whether debit cards can generate any profits at all.[14]

One alternative is the prepaid debit card, which again is already widely used in other parts of the world, especially Europe and Japan.[15] With this type of debit card, the individual deposits a given amount in an account and that account is then debited, up to the amount deposited, each time the card is used. The magnetic (or electronic) strip on the card records the initial face value and then makes deductions as the card is used.

In the United States, such cards are at the moment largely restricted to single-purpose uses like vending machines, copying machines, telephones, cafeterias, transit systems, and toll-booths.[16] But they can and will be used more frequently in the future and for a wider range of activities.[17] For example, a big growth area is the use of prepaid debit cards for electronic benefit transfers (EBTs) such as welfare, Medicaid, and food stamps. Instead of being given checks or stamps, people will be given debit cards that they can use to obtain money at an ATM or buy food at grocery stores with the necessary equipment. Plans are afoot to transfer the entire $17 billion national food stamp program to such debit cards.[18]

The big attraction of prepaid debit cards from a customer's perspective is that pulling one out is easier than fumbling for needed change and small bills. On the other hand, in Japan it has been found that people using prepaid debit cards make longer and costlier telephone calls because they do not need to keep feeding the telephone with coins. Extrapolating from this experience, we can predict that people may end up spending more with prepaid debit cards than they would if they used cash. In the experimental use of debit cards in an American fast-food restaurant, the average for a debit transaction was $2 to $3 more than the average cash transaction.[19] Another liability of this type of card from customers' viewpoint is that the money they initially invest in the card constitutes a free loan to the issuing companies.

The latest, but certainly not the last, innovation in this area is the wedding of the prepaid debit card and smart-card technology. In 1994 Visa announced that it would be creating an "electronic purse," a prepaid debit card whose "internal computer chip would store and keep track of value that can be loaded or reloaded at automatic teller machines or other electronic devices, and debited at vending machines, telephones, gas stations, fast-food restaurants, and other cash-oriented locations."[20]

We are going to see more innovations with debit cards in the coming years. Thus, in spite of all the reservations and the problems of the past two decades, debit cards do finally seem to be taking off. Said one observer, "Most banks realize that sooner or later they'll be offering a debit card. . . . In the '70s, it was 'will we or won't we?' Now, it's a question of when."[21]

Electronic Funds Transfers

Debit cards (as well as credit cards) involve electronic funds transfers, but other kinds of transactions entail EFTs as well. Thus, the American Bankers Association uses the idea of EFT very broadly to encompass "modern banking—the use of modern techniques for the transfer of value."[22] It includes under the EFT heading a variety of "transaction modes," including POS machines that accept debit cards, ATM machines, automated clearinghouses, telephone bill-payer services, and the like. Other, more sophisticated EFT methods, such as "smart" telephones and payment systems that operate like video games, are in the tryout or planning stage.

The Electronic Funds Transfer Association (EFTA) has identified five key areas in EFT:

♦ The first area, the use of credit and debit cards at retail POS terminals, has already been discussed here, in Chapter 2, and throughout this book.

♦ The second key area is the use of smart telephones and personal computers for home electronic services like bill paying, catalog ordering, travel arranging, and ticket ordering. For example, in telephone bill paying, customers use a touch-tone telephone to enter account numbers and amounts, and the bank automatically transfers the payments. Citicorp in New York City has set up a service, at a charge of $6.50 per month, that allows customers to pay virtually any kind of bill by telephone (the bank already offers home banking via personal computer). A customer must first provide the bank with a list of potential payees. The customer then may pay these bills by calling the customer service line. Citicorp writes checks on behalf of the customer to individuals and small businesses and transfers funds electronically to those firms that accept EFT.[23] From the bank's point of view, telephone bill paying works best with large companies that maintain their own accounts with the bank and less well when small merchants or individuals without accounts are to be paid. In the latter cases, the bank may have to write its own checks. As of now, only about 4% to 5% of all U.S. households pay by telephone (such a system is potentially available to a third of all households).[24] The major barrier appears to be, as usual, resistance to new technologies. The president of one research firm in this area said that in order to achieve wider acceptance banks "will have to come up with a product that offers some kind of receipt or screen so people can see what they are doing."[25] Whatever the potential of payment by telephone, home banking and EFTs by computer will increase. The Prodigy computer network already offers bill-paying capacity to its subscribers. Said an executive vice president of Banc One: "We believe that it's still very early in the curve of electronic bill payment, . . . whether it's PC-based or telephone. . . . We think it will be at least the middle of the decade [1990s] before we start to see the growth."[26]

◆ The third EFT area is the use of credit, debit, and prepaid debit cards for various forms of transportation. EFTs can be used for air, bus, and rail tickets, on toll roads, in parking lots, in taxis, and so on.

◆ What EFTA considers the biggest potential growth area is the increased use of EFTs in health care. Among other possibilities are the use of health-care credit cards and pharmacy cards and greater use of EFTs in insurance and patient payment processes.

◆ The fifth key area is electronic benefit transfers (EBTs) from the federal and state governments to nearly a third of the United States population. The U.S. government is planning to move toward an EBT system as early as 1996.[27] Various states are also moving in this direction, and the state of Maryland already has an EBT system in place. The electronic payment of welfare benefits offers a number of advantages. First, it is faster and less costly than paper-based systems, which involve stamps, checks, eligibility forms, and records. For example, the federal government spends $400 million a year to "print, distribute and eventually destroy" the food stamps it sends out to over 26 million people each month.[28] It is estimated that $1 billion could be saved over a five-year period on food stamps alone by switching to EBT. As of 1992, only eight states were reimbursing Medicaid providers through EFTs, but the practice has considerable appeal to financially strapped state governments.[29] For one reason, it is much less expensive. An EFT costs between 3¢ and 10¢, whereas the cost of a stamp is, at the moment, 29¢. Another cost benefit is the elimination of lost checks. In at least one state, a single lost check costs $47 to replace. Second, EBT can help cut down on the theft and fraudulent use of welfare checks and food stamps. For example, stamps may be sold to third parties who then use them to make prohibited nonfood purchases. Third, EBT reduces the stigma associated with cashing a welfare check or with using food stamps in the grocery store. Here is the way one welfare recipient described the difference between Minnesota's EBT system (which replaces food stamps and monthly welfare checks) and the system in her previous state of residence:

> We happened to live in a more affluent city and most of the people in the grocery store were not me. And I wanted to get out my food stamp coupons and, kind of trembling, tear them out. I wanted to get this done with, and then they had to stamp every one of them. And it was very embarrassing and I didn't like it at all and I ended up going to other stores where I wouldn't be known.
>
> Coming to Minnesota it is entirely different. No one knows, it seems, that I'm even on welfare. They think it's a credit card.[30]

Finally and more generally, EBTs help familiarize poor people with electronic payment systems.[31] However, as with all such changes, there are barriers to be overcome. States worry about the start-up costs, the potential for fraud, and the loss of control over their bank balances (because money is transferred more quickly than they would like, with a consequent loss of interest income).

In some cases EFTs are being combined with the electronic transfer of data. This practice is particularly attractive in the health field, which is being overwhelmed by paperwork. In 1990 Americans spent $162 billion on health care; of that amount, 20% went to administrative expenses. Banc One has a pilot program involving the electronic transfer of both payments and information. Patients are given cards with embedded information on insurance deductibles, copayments, and the like. The physician electronically completes the claim form and transmits it to the insurance company.

The insurance company then credits the doctor's account with the appropriate payment and sends a confirmation statement to the cardholder.[32]

There is also a trend toward automated EFTs for recurring bills such as mortgage payments, utility bills, and telephone bills. The customer authorizes such creditors to withdraw money from his or her account on a regular basis. In 1990, about 400 million of a total of 15 billion paid bills were settled in this way. It is estimated that automated payments are increasing at a rate of 20 percent per year.[33] It is also possible to invest money automatically by having a fixed sum transferred each month from, say, a bank account to a mutual fund account.

Automated payment systems offer advantages to all concerned parties. Banks save between 5.5¢ and 7¢ per item on processing automated payments in comparison to checks. The creditors to whom bills are being paid are assessed lower check-processing fees, do not have to pay for the generation of a bill, are assured that bills will be paid on time, and therefore save on collection costs associated with late or delinquent payments. Consumers reap a number of advantages, such as savings on postage, envelopes, checks, check-processing fees (when charged), and late charges. In addition, some financial institutions charge a lower interest rate (on mortgages, for example) if payments are deducted automatically. Some in the banking industry are urging that charges be increased for checks so that people will feel more compelled to use automated payment systems, as well as pay-by-telephone systems.[34] However, automated payments do present some dangers to consumers, such as a greater risk of being overdrawn on one's checking account and of overlooking bank errors in automated payments.

Smart cards also have implications for EFT. Most important is the promise of a true multipurpose card, one that can be used not only as a credit and debit card but also to expedite all sorts of EFTs, such as health-care payments, frequent-flier miles, frequent-shopper programs, and even lottery bets (by storing a gambler's favorite numbers so that the same bets can be made over and over again).[35]

Despite the excitement about new EFT systems, they have yet to produce the same kind of revolutionary change that was introduced by credit cards. The chief executive officer of one of the largest regional banks offers a dose of realism: "Dreams get ahead of reality. If you look at what might happen through the '90s, banking is going to still look an awful lot like it does today."[36] But even if the EFT revolution does not occur in this decade, it nonetheless will come. Consider the initially slow adaptation to ATM machines. Today, 25% to 50% of bank customers still do not use their ATM cards. But the use of ATM systems appears to be age related and thus sure to increase as younger generations mature. Said the chief executive officer of another large bank, "My mother is 78 and she does not want to use one of those ATM machines. . . . I'm 47 and it's OK. My daughter is 19 and she asks why anyone would ever go to a bank."[37] In fact, ATM use has already achieved wide acceptance. According to a Visa vice president:

> Fifteen years ago, it was enough of a struggle to get consumers to use their ATM card at the ATM. Many people had to break the comfortable habit of seeing their bank teller for cash. . . . The banking industry has gone through that evolution and we've broken many barriers with those in the population initially opposed to using electronics. Most people today have a comfortable pattern of ATM use. We're no longer in an education phase.[38]

It seems clear, given this reality, that resistance to EFT systems will decline rapidly in the future.

Automated Clearinghouses

Consumers are likely to be familiar with credit cards, debit cards, and to a lesser degree with at least some of the other forms of EFT, but they are less likely to be acquainted with automated clearinghouses (ACHs). This lack of familiarity is traceable to the fact that consumers are less directly involved in ACH transactions. As mentioned in Chapter 2, ACH transactions take place largely among and between financial institutions and corporations—for example, savings and loan institutions, utilities, and the federal government. As a central clearing (that is, distribution and settlement) facility, an ACH receives batches of paperless, electronic entries from various financial institutions and then distributes them, usually through ACHs in other locales, to the receiving banks. Thus an ACH is nothing more than an efficient means to electronically exchange money. In other words, an ACH is a means for handling EFTs among large-scale systems.

Most processing of ACH transactions—the debiting of one account and the crediting of another—is done (as is the case with paper checks) by the Federal Reserve. In 1990 the "Fed" controlled all national processing of ACH transactions. However, in the past few years Visa has begun to compete with the Fed. By 1992 Visa had about 20% of the market. One reason for Visa's growth is that its processing charges are lower than the Fed's.[39]

The best-known example of an ACH transaction is direct deposit, especially of payroll checks. Direct deposit can also involve other kinds of transfers of funds, including dividends, interest, annuities, pension payments, and expense reimbursements. Similarly, the United States government makes a variety of payments through the ACH network, including a large proportion of Social Security benefits, payrolls for the military and for civilian employees, and retirement benefits. Another example is corporate-to-corporate payments, in which one company pays another electronically through the ACH network.

Automated clearinghouses had their origins in the late 1960s. As of January 1993, the National Automated Clearing House Association (NACHA) had 40 member ACH associations (for example, the Arizona Clearing House Association and the Mellon Automated Clearing House Association). These member associations represent approximately 14,000 financial institutions. ACH services are provided to about 150,000 companies and millions of consumers. Total ACH dollar volume grew from $2.2 trillion in 1986 to $7.8 trillion in 1992.[40]

Many ACH activities, at least until recently, have been animated by the desire to replace relatively slow and costly check transactions with faster and less expensive electronic transactions. In other words, the goal is the creation, at least as far as possible, of a "checkless society." In the traditional payroll procedure, for example, a check is handed to an employee, who goes to her bank, the check is cashed and processed by the bank, is then processed through the banking system, and is finally returned to the employer. All this handling and processing of a paper check is expensive, cumbersome, and time consuming. According to NACHA, an average of 12 sets of hands are involved in each deposit of a paper check.[41] It costs the bank 70¢ less per transaction to process the payment electronically. Corporations can also save between 10¢ and $1.25 on each payroll check that is handled electronically. Furthermore, NACHA contends, employee productivity increases dramatically when employees no longer need to go to the bank every week or two to cash their checks. Employees gain too, because they no longer need to make such treks and they face no risk of losing their paychecks or having them stolen. Employees also gain, at least minimally, because pay begins earning interest from the start of payday.

Participation in direct deposit of payroll checks has grown in the United States from about 10% of the workforce in 1988 to about 30% of the workforce today. (Over 50% of Social Security payments were made by direct deposit in 1993.) However, almost all Japanese workers use direct deposit, and over 90% of European workers use this system.

A less well-known ACH activity is electronic check truncation (ECT). In ECT, the paper check is replaced by an electronic message that clears and settles a payment. Instead of receiving the canceled check at the end of the month, the consumer (or business) receives a monthly statement listing each item that was paid and the amount. Again, ECT has all sorts of benefits in comparison to the use of paper checks: It is quicker and more efficient, processing costs less, and risks due to theft or inadequate funds are reduced. According to NACHA, only 10% of all checks are currently handled by ECT. However, given the benefits, this too is likely to be a growth area.

Another type of ACH transaction is cash concentration, in which funds are rapidly moved from outlying locations to a company's central account. For example, a retail chain might use ECT to bring in funds from its company-owned outlets around the country. Still another ACH application for organizations is preauthorized bill payments. Recurring bills might be automatically deducted from a central account and paid to the suppliers.

ACHs are also pushing electronic data interchange (EDI). EDI combines the electronic exchange of payments with the exchange of a wide array of information that can be processed by computer. For example, payment and invoice information can be transmitted at the same time that money is transferred. Said one industry leader: "If I want to send invoices along with electronic payments to the banks of my customers' suppliers, these banks better have EDI systems that can handle this."[42] More generally, of course, EDI can be used to transmit such business documents as shipping notices, purchase orders, and invoices, thereby eliminating the need for paper transmittal. Transferring information electronically is far cheaper than transferring it by paper. Said an EDI manager at DuPont, "It will soon be a mandatory condition of doing business, just as having a telephone is today. . . . There are no technical barriers. EDI implementation is simply a question of when."[43] The U.S. Customs Service has been in the forefront, using EDI to keep "track of every sweater, banana, Toyota and machine tool that crossed the nation's borders."[44] At the same time that relevant data are being transmitted, tariffs and duties are being paid electronically. An EFT component of the system allows brokers to make one overall money transfer per day rather than having a check accompany each shipment.

Since its inception, the ACH system has combined electronic and paper-based systems. However, over the years the paper-based component has declined and the electronic component has increased. In 1991 the Federal Reserve mandated that the system become totally electronic. In June 1991 it was only one-third electronic, but by June 1992 it had increased to 73% electronic.[45] The Fed achieved its goal of an all-electronic ACH system by the target date of July 1, 1993.

ACHs are just one of several major methods for moving funds among accounts in the banking system.[46] Fedwire is a real-time method of transferring money from one bank's Federal Reserve account to that of another bank.[47] CHIPS (Clearing House for Interbank Payment Systems), operating out of New York City, includes 135 of the city's financial institutions, although many other institutions have access to the system. CHIPS handles over $500 billion in transactions each day and approximately 90% of all international interbank transactions in dollars. Another international system is SWIFT (Society for Worldwide Interbank Financial Telecommunications). A million messages a day flow through SWIFT to its over 1,600 member banks in 54 countries. Among other things, SWIFT handles letters of credit, trade information, transaction confirmations, and balance reports.

Many in the CREDEBEL industry are just beginning to look into international electronic payments and data interchanges.[48] For example, NACHA reports a vast untapped market for electronic payments between the United States and Canada, among Canadians who retire to the Sunbelt states or citizens of both countries who live in one and work in the other.[49] There are also a variety of corporate-to-corporate applications, such as making trade payments and concentrating cash from outlets in the other country. Similarly, efforts are underway to expedite the electronic exchange of money and information among the nations of Europe.[50]

The different types of electronic payment systems overlap to some degree. Perhaps briefly discussing one company, CoreStates Financial Corp., would help to clarify the relationship among these systems.[51] CoreStates is a bank holding company that provides customers with a range of banking and electronic services:

- It owns and operates Money Access System (MAC), a system of ATMs.
- MAC supports a large number of POS machines in gas stations, supermarkets, and the like, in which people can use their debit cards.
- MAC also supports MAC Medical Payment Service, a POS system for the health-care industry.
- CoreStates is involved in EFT and EDI, allowing customers to send information and submit payments to their suppliers' banks electronically.
- The actual payment of such bills is done through the ACH system to which CoreStates transmits directly and electronically.

As you can see, the CREDEBEL industry encompasses far more than credit cards. However, credit cards are the most important aspect of the CREDEBEL system, and they are likely to instigate, at least for the foreseeable future, the greatest personal troubles and public issues. Yet, the other CREDEBELS also create many of the problems discussed throughout this book.

Personal Troubles, Public Issues, and the Other CREDEBELS

The credit card clearly presents the greatest temptation to imprudence of all the CREDEBELS, but that is not to say that the other CREDEBELS help one resist temptation. In comparison to cash, CREDEBELS permit more, and more rapid, transactions. CREDEBELS also carry with them a greater risk of impulse buying than if one is limited to cash on hand. As you saw earlier, people tend to spend more with debit cards than they do with cash. Furthermore, it has been argued that ATMs can contribute to "impulsive cash withdrawals."[52] However, because the other CREDE-BELS do not generally carry credit with them, they do not pose anything approaching the danger of imprudence that is associated with credit cards.

Nevertheless, the temptation to imprudence can be magnified greatly in at least some of the other CREDEBEL systems because they involve institutions, not individuals. A single imprudent act by an institution can involve far more money than the imprudence of thousands of individuals.

Many of the types of fraud associated with credit cards also apply to the other CREDEBELS. In addition, the other CREDE-BELS are subjected to many idiosyncratic fraudulent activities. Consider the types of fraud perpetrated against those who utilize ATMs. One noteworthy instance occurred in a shopping mall near Hartford, Connecticut.[53] Thieves installed an ordinary-looking but bogus ATM in the mall. When customers inserted their cards into the fake ATM, they received receipts apologizing for the fact that transactions were not possible at the moment. However, unknown to the customers, the machines were recording their card and PIN numbers. The criminals used these numbers to produce counterfeit bank cards and then used the cards to extract large sums of money from ATMs in at least six states.[54] After being in place for about two weeks, the bogus ATM disappeared, spirited from the mall on Mother's Day, ostensibly for repairs, by the thieves dressed in appropriate uniforms. The two men who masterminded the crime eventually pleaded guilty, and each received a sentence of two and one-half years in prison. They were also ordered to pay $464,000 in restitution to the victims. Fraud against CREDEBELS other than credit cards has heretofore not been a significant concern, but the case of the fake ATM has changed all that. Said the president of the Electronic Funds Association:

> In the past, ATM fraud has not been a problem and there is growing anxiety that it could become a problem. . . . It's not just the problem created by the loss of money by financial institutions in the event these kinds of scams become more frequent; more important is the loss of confidence in the system.[55]

ATMs have also become a magnet for many petty thieves, who find the users of those machines easy victims. Said a security consultant,

ATMs have become a criminal's dream and a customer's security nightmare. . . . The reality is that tens of thousands of ATM-related crimes occur across the country. . . . In recent years at least 25 people have been killed in the United States in ATM-related robberies. Hundreds of other ATM victims have been kidnapped, raped, or wounded.[56]

In one case, a couple was kidnapped and taken to several bank machines to withdraw cash. Then the couple was held overnight in a motel, and their cards were used again the next day. (Most banks limit the amount of cash that can be withdrawn by an ATM card on a single day.) Of course, holding victims overnight creates an opportunity for the commission of even worse crimes than the illegal withdrawal of cash. More severe crimes did occur in another case, in which a teenager was accused of raping three women at gunpoint.[57] In the three instances, the women were abducted, forced to drive to an ATM to withdraw money, and raped either before or after the money was stolen. It should be noted, however, that these are highly unusual types of ATM theft. More frequently, thieves simply lurk near an ATM and rob customers after they have gotten their cash or simply collect discarded ATM receipts in order to obtain information needed to illegally withdraw funds.[58]

The problem has become so bad in some areas that extraordinary steps have been taken. On the south side of Chicago, one bank has installed an ATM inside a local police station. A sign above the Chicago machine reads, "Now you can feel secure withdrawing cash from an automatic teller machine knowing it's police protected 24 hours a day, 7 days a week." But even here, one customer clutched her purse and looked about anxiously. "No matter where you are nowadays," she said, "you got to be on your guard every minute."[59] The Los Angeles City Council has also approved the installation of 30 ATMs in police stations. In some other areas ATMs are being moved into supermarkets. And in Oakland, California, some ATMs have red emergency buttons that allow users to signal the police directly if there is trouble.

Crime is not the only trouble afflicting ATMs. Confidence in ATMs may also have been shaken by an incident in which one bank's ATMs made all withdrawals twice, costing (at least until the problem was caught) over 100,000 customers about $16 million.[60] It is this issue of the "loss of confidence in the system" that is behind the obsession of issuers of ATM cards, indeed of all types of cards, with fraud.[61] However, as Chapter 4 explains, the card companies do not seem similarly concerned with the loss of confidence that could result from their own questionable activities. Either because other CREDEBELS are used less than credit cards or are used less publicly, the danger of fraud is less, at least at the moment. Nonetheless, it should be noted that an individual's losses from credit card fraud are limited to $50 but protection is less for the other CREDEBELS. For example, if an ATM or debit card is lost or stolen and the card issuer is notified within two business days, then the victim's loss is limited to $50; a victim who does not notify the card issuer could be liable up to $500 if the company can prove that the victim knew the card was missing. However, someone who receives an ATM or debit statement that contains fraudulent charges but does not notify the card issuer within 60 days of mailing has no protection from further use of the card by the thief. All the funds in the ATM or debit account could be lost, as well as the amount of any overdraft protection associated with that account.[62]

There is less likelihood of fraudulent losses with large EFT and ACH settlements than with credit card transactions. However, given the large amounts involved in many of these transactions, one massive EFT or ACH fraud could potentially cost as much as, or more than, the defrauding of a large number of individual credit card holders. The same point applies to the possibility of a threat to privacy. Although large EFT and ACH systems are likely to be more secure than individual credit card accounts, access to such systems could instantly yield very private information on large numbers of people.

The increasingly widespread use of debit (and ATM) cards to make everyday purchases for food, gasoline, medications, and so on. poses an interesting threat to an individual's right to make purchases privately. Computers will be able to follow purchases and companies can use the information to send out mailing coupons and money-saving offers. Worse, "you can imagine getting a note from Coke, a day or two after you buy ten twelve-packs of Pepsi for a party, asking you to mend your errant ways and consider the Real Thing for your next barbecue."[63]

On the issue of rationalization and the attendant dehumanization, the other CREDEBELS are certainly part of this historic process. That is, their expansion will bring more efficiency, calculability, predictability, and control through the continued replacement of human with nonhuman technology. Just as credit cards rationalized the consumer loan business, the other CREDEBELS have in various ways rationalized the movement of money:

- Using a debit card is a more rational way of paying bills than writing checks or paying in cash.
- Visiting an ATM is more rational than dealing with a human bank teller.
- EFT by telephone or computer is more rational than check writing.
- ACH transactions are rationalized methods for moving large sums of money between financial institutions, and they are more efficient than the available alternatives.

The rationalization process is linked to many factors, but it is associated above all with the computerization of money and, more generally, value. Computerization simultaneously brings many new advantages and many new irrationalities of rationality. Most notable is a further increase in dehumanization in a society increasingly dominated by computers. In the future, computers will be more and more likely to make the decisions about people that were formerly in the hands of other people.

Increasing computerization will also bring more Americanization and the homogenization that comes with it. However, at some future point it will become more accurate to talk of a multidirectional process of globalization. For example, debit cards are already far more popular in many parts of the world than they are in the United States, and their increasing popularity in the United States is indicative of the influence of other nations. At the same time, the recent strong movement of Visa and MasterCard into the debit card business may indicate that the United States will usurp control and then export debit cards to nations in which they have not yet taken hold. In this way, these companies may succeed in Americanizing debit cards and then using the debit card to help Americanize other nations.

Credit cards are the focus of most of this book. However, soon the other CREDEBELS will become far more important and themselves worthy of more detailed sociological analysis and critique.

Endnotes

Chapter 1

1. Bryan S. Turner. "Simmel, Rationalisation and the Sociology of Money." *Sociological Review* 34(1986):95.

2. For more on what I have elsewhere termed "methodological relationism," see George Ritzer and Pamela Gindoff. "Methodological Relationism: Lessons for and from Social Psychology." *Social Psychology Quarterly* 55(1992):128–140.

3. Terry Galanoy. *Charge It: Inside the Credit Card Conspiracy*. New York: Putnam, 1980, p. 33.

4. Terry Galanoy. *Charge It: Inside the Credit Card Conspiracy*. New York: Putnam, 1980, p. 15.

5. Georg Simmel. "Money in Modern Culture." *Theory, Culture and Society* 8(1991):20.

6. Terry Galanoy. *Charge It: Inside the Credit Card Conspiracy*. New York: Putnam, 1980.

7. Terry Galanoy. *Charge It: Inside the Credit Card Conspiracy*. New York: Putnam, 1980, p. 53.

8. Francis Williams. *The American Invasion*. New York: Crown, 1962, p. 53. It is interesting to note that Williams was making this point when credit cards were of minuscule significance in comparison to their importance today.

9. Board of Governors of the Federal Reserve System. *Federal Reserve Bulletin*, vol. 80 no. 5, 1994. "Selected Measures," pp. A30, A51.

10. Fred R. Bleakley. "Consumers Loading up on Debt Again, But Many View Trend as Positive Sign." *Wall Street Journal*, March 30, 1994, pp. A2, A6.

11. U.S. Bureau of the Census. *Statistical Abstracts of the United States: 1993* (113th ed.). Washington, DC: Government Printing Office, 1993, p. 506.

12. U.S. Bureau of the Census. *Statistical Abstracts of the United States: 1992* (112th ed.). Washington, DC: Government Printing Office, 1992, p. 504.

13. Peter Conrad and Joseph Schneider. *Deviance and Medicalization: From Badness to Sickness.* St. Louis: Mosby, 1980.

14. Russell Ben-Ali. "Urge to Spend Money Can Lead to Ruin, Therapy." *Los Angeles Times,* May 6, 1991, p. B5.

15. Joseph Nocera. *A Piece of the Action: How the Middle Class Joined the Money Class.* New York: Simon & Schuster, 1994, p. 96.

16. Andree Brooks. "Lessons for Teen-Agers: Facts of Credit-Card Life." *New York Times,* November 5, 1994, p. 40.

17. "Credit Cards Become Big Part of Campus Life." *New York Times,* February 9, 1991, pp. 16, 48.

18. Albert Crenshaw. "A Crash Course in Credit." *Washington Post,* November 7, 1993, p. H3.

19. Cecilia Cassidy. "Chaarrrge!: America's Card-Carrying Teens." *Washington Post,* June 25, 1991, p. D5.

20. "Credit Card Wars on Campus." *Fortune,* April 10, 1989, p. 18.

21. Albert Crenshaw. "A Crash Course in Credit." *Washington Post,* November 7, 1993, p. H3.

22. Albert Crenshaw. "A Crash Course in Credit." *Washington Post,* November 7, 1993, p. H3.

23. Barry Meier. "Credit Cards on the Rise in High Schools." *New York Times,* September 5, 1992, p. 9; Andree Brooks. "Lessons for Teen-Agers: Facts of Credit-Card Life." *New York Times,* November 5, 1994, p. 40.

24. Barry Meier. "Credit Cards on the Rise in High Schools." *New York Times,* September 5, 1992, p. 9.

25. Barry Meier. "Credit Cards on the Rise in High Schools." *New York Times,* September 5, 1992, p. 9.

26. George Ritzer. "The 1980s: Micro-Macro (and Agency-Structure) Integration in Sociological Theory," in George Ritzer, *Metatheorizing in Sociology.* Lexington, MA: Lexington Books, 1991, pp. 207–234; George Ritzer. "The Recent History and the Emerging Reality

of American Sociological Theory: A Metatheoretical Interpretation." *Sociological Forum* 6(1991): 269–287.

27. For an application of a micro-macro approach to the sociological analysis of money, see Wayne E. Baker and Jason B. Jimerson. "The Sociology of Money." *American Behavioral Scientist*, July/August (1992):678–693.

28. For an overview of the sociological study of social problems, see George Ritzer. "Social Problems Theory," in Craig Calhoun and George Ritzer (eds.), *Introduction to Social Problems*. New York: McGraw-Hill Primis, 1993.

29. Hans Gerth and C. Wright Mills. *Character and Social Structure*. New York: Harcourt Brace and World, 1953, p. xvi.

30. For a discussion of Gerth and Mills's *Character and Social Structure* in light of the recent movement toward more integrative theoretical perspectives, see George Ritzer. *Toward an Integrated Sociological Paradigm: The Search for an Exemplar and an Image of the Subject Matter.* Boston: Allyn & Bacon, 1981, pp. 193–198.

31. C. Wright Mills. *The Sociological Imagination.* New York: Oxford University Press, 1959.

32. Richard Munch and Neil Smelser. "Relating the Micro and Macro," in Jeffrey C. Alexander et al. (eds.), *The Micro-Macro Link*. Berkeley: University of California Press, 1987, pp. 356–387.

33. Terry Galanoy. *Charge It: Inside the Credit Card Conspiracy.* New York: Putnam, 1980, p. 110.

34. Paul Baran and Paul Sweezy. *Monopoly Capital: An Essay on the American Economic and Social Order.* New York: Monthly Review Press, 1966.

35. Georg Simmel. *The Philosophy of Money.* London: Routledge & Kegan Paul, 1907/1978. In fact, Simmel did have a few things to say about credit (see pp. 479–481).

36. For an explication of the way that the fast-food restaurant rationalized the way food is made and obtained, see George Ritzer. *The McDonaldization of Society.* Thousand Oaks, CA: Pine Forge Press, 1993.

37. Max Weber. *Economy and Society* (3 vols.). Totowa, NJ: Bedminster Press, 1968; Stephen Kalberg. "Max Weber's Types of Rationality: Cornerstones for the Analysis of Rationalization Processes in History." *American Journal of Sociology* 85(1980):1145–1179.

38. See also Hans Gerth and C. Wright Mills. *Character and Social Structure.* New York: Harcourt Brace and World, 1953.

39. Rolf Wiggershaus. *The Frankfurt School: Its History, Theories, and Political Significance.* Cambridge, MA: The MIT Press, 1994.

40. Roland Robertson. *Globalization: Social Theory and Global Culture.* London: Sage, 1992; Mike Featherstone (ed.). *Global Culture: Nationalism, Globalization and Modernity.* London: Sage, 1990.

41. Richard Kuisel. *The Seduction of the French: The Dilemma of Americanization.* Berkeley: University of California Press, 1993.

42. Dr. Ernest Dichter, cited in Francis Williams. *The American Invasion.* New York: Crown, 1962, p. 60.

43. Viviana A. Zelizer. *The Social Meaning of Money.* New York: Basic Books, 1994; Kenneth O. Doyle (ed.), "The Meanings of Money." *American Behavioral Scientist,* July/August (1992):637–840.

44. Robert A. Hendrickson. *The Cashless Society.* New York: Dodd, Mead, 1972.

45. Terry Galanoy. *Charge It: Inside the Credit Card Conspiracy.* New York: Putnam, 1980, p. 212.

46. Joel Kurtzman. *The Death of Money.* New York: Simon & Schuster, 1993, pp. 82–83.

47. Joseph Nocera. *A Piece of the Action: How the Middle Class Joined the Money Class.* New York: Simon & Schuster, 1994, pp. 100–105.

48. James Sterngold. "Thrift Is Under Siege in Japan as Use of Credit Cards Soars." *New York Times,* June 16, 1992, pp. A1, D9.

49. "1993—Banner Year." *Bankcard Update,* March 1994, pp. 1, 12.

50. William Dunn. "Debit It! New Breed of Cards an Alternative to Cash, Checks, Credit." *Chicago Tribune,* November 18, 1993, p. N1.

51. "Credit Card Issuer's Guide: 1995 Edition." *Credit Card News,* August 15, 1994, p. 5; "The Big Squeeze." *The Economist,* November 2, 1991, pp. 69–70; Adam Bryant. "Raising the Stakes in a War of Plastic." *New York Times,* September 13, 1992, p. F13.

52. Peter Lucas. "Buy Now, Borrow Later." *Credit Card Management,* April 1994: 74.

53. *Credit Card News,* May 15, 1994, p. 7; Jeffrey Kutler. "Uncertainty Emerges on Bank Card Industry Future." *American Banker,* September 19, 1979, p. 1; "The Big Squeeze." *The Economist,* November 2, 1991, pp. 69–70; Janice Castro. "Charge It Your Way." *Time,* July 1,

1991, pp. 50–51; "Plastic Profits Go Pop." *The Economist*, September 12, 1992, p. 92.

54. Steve Lipin, Brian Coleman and Jeremy Mark. "Visa, American Express and MasterCard Vie in Overseas Strategies." *Wall Street Journal*, February 15, 1994, p. A1.

55. Marguerite Smith and Jordan E. Goodman. "Betting on the Value of Regional Banks' Plastic Portfolios." *Money*, January 1990, pp. 57–58.

56. Bill Saporito. "Melting Point in the Plastic War." *Forbes*, May 20, 1991, p. 72.

57. Robert A. Hendrickson. *The Cashless Society*. New York: Dodd, Mead, 1972, p. 46.

58. Peter Berger. *Invitation to Sociology: A Humanistic Perspective*. Garden City, NY: Anchor Books, 1963, p. 41.

59. Robert A. Hendrickson. *The Cashless Society*. New York: Dodd, Mead, 1972, p. 45.

60. Lewis Mandell. *Credit Card Use in the United States*. Ann Arbor: University of Michigan, 1972; Lewis Mandell. *The Credit Card Industry: A History*. Boston: Twayne, 1990; Thomas Russell. *The Economics of Bank Credit Cards*. New York: Praeger, 1975; Lawrence M. Ausubel. "The Failure of Competition in the Credit Card Market." *American Economic Review* 81(1991):50–80.

61. One exception is sociologist Steven L. Nock who in his recent book, *The Costs of Privacy: Surveillance and Reputation in America* (New York: Aldine De Gruyter, 1993), has devoted some attention to credit cards as one means of surveillance necessary to establish reputations in our contemporary world of strangers.

Chapter 2

1. "Co-Branding Redefines an Industry." *Adweek L.P.*, October 18, 1993, p. S80.

2. James J. Flink. *The Automobile Age*. Cambridge, MA: MIT Press, 1988; Daniel Yergin. *The Prize: The Epic Quest for Oil, Money and Power*. New York: Simon & Schuster, 1991.

3. Isabel Wilkerson. "For Shoppers, a Fast Flight to Paradise." *New York Times*, December 20, 1993, p. D9.

4. Linda Punch. "The Jackpot in New Markets." *Credit Card Management*, April 1991, p. 30.

5. This discussion draws heavily on Lewis Mandell. *The Credit Card Industry: A History*. Boston: Twayne, 1990.

6. Adam Bryant. "It Pays to Stick to Basics in Credit Cards." *New York Times*, October 31, 1992, p. 35.

7. American Bankers Association. *Bank Card Fact Book*. Washington, DC: American Bankers Association, 1990, p. 2.

8. "The Big Squeeze." *The Economist*, November 2, 1991, pp. 69–70.

9. Bill Saporito. "Melting Point in the Plastic War." *Forbes*, May 20, 1991, p. 72.

10. Linda Punch. "The Knockdown Battle in Corporate Cards." *Credit Card Management*, November 1992, pp. 37ff.

11. Adam Bryant. "Raising the Stakes in a War of Plastic." *New York Times*, September 13, 1992, p. F13.

12. American Bankers Association. *Bank Card Fact Book*. Washington, DC: American Bankers Association, 1990, p. 19.

13. Joseph Nocera. *A Piece of the Action: How the Middle Class Joined the Money Class*. New York: Simon & Schuster, 1994, p. 56.

14. Adam Bryant. "Raising the Stakes in a War of Plastic." *New York Times*, September 13, 1992, p. F13.

15. Pat Widder. "Credit Cards Slipping From Banks' Grasp." *Chicago Tribune*, March 3, 1991, p. B1.

16. Adam Bryant. "Raising the Stakes in a War of Plastic." *New York Times*, September 13, 1992, p. F13.

17. Saul Hansell. "Dean Witter Gets Entry to MasterCard." *New York Times*, November 23, 1993, pp. D1, D16.

18. Leah Nathans Spiro. "More Cards in the Deck." *Business Week*, December 16, 1991, pp. 100ff.

19. Adam Bryant. "G.M.'s Bold Move Into Credit Cards." *New York Times*, September 10, 1992, p. D5.

20. "CoBranding, Affinity Cards Remain Tools to Spur Use." *Card News*, January 23, 1993, pp. 1–3.

21. Charles Kraul. "Co-Branded Cards Charge Full Speed Ahead." *Los Angeles Times*, November 26, 1993, p. D1.

22. "How Cobranding Changed the Card Associations." *Credit Card News*, July 15, 1993, p. 3.

23. G. Bruce Knecht. "American Express Embraces Co-Brands." *Wall Street Journal*, February 17, 1994, p. B1.

24. John Waggoner. "A Credit to GM." *USA Today*, October 8, 1992, p. 1B; Mickey Meece. "GE's Rewards Card Grows in Shadow of Giants." *American Banker*, March 17, 1994, p. 14.

25. Adam Bryant. "Raising the Stakes in a War of Plastic." *New York Times*, September 13, 1992, p. F13; Adam Bryant. "G.M.'s Bold Move Into Credit Cards." *New York Times*, September 10, 1992, p. D5.

26. Cited in Albert Crenshaw. "Credit Cards in Combat." *Washington Post*, July 11, 1991, p. A33.

27. Jon Friedman and John Meehan. *House of Cards: Inside the Troubled Empire of American Express*. New York: Putnam, 1992.

28. "Credit Card Issuer's Guide: 1995 Edition." *Credit Card News*, August 15, 1994, p. 3; G. Bruce Knecht. "American Express Embraces Co-Brands." *Wall Street Journal*, February 17, 1994, p. B1.

29. Janice Castro. "Charge It Your Way." *Time*, July 1, 1991, p. 50.

30. Gerri Detweiler. *The Ultimate Credit Handbook*. New York: Plume, 1993.

31. Eric Gelman. "Feeding the Card Habit." *Newsweek*, July 8, 1985, p. 52.

32. Mark Arend. "Card Profits: How Far Will They Slide?" *ABA Banking Journal*, September 1992, p. 82.

33. Jon Friedman and John Meehan. *House of Cards: Inside the Troubled Empire of American Express*. New York: Putnam, 1992, p. 110.

34. Joseph DiStefano. "Card Companies Try to Spur Holiday Spending." *Wilmington News Journal*, November 26, 1993, p. B10.

35. Leonard Sloane. "Secured Credit Cards: Ask Before You Leap." *New York Times*, March 16, 1991, pp. 13, 48.

36. "Once-Shunned Secured Cards Gain a Following." *Credit Card News*, June 1, 1993, pp. 1–7.

37. Suzanne Wooley. "Plastic—For a Pretty Penny." *Business Week*, May 18, 1992, p. 118.

38. Dona Wong and Vivien Kellerman. "No Credit History? No Problem With a Secured Card." *New York Times*, January 8, 1994, p. 38.

39. "New Markets for Credit Cards: Seek and Ye Shall Find." *Card News*, October 4, 1993, pp. 1–4; Linda Punch. "The Knockdown Battle in Corporate Cards." *Credit Card Management*, November 1992, pp. 37ff.

40. "American Express Adds a New Card." *New York Times*, January 13, 1994, p. D4.

41. Lauryn Franzoni. "Card Use Growing Rapidly for Industry Transactions." *American Banker*, May 8, 1991, p. 12.

42. "GSA's Word of Advice on Buying: Plastic." *Washington Post*, February 25, 1994, p. A19.

43. Peter Steinfels. "For Catholic Charities: A New Credit Card." *New York Times*, February 4, 1989, p. 52; Debra Rowland. "Charge Card Gives Peace a Chance." *Chicago Tribune*, March 3, 1991, p. B2.

44. Adam Bryant. "It Pays to Stick to Basics in Credit Cards." *New York Times*, October 31, 1992, p. 35. However, some banks remain interested; see *Credit Card News*, vol. 4, no. 21, 1992 for a discussion of MBNAs continuing interest in affinity cards.

45. "Co-Branding, Affinity Cards Remain Tools to Spur Use." *Card News*, January 25, 1993, pp. 1–3.

46. James Sterngold. "Thrift Is Under Siege in Japan as Use of Credit Cards Soars." *New York Times*, June 16, 1992, pp. A1, D9.

47. Steven Lipin, Brian Coleman and Jeremy Mark. "Visa, American Express and MasterCard Vie in Overseas Strategies." *Wall Street Journal*, February 15, 1994, p. A10.

48. Ferdinand Protzman. "Germans Sigh and Say, 'Charge It.'" *New York Times*, July 13, 1991, p. 37.

49. "Credit Card Issuer's Guide: 1995 Edition." *Credit Card News*, August 15, 1994, p. 3.

50. For more on why credit card companies have been tightening restrictions and backing away from these plans, see Leonard Wiener. "Backing Away From a Providential Perk." *U.S. News & World Report*, June 1, 1992, p. 67; see also "Remember the One About the Ape and the Camcorder?" *Consumer Reports*, July 1992, pp. 432–433.

51. Margaret Mannix, Diane Duke, and Marc Silver. "Match That Price." *U.S. News & World Report*, April 15, 1991, p. 74.

52. Janice Castro. "Charge It Your Way." *Time*, July 1, 1991, pp. 50–51.

53. Joseph DiStefano. "Card Companies Try to Spur Holiday Spending." *Wilmington News Journal*, November 26, 1993, p. B10.

54. "Nationsbank Card Features Savings Plan." *New York Times*, January 7, 1993, p. D4.

55. Michael Quint. "Credit Card Issuers Seeking New Ways to Keep Business." *New York Times*, April 20, 1992, p. C1.

56. Denise Gellene. "B of A Changing Its Credit Card Insurance Option." *Los Angeles Times*, October 29, 1993, p. D3; "Card Issuers Test and Offer Fee-Based Enhancement Packages." *Bank Letter* 17 (1993):1.

57. Albert B. Crenshaw. "Taking Credit for a Card-Using Boom." *Washington Post*, October 17, 1993, pp. H1, H3.

58. George White. "More Americans Turning to Their Credit Cards to Purchase Groceries." *Los Angeles Times*, August 8, 1992, p. D3.

59. Albert B. Crenshaw. "Giant Begins Accepting Credit and Debit Cards." *Washington Post*, November 14, 1992, p. C1.

60. "Tapping the $4 Billion-a-Year Magazine Renewal Market." *Credit Card News*, February 15, 1991; "A Taxing New Use for Credit Cards: Paying Your Income Taxes." *Credit Card News*, July 15, 1991, p. 6; *Credit Card News*, August 1, 1992; "New Markets For Credit Cards: Seek and Ye Shall Find." *Card News*, October 4, 1993, pp. 1–4.

61. Jeanne Ilda. "Mellon, Port Authority in Card Deal." *American Banker*, July 25, 1991, p. 3; "The Cashless Garage: Parking Your Parking Charges on Plastic." *Credit Card News*, April 1, 1991, p. 6; Linda Punch. "The Jackpot in New Markets." *Credit Card Management*, April 1991, pp. 23–31; Jody K. Hancock. "Card Use for Fast, Small-Ticket Purchases." *American Banker*, September 10, 1991, p. 8A; *Credit Card News*, January 15, 1991; John McManus and Scott Hume. "Arby's Takes Fast-Food Lead in Credit Cards." *Advertising Age*, October 8, 1990, p. 20.

62. Jeanne Dugan Cooper. "Burger King Program in Oregon Allows Customers to Pay by Credit Card or Check." *American Banker*, October 4, 1989, p. 10.

63. Calvin Sims. "Ride on Credit: Make It J.F.K. and Don't Spare the Plastic!" *New York Times*, June 8, 1991, pp. 25, 27.

64. Linda Punch. "Credit Cards and the Health Care Crisis." *Credit Card Management*, July 1992, pp. 29ff.

65. "A New Way to Pay for Your Pearly Whites." *Changing Times*, October 1990, p. 102.

66. Leah Nathans Spiro. "Behind the Bombshell From Amex." *Business Week*, October 21, 1991, pp. 124–126.

67. Saul Hansell. "A Mighty Giant's Dressing-Down." *New York Times*, May 17, 1993, p. D1.

68. "How the Gold Card's Identity Crisis Is Deepening." *Credit Card News*, December 1, 1992, p. 1.

69. James K. Glassman. "American Express Charges Ahead With 'Cause' Marketing." *Washington Post,* December 24, 1993, p. D10.

70. John Stewart. "Goodbye, Fat City." *Credit Card Management,* March 1992, pp. 70ff.

71. Andree Brooks. "Plenty of New Offerings, but Read the Fine Print." *New York Times,* May 15, 1993, p. 34.

72. Lawrence M. Ausubel. "The Failure of Competition in the Credit Card Market." *American Economic Review* 81(1991):50–81.

73. John Stewart. "The New Frugality." *Credit Card Management,* May 1992, pp. 28–29.

74. Peter Lucas. "Say So Long to Booming Balances." *Credit Card Management,* April 1992, pp. 55ff.

75. "Issuers Consider a World Without Grace Periods." *Credit Card News,* June 1, 1992; "Remember the One About the Ape and the Camcorder?" *Consumer Reports,* July 1992, pp. 432–433.

76. "The Pressure Builds to Make Convenience Users Pay." *Credit Card News,* May 15, 1993, pp. 1–2.

77. American Bankers Association. *Bank Card Fact Book.* Washington, DC: American Bankers Association, 1990, p. 13.

78. American Bankers Association. *Bank Card Fact Book.* Washington, DC: American Bankers Association, 1990, p. 13.

79. Robert J. Klein. "Want Fair Treatment from Lenders? Know Your Rights." *Money,* December 1988, pp. 183–184.

80. "Access by Plastic Increasing; Cards May Soon Tap Investment Accounts." *Houston Chronicle/Business,* November 21, 1993, p. 3.

81. Based on Sandra Lowe. "Americard Banking Cashes In on Debit Card System." *San Antonio Business Journal* 6 (1992):13.

82. "A History of Debit and Credit: How Plastic Cards Forever Changed Our Lives." *Chain Store Executive,* September 1992, p. 22.

83. S. J. Diamond. "Debit Cards Pay Off—and Do It Really Fast." *Los Angeles Times,* April 22, 1985, section 4, p. 1.

84. William F. Powers. "For More Customers, Electronic Money Is the Way to Pay." *Washington Post/Business,* January 10, 1994, p. 7.

85. *Credit Card Management: Card Industry Directory, 1994 Edition.* New York: Faulkner and Gray, 1993, p. 39.

86. William F. Powers. "For More Customers, Electronic Money Is the Way to Pay." *Washington Post/Business,* January 10, 1994, p. 7.

87. *Credit Card Management: Card Industry Directory, 1994 Edition.* New York: Faulkner and Gray, 1993.

88. "Multiple Application Cards Show Their Smarts." *Card News*, December 28, 1992, pp. 3–5.

89. *Credit Card Management: Card Industry Directory, 1994 Edition.* New York: Faulkner and Gray, 1993, p. 39.

90. Albert G. Crenshaw. "Giant Begins Accepting Credit and Debit Cards." *Washington Post*, November 14, 1992, p. C1.

91. American Bankers Association. *Statistical Information on the Financial Services Industry* (6th ed.). Washington, DC: American Bankers Association, 1993, p. 197.

92. Janice Castro. "Charge It Your Way." *Time*, July 1, 1991, p. 51.

93. American Bankers Association. *Statistical Information on the Financial Services Industry* (6th ed.). Washington, DC: American Bankers Association, 1993, p. 197.

Chapter 3

1. Andrew Tobias. "Beware the Plastic Loan Shark." *Time*, January 10, 1994, p.20.

2. Georg Simmel. *The Philosophy of Money.* London: Routledge & Kegan Paul, 1907/1978, p.479.

3. Georg Simmel. *The Philosophy of Money.* London: Routledge & Kegan Paul, 1907/1978, p.194.

4. Linda Punch. "The Jackpot in New Markets." *Credit Card Management*, April 1991, p.29.

5. Gene Yasuda. "The Big Cards on Campus." *Orlando Sentinel*, November 1, 1993, p. D1.

6. Janice Castro. "Charge It Your Way." *Time*, July 1, 1991, p. 51.

7. American Bankers Association. *Bank Card Fact Book.* Washington, DC: American Bankers Association, 1990, p. 9.

8. Erik Lundegaard. "About Men: Card Sharks." *New York Times Magazine*, May 22, 1994, p. 24.

9. Albert B. Crenshaw. "Rising Debit Card Use Heralds Change in Spending Habits." *Washington Post*, September 18, 1991, p. D1.

10. Kathy M. Kristof. "Beware the Pitfalls of Using a Debit Card." *Los Angeles Times*, July 5, 1991, p. D2.

11. Jane Bryant Quinn. "Automated Monthly Payments Offer Convenience and Savings." *Washington Post*, October 13, 1991, p. H3.

12. "Credit Card Issuer's Guide: 1995 Edition." *Credit Card News*, August 15, 1994, p. 4.

13. American Bankers Association. *Statistical Information on the Financial Services Industry* (6th ed.). Washington, DC: American Bankers Association, 1993, p. 35.

14. Albert Crenshaw. "Battling the High Costs of Borrowing." *Washington Post*, January 27, 1992, p. A5.

15. Dana Milbank. "Hooked on Plastic: Middle-Class Family Takes a Harsh Cure for Credit-Card Abuse." *Wall Street Journal*, January 8, 1991, pp. A1, A11.

16. John Stewart. "Collections Feels the Heat." *Credit Card Management*, October 1992, pp. 39ff; "Bankruptcy Baffles the Experts." *Credit Card Management*, December 1993, p. 10; A. Charlene Sullivan. "Do Consumers Want More Debt?" *Credit Card Management*, April 1994, pp. 22–26.

17. Linda Punch. "The Land of Milk and Honey." *Credit Card Management*, August 1994, p. 51.

18. The Wards' story is told in Dana Milbank. "Hooked on Plastic: Middle-Class Family Takes a Harsh Cure for Credit-Card Abuse." *Wall Street Journal*, January 8, 1991, pp. A1, A11.

19. Eric K. Tyson. "Credit Crackdown: Control Your Spending Before It Controls You." *San Francisco Examiner*, November 28, 1993, p. E1.

20. David E. Rosenbaum. "High Credit Card Rates: A Luxurious Necessity?" *New York Times*, December 24, 1991, p. 2.

21. Dennis Romero. "Piling Up Debt: Easy Credit Luring College Students." *Chicago Tribune*, December 20, 1993, p. C1.

22. Mark Potts. "The Ghosts of Debt to Come." *Washington Post*, January 1, 1993, p. F1.

23. Jan M. Rosen. "'Maxed' Credit Cards and Other Red Flags." *New York Times*, December 26, 1992, p. 36.

24. Ronald J. Faber. "Money Changes Everything: Compulsive Buying from a Biopsychosocial Perspective." *American Behavioral Scientist*, July/August (1992):809–819; Daniel Goleman. "A Constant Urge to Buy: Battling a Compulsion." *New York Times*, July 7, 1991, p. C12.

25. Russell Ben-Ali. "Urge to Spend Money Can Lead to Ruin, Therapy." *Los Angeles Times*, May 6, 1991, p. B5.

26. Terry Galanoy. *Charge It: Inside the Credit Card Conspiracy*. New York: Putnam, 1980, p. 183.

27. Daniel Goleman. "A Constant Urge to Buy: Battling a Compulsion." *New York Times*, July 7, 1991, p. C12.

28. "Shopping Addiction: Abused Substance Is Money." *New York Times*, June 16, 1986, p. C11.

29. Eric K. Tyson. "Credit Crackdown: Control Your Spending Before It Controls You." *San Francisco Examiner*, November 28, 1993, p. E1.

30. George White. "More Americans Turning to Their Credit Cards to Purchase Groceries." *Los Angeles Times*, August 8, 1992, p. D3.

31. "Credit-Card War Moves Into High Gear." *U.S. News & World Report*, March 5, 1979, p. 73.

32. A. Gary Shilling. "Plastic Bombs." *Forbes*, July 22, 1991, p. 326.

33. Yvette D. Kantrow. "Banks Press Cardholders to Take Cash Advances." *American Banker*, January 28, 1992, pp. 1, 6.

34. John Crudele. "Hey, Big Spenders: Living Beyond One's Means." *New York Magazine*, February 20, 1989, p. 19.

35. "The Cost of Instant Cash." *Changing Times*, June 30, 1990, p. 96.

36. Albert B. Crenshaw. "It Can Be Easy to Cut Credit Cards' Costs." *Washington Post*, December 15, 1991, p. H3.

37. Karen De Witt. "Using Credit Cards, Students Learn a Hard Lesson." *New York Times*, August 26, 1991, p. A17.

38. Jan M. Rosen. "'Maxed' Charge Cards and Other Red Flags." *New York Times*, December 26, 1992, p. 36.

39. Jerrold Mundis. *How to Get Out of Debt, Stay Out of Debt and Live Prosperously*. Toronto: Bantam Books, 1988.

40. Jeanine Stein. "Is There Life After Credit?" *Los Angeles Times*, October 12, 1987, p. V1.

41. Jerrold Mundis. *How to Get Out of Debt, Stay Out of Debt and Live Prosperously*. Toronto: Bantam Books, 1988, pp. 118, 123, 124.

42. Terry Galanoy. *Charge It: Inside the Credit Card Conspiracy*. New York: Putnam, 1980, p. 218.

43. Terry Galanoy. *Charge It: Inside the Credit Card Conspiracy*. New York: Putnam, 1980, p. 219.

44. Marjorie Marks. "Stopping the Shopping Juggernaut." *Los Angeles Times*, December 3, 1987, p. V1.

45. Kathy Kristof. " 'Disguised' Interest on Credit Cards Is Decried." *Los Angeles Times*, June 18, 1992, pp. D2, D3.

46. Denise Gellene. "Consumers Taking Hard Look at Credit Cards." *Los Angeles Times*, November 20, 1991, p. D4.

47. Mary Beth Libbey. "Consumers Say They'll Switch, But Do They?" *American Banker*, September 10, 1991, p. 3A.

48. Peter Pae. "Credit Junkies: Many Keep on Paying High Rates on Cards, Through Bad Planning." *Wall Street Journal*, December 26, 1991, pp. A1, A2.

49. Saul Hansell. "Consumers Finally Respond to High Credit Card Interest." *New York Times*, March 29, 1993, p. D7.

50. Peter Pae. "Credit Junkies: Many Keep on Paying High Rates on Cards, Through Bad Planning." *Wall Street Journal*, December 26, 1991, pp. A1, A2.

51. Albert B. Crenshaw. "Pressures on 'Plastic.' " *Washington Post/Business*, April 18, 1993, p. H1.

52. Glenn Burkins. "Low-Interest Credit Cards Easy to Find, Hard to Get." *Washington Post*, April 11, 1993, p. H5.

53. Albert Crenshaw. "Battling the High Costs of Borrowing." *Washington Post*, January 27, 1992, p. A1.

54. Bill Sing. "Good Credit Counselor Can Be Godsend." *Los Angeles Times*, September 24, 1988, pp. IV3–IV4.

55. "Easing Borrowers Off the Road to Bankruptcy." *ABA Banking Journal*, February 1990, p. 42.

56. "Shopping Addiction: Abused Substance Is Money." *New York Times*. June 16, 1986: C11; Carol Krucoff. "MONEY: A Club That Could Save You From Yourself." *Washington Post*, March 25, 1980, p. C5; Margaret K. Webb. "Out of Control." *Washington Post*, December 18, 1992, p. D5.

57. Carol Krucoff. "MONEY: A Club That Could Save You From Yourself." *Washington Post*, March 25, 1980, p. C5.

58. Katy Butler. "Big Spenders Learn to Set Limits." *San Francisco Chronicle*, September 17, 1991, p. A1.

59. Michael Schrage. "It's Time to Put a Transaction Tax on Credit Card Purchases." *Washington Post*, October 12, 1990, p. F3.

60. "Easing Borrowers Off the Road to Bankruptcy." *ABA Banking Journal*, February 1990, p. 42.

61. Marjorie Marks. "Stopping the Shopping Juggernaut." *Los Angeles Times*, December 3, 1987, p. V1.

Chapter 4

1. Terry Galanoy. *Charge it: Inside the Credit Card Conspiracy*. New York: Putnam, 1980, p. 193.

2. Georg Simmel. *The Philosophy of Money*. London: Routledge & Kegan Paul, 1907/1978, p. 432.

3. Georg Simmel. "Money in Modern Culture." *Theory, Culture and Society* 8(1991):29.

4. James William Coleman. "Crime and Money: Motivation and Opportunity in a Monetarized Economy." *American Behavioral Scientist*, July/August (1992):835.

5. David R. Warwick. *Reducing Crime by Eliminating Cash*. San Francisco: National Council on Crime and Delinquency, 1993, pp. 8, 10.

6. Joel Lisker. "The Card Is Not in the Mail." *Credit Card Management*, March 1993, pp. 90ff.

7. "Credit Card Issuer's Guide: 1995 Edition." *Credit Card News*, August 15, 1994, p. 6.

8. Serge F. Kovaleski. "Credit Scam Targets Mailboxes." *Washington Post*, December 2, 1993, p. A4.

9. Peter Pae. "Citicorp Plans to Put Customers' Pictures on Its Credit Cards." *Wall Street Journal*, April 20, 1992, p. A1.

10. Gail DeGeorge. "When Knaves Play With Credit Cards." *Business Week*, November 5, 1990, p. 163.

11. Serge F. Kovaleski. "Credit Scam Targets Mailboxes." *Washington Post*, December 2, 1993, pp. A1, A4.

12. *Credit Card News*, February 1, 1990, p. 1.

13. Serge F. Kovaleski. "Credit Scam Targets Mailboxes." *Washington Post*, December 2, 1993, pp. A1, A4.

14. "A Criminal Element Begins to Siphon Off Credit Card Gasoline Purchases." *Credit Card News*, October 1, 1992, p. 8.

15. Ellen E. Schultz. "Plastic Explosives: Ways to Defuse Credit-Card Fraud." *Wall Street Journal*, November 16, 1990, p. C1.

16. "A Nationwide Computer-Fraud Ring Is Broken Up." *New York Times*, April 19, 1992, p. B3.

17. Serge F. Kovaleski. "Credit Scam Targets Mailboxes." *Washington Post*, December 2, 1993, p. A4.

18. Bill Sing. "Protect Your Credit Cards From Retail Practices." *Los Angeles Times*, April 8, 1990, p. D4.

19. Stephen J. Shaw. "The Credit Thieves." *Washington Post*, November 9, 1992, p. D5.

20. Ellen E. Schultz. "Credit Card Crooks Devise New Scams." *Wall Street Journal*, July 17, 1992, pp. C1, C11.

21. Bob Drogin. "Losing Millions in Asia's Notorious 'Plastic Triangle.'" *Los Angeles Times*, June 23, 1992, pp. H1, H8.

22. "Credit Card Fraud Continues to Plague the Industry." *Card News*, June 28, 1993, p. 4.

23. Julie Tamaki and Michael Connelly. "Computer Skills Aid '90s Credit Card Scam." *Los Angeles Times*, August 23, 1992, p. B5.

24. Julie Tamaki and Michael Connelly. "Computer Skills Aid '90s Credit Card Scam." *Los Angeles Times*, August 23, 1992, p. B5.

25. "Credit Card Fraud Continues to Plague the Industry." *Card News*, June 28, 1993, p. 4.

26. Michael deCourcy Hinds. "The New-Fashioned Way to Steal Money: Fake Credit." *New York Times*, December 31, 1988, p. 28.

27. Robert Hanley. "U.S. Writing 2,500 Possible Credit-Fraud Victims." *New York Times*, December 9, 1993, pp. B1, B6.

28. Serge F. Kovaleski. "Credit Scam Targets Mailboxes." *Washington Post*, December 2, 1993, pp. A1, A4.

29. "New Hope in the Battle Against Draft Laundering." *Credit Card News*, January 15, 1992, p. 93.

30. Larry Schwartz and Pearl Sax. "Risk Management for Survival." *Direct Marketing*, February 1991, pp. 37ff.

31. Richard B. Schmitt. "Visa, MasterCard Sue Telemarketers, Alleging Card Scam." *Wall Street Journal*, April 16, 1991, pp. B2, B7.

32. Barry Meier. "Sharing Credit Card Numbers by Merchants Brings New Fears of Fraud." *New York Times*, March 28, 1992, p. 50; Barry Meier. "$1.50 Worth of Help for $200, but No Credit." *New York Times*, February 9, 1991, p. 48.

33. "Card Launderers Stay One Step Ahead of the Law." *Credit Card News*, February 1, 1993, p. 6; "Telemarketing-Curbs Plan Gets Support." *Los Angeles Times*, January 1, 1992, pp. D2, D3.

34. "Card Launderers Stay One Step Ahead of the Law." *Credit Card News*, February 1, 1993, p. 6.

35. Jane Bryant Quinn. "Credit Card Protection and Other Bad Ideas." *Washington Post*, April 28, 1991, p. H3.

36. Chris Woodyard. "Firm's Claim of 'Credit Repair' Sparks State Suit." *Los Angeles Times*, August 1, 1991, p. D7.

37. Leonard Sloane. "Secured Credit Cards: Ask Before You Leap." *New York Times*, March 16, 1991, p. 48.

38. Bill Sing. "Credit Repair Clinics Could Clean You Out." *Los Angeles Times/Business*, July 8, 1989, p. 3.

39. Barton Crockett. "Banks Unlikely to Find a Bonanza in Debit Cards." *American Banker*, September 2, 1992, pp. 1, 10; John Meehan. "Pushing Plastic Is Still One Juicy Game." *Business Week*, September 21, 1992, pp. 76–78.

40. Albert B. Crenshaw. "Credit Card Rate 'Spreads' Keep Growing." *Washington Post*, October 13, 1991, p. H3; Elgie Holstein. "The Hidden Costs of Credit Cards." *USA Today*, November 1989, pp. 82–83.

41. John Meehan. "Pushing Plastic Is Still One Juicy Game." *Business Week*, September 21, 1992, p. 76.

42. Albert B. Crenshaw. "Credit Card Rate 'Spreads' Keep Growing." *Washington Post*, October 13, 1991, p. H3.

43. David R. Sands. "Senate Votes to Cap Credit Card Rates." *Washington Times*, November 14, 1991, pp. C1, C10.

44. Elgie Holstein. "The Hidden Costs of Credit Cards." *USA Today*, November 1989, p. 82.

45. Albert Crenshaw. "Complex Charges on Credit Cards Can Push Rates Higher, Study Says." *Washington Post*, June 19, 1992, p. C4.

46. "Credit Card Users Misled By Banks, Study Charges." *Wall Street Journal*, June 18, 1992, p. A5.

47. Albert Crenshaw. "Complex Charges on Credit Cards Can Push Rates Higher, Study Says." *Washington Post*, June 19, 1992, pp. C1, C4.

48. Don Dunn. "When Credit-Card Issuers Say 'Relax,' Don't." *Business Week*, January 13, 1992, p. 146.

49. Kathy Kristof. "'Disguised' Interest on Credit Cards Is Decried." *Los Angeles Times*, June 18, 1992, pp. D2, D3.

50. Gerri Detweiler. *The Ultimate Credit Handbook*. New York: Plume, 1993, p. 67.

51. *Credit Card News*, February 1, 1990.

52. Leonard Sloane. "Low Interest Rates in Credit Card Offers Are Often Just Teasers." *New York Times*, January 15, 1994, p. 35.

53. Suzanne Woolley. "Plastic—For a Pretty Penny." *Business Week*, May 18, 1992, p. 118.

54. Terry Galanoy. *Charge It: Inside the Credit Card Conspiracy*. New York: Putnam, 1980, p. 193.

55. Denise Gellene. "A Case of Phony Identity." *Los Angeles Times*, August 26, 1992, p. A1.

56. Joel Lisker. "The Card Is Not in the Mail." *Credit Card Management*, March 1993, pp. 90ff; Dwane Krumme. *Bank Card Fraud*. Washington, DC: American Bankers Association, 1988; Linda Punch. "A High-Tech Arsenal Against Fraud." *Credit Card Management*, March 1993, pp. 20ff.

57. "Card Associations Play Pivotal Role in War on Fraud." *Card News*, July 26, 1993, pp. 3–5.

58. Stuart Elliott. "Phone Promotion Miscue Raises Concerns of Fraud." *New York Times*, April 7, 1994, pp. A1, D20.

59. "Rise in Fraud Prompts Call for New Credit Card ID." *Los Angeles Times*, September 9, 1992, p. D2.

60. Yvette Kantrow. "Citibank Offers Photo ID on Cards." *American Banker*, April 21, 1992, p. 7.

61. "Credit Card Issuers Find Technology Packs a Punch in Battle Against Fraud." *Card News*, July 12, 1993, pp. 3–5.

62. "Card Associations Play Pivotal Role in War on Fraud." *Card News*, July 26, 1993, pp. 3–5.

63. Jeffrey Kutler. "Is Banking Finally Ready for Smart Cards?" *American Banker*, July 7, 1992, p. 7.

64. William T. Neumann. "Busting Credit Card Crime Is Tough." *American Banker*, September 18, 1989, pp. 26–27.

65. "The Card Companies to Scrub Laundering." *Credit Card News*, June 1, 1993, p. 4.

66. William T. Neumann. "Busting Credit Card Crime Is Tough." *American Banker*, September 18, 1989, pp. 26–27.

67. Michael deCourcy Hinds. "The New-Fashioned Way to Steal Money: Fake Credit." *New York Times,* December 31, 1988, p. 28.

68. "A New Merchant-Fraud Fighter: Neural Networks." *Credit Card News,* September 11, 1993, pp. 4–5.

69. Tony Robinson. "Firms Say Fight Against Credit-Card Fraud Is Paying Off." *Los Angeles Times,* January 7, 1985, pp. IV1, IV2.

70. Jane Bryant Quinn. "Credit Card Protection and Other Bad Ideas." *Washington Post,* April 28, 1991, p. H3.

71. David Warsh. "Credit Rate Cap Is One Way to Treat an Addiction." *Washington Post,* November 27, 1991, p. C3.

72. Paul S. Nadler. "Politicians Create Credit Card Furor." *Bankers Monthly,* February, 1992, p. 8.

73. John Waggoner. "Lower Rates and Demand Pinch Issuers." *USA Today,* March 24, 1992, pp. 1B, 2B.

74. "Creditors May Lose Big If New Bill Passes." *Card News,* May 17, 1993, p. 1.

Chapter 5

1. Georg Simmel. *The Philosophy of Money.* London: Routledge & Kegan Paul, 1907/1978, p. 385.

2. "Call Boy Probe Chronology." *Washington Times,* October 20, 1989, p. A10; "Washington Lobbyist Craig Spence." *Chicago Tribune,* November 10, 1989, p. 10.

3. James Rule, Douglas McAdam, Linda Stearns, and David Uglow. *The Politics of Privacy.* New York: Elsevier, 1980.

4. Terry Galanoy. *Charge It: Inside the Credit Card Conspiracy.* New York: Putnam, 1980, p. 18.

5. Stephen Kleege. "Privacy a Concern with Marketing Based on Card Data." *American Banker,* March 14, 1994, p. 15.

6. John Stewart. "The Credit-Reporting Mess." *Credit Card Management,* July 1991, pp. 55ff.

7. Stephen Kleege. "Privacy a Concern With Marketing Based on Card Data." *American Banker,* March 14, 1994, p. 15.

8. Evan Schwartz. "Credit Bureaus: Consumers Are Stewing and Suing." *Business Week,* July 29, 1991, pp. 69–70; "Your Credit Rating." *Consumer Reports,* October, 1990, p. 648.

9. Gerri Detweiler. "Congress Takes Aim at Credit Reporting." *American Banker,* September 10, 1991, p. 7A.

10. "Credit Bureaus Adopt Policy to Improve Accuracy." *Card News,* May 31, 1993, p. 8.

11. Amy Dunkin. "Getting the Kinks Out of Your Credit Report." *Business Week,* May 25, 1992, pp. 132–133; Robert A. Rosenblatt. "Better Consumer Guards in Credit Reports Urged." *Los Angeles Times,* June 7, 1991, pp. D1, D14; "Your Credit Rating." *Consumer Reports,* October 1990, p. 648.

12. S. J. Diamond. "Credit Bureaus' Tardy Rush to Aid Consumer." *Los Angeles Times,* October 11, 1991, p. D12.

13. Evan I. Schwartz. "It's Time to Clean Up Credit Reporting." *Business Week,* May 18, 1992, p. 52.

14. Michael G. Riley. "Sorry, Your Card Is No Good." *Time,* April 9, 1990, p. 62.

15. Michael G. Riley. "Sorry, Your Card Is No Good." *Time,* April 9, 1990, p. 62.

16. Leonard Sloane. "Credit Reports: The Overhaul Rolls On." *New York Times,* January 4, 1992, p. B10.

17. Robert Naylor, Jr. "House May Tighten Credit Report Rules." *Los Angeles Times,* September 24, 1991, p. D2.

18. Albert B. Crenshaw. "Checking the Credit Bureau Industry." *Washington Post,* June 9, 1991, p. H3.

19. Amy Dunkin. "Getting the Kinks Out of Your Credit Report." *Business Week,* May 25, 1992, p. 132.

20. "TRW to Offer Free Reports." *American Banker,* January 2, 1992, p. 5.

21. Chris Woodyard. "Bill May Curb Credit Reporting Abuses." *Los Angeles Times,* June 13, 1990, p. D6.

22. Jane Bryant Quinn. "Bank Balks at Disclosing Charities' Credit Card Cut." *Washington Post,* December 8, 1991, p. H3.

23. Jane Bryant Quinn. "Bank Balks at Disclosing Charities' Credit Card Cut." *Washington Post,* December 8, 1991, p. H3.

24. Jane Bryant Quinn. "Bank Balks at Disclosing Charities' Credit Card Cut." *Washington Post,* December 8, 1991, p. H3.

25. William T. Tener. "Keeping a Computer's Secrets." *Los Angeles Times,* December 5, 1988, p. IV6.

26. Daniel Mendel-Black and Evelyn Richard. "Peering Into Private Lives." *Washington Post,* January 20, 1991, pp. H1, H6.

27. Daniel Mendel-Black and Evelyn Richard. "Peering Into Private Lives." *Washington Post,* January 20, 1991, pp. H1, H6.

28. Daniel Mendel-Black and Evelyn Richard. "Peering Into Private Lives." *Washington Post,* January 20, 1991, p. H1.

29. Michael W. Miller. "Citicorp Creates Controversy With Plan to Sell Data on Credit-Card Purchases." *Wall Street Journal,* August 21, 1991, p. B7.

30. "The 10 Big Businesses That Have Your Numbers." *Money,* March, 1992, p. 102.

31. "The 10 Big Businesses That Have Your Numbers." *Money,* March, 1992, p. 102.

32. "The 10 Big Businesses That Have Your Numbers." *Money,* March, 1992, p. 102.

33. Ellen Schultz. "It's Tough to Safeguard Financial Privacy." *Wall Street Journal,* July 9, 1991, pp. C1, C14.

34. Bill Sing. "Protect Your Credit Cards from Retail Practices." *Los Angeles Times,* April 8, 1990, p. B1 .

35. Albert B. Crenshaw. "Protecting Credit Card Privacy." *Washington Post,* October 22, 1989, p. H13.

36. Sam Fulwood III. "Data Crunchers: Marketing Boon or Threat to Privacy?" *Los Angeles Times,* May 19, 1991, p. D18.

37. Jeffrey Rothfeder. *Privacy for Sale: How Computerization Has Made Everyone's Life an Open Secret.* New York: Simon & Schuster, 1992.

38. "Credit Report Cases Settled." *New York Times,* October 10, 1991, p. A1.

39. Kenneth N. Gilpin. "Three Credit-Data Concerns Settle Charges." *New York Times,* August 19, 1992, p. D4.

40. Jeffrey Rothfeder. *Privacy for Sale: How Computerization Has Made Everyone's Life an Open Secret.* New York: Simon & Schuster, 1992.

41. Michael Isikoff. "Theft of U.S. Data Seen as Growing Threat." *Washington Post,* December 28, 1991, pp. A1, A4.

42. Leonard Sloane. "Credit Bureaus Draw Fire for Misuse of Data." *New York Times,* June 22, 1991, p. 48.

43. Jeffrey Kutler. "Is Banking Finally Ready for Smart Cards?" *American Banker,* July 7, 1992, pp. 1, 7.

44. Karen Timmons. "Study Finds Credit Report Errors." *Los Angeles Times*, April 30, 1991, p. D9F.

45. Sam Fulwood III. "Data Crunchers: Marketing Boon or Threat to Privacy?" *Los Angeles Times*, May 19, 1991, p. D18.

46. Dana Priest. "How Direct Mailers Get New Addresses." *Washington Post*, May 15, 1992, p. A23.

47. Saul Hansell. "Getting to Know You." *Institutional Investor*, June, 1991, p. 72.

48. Saul Hansell. "Getting to Know You." *Institutional Investor*, June, 1991, p. 73.

49. Don G. Campbell. "Those 'Pre-Approved' Credit Card Come-Ons." *Los Angeles Times*, June 7, 1989, p. V3.

50. Walecia Konrad and Zachary Schiller. "Credit Reports—With a Smile." *Business Week*, October 21, 1991, pp. 100, 102; Kathy M. Kristof. "Equifax Agrees to Reforms in Credit Reports." *Los Angeles Times*, July 1, 1992, pp. D1, D5.

51. Albert B. Crenshaw. "Credit Card Holders to Be Warned of Lists." *Washington Post*, May 14, 1992, pp. D11, D14; For a lampooning of American Express on this revelation, see Art Buchwald. "Credit Card Sharks." *Washington Post*, June 25, 1992, p. C1.

52. S. J. Diamond. "Credit Bureaus' Tardy Rush to Aid Consumer." *Los Angeles Times*, October 11, 1991, p. D12.

53. Stephen Kleege. "Privacy a Concern With Marketing Based on Card Data." *American Banker*, March 14, 1994, p. 15.

54. John Markoff. "More Threats to Privacy Seen as Computer Links Broaden." *New York Times*, June 1, 1988, pp. A1, C1.

55. Leonard Sloane. "Credit Reports: The Overhaul Rolls On." *New York Times*, January 4, 1992, p. B10.

56. Albert B. Crenshaw. "Credit Card Holders to be Warned of Lists." *Washington Post*, May 14, 1992, p. D14.

57. Albert B. Crenshaw. "Credit Card Holders to be Warned of Lists." *Washington Post*, May 14, 1992, p. D14.

58. Sam Fulwood III. "Data Crunchers: Marketing Boon or Threat to Privacy?" *Los Angeles Times*, May 19, 1991, p. D18.

59. David F. Linowes. "The Privacy Crisis." *Newsweek*, June 26, 1978, p. 19.

60. Richard Lacayo. "Nowhere to Hide." *Time*, November 11, 1991, p. 36.

61. "Your Credit Report." *Money*, September, 1984, p. 124.

62. Jeffrey Rothfeder. *Privacy for Sale: How Computerization Has Made Everyone's Life an Open Secret*. New York: Simon & Schuster, 1992, p. 30.

63. Chris Woodyard. "Losing Faith in Credit Files." *Los Angeles Times*, July 22, 1991, pp. A1, A16.

64. "One-Stop Shopping for Credit Reports." *Consumer Reports*, December, 1992, p. 745.

65. Evan Schwartz. "Credit Bureaus: Consumers Are Stewing and Suing." *Business Week*, July 29, 1991, pp. 69–70; Walecia Konrad and Zachary Schiller. "Credit Reports—With a Smile." *Business Week*, October 21, 1991, pp. 100, 102.

66. Chris Woodyard. "Losing Faith in Credit Files." *Los Angeles Times*, July 22, 1991, p. A16.

67. Leonard Sloane. "Unraveling of Measure to Revamp Consumer-Credit Reporting." *New York Times*, October 17, 1992, p. 34.

68. "Credit Bureaus Adopt Policy to Improve Accuracy." *Card News*, May 31, 1993, p. 8.

69. "The 10 Big Businesses That Have Your Numbers." *Money*, March, 1992, p. 102.

70. William T. Tener. "Keeping a Computer's Secrets." *Los Angeles Times*, December 5, 1988, p. IV6.

71. "Credit Bureaus Adopt Policy to Improve Accuracy." *Card News*, May 31, 1993, p. 8.

72. Jeffrey Rothfeder. "What Happened to Privacy?" *New York Times*, April 13, 1993, p. A21.

Chapter 6

1. Lewis Mandell. *The Credit Card Industry: A History*. Boston: Twayne, 1990, p. 11.

2. George Ritzer. *The McDonaldization of Society*. Thousand Oaks, CA: Pine Forge Press, 1993, pp. 31–32.

3. Lewis Mandell. *The Credit Card Industry: A History*. Boston: Twayne, 1990, p. 11.

4. Jon Friedman and John Meehan. *House of Cards: Inside the Troubled Empire of American Express*. New York: Putnam, 1992.

5. Jon Friedman and John Meehan. *House of Cards: Inside the Troubled Empire of American Express.* New York: Putnam, p. 110.

6. Debra Whitefield. "Money Talk: Credit Vendors Target the Colleges." *Los Angeles Times,* May 21, 1987, p. IV3; Barry Meier. "Credit Cards on the Rise in High Schools." *New York Times,* September 5, 1992, p. 9.

7. American Express advertisement, *New York Times,* November 23, 1993, p. A17.

8. "American Express Tries Its Hand at a Cause-Related Campaign." *Credit Card News,* November 1, 1993, p. 7.

9. James K. Glassman. "American Express Charges Ahead With 'Cause' Marketing." *Washington Post,* December 24, 1993, pp. D9–D10.

10. For an overview of Weber's theory of rationalization, see Stephen Kalberg. "Max Weber's Types of Rationality: Cornerstones for the Analysis of Rationalization Processes in History." *American Journal of Sociology* 85(1980):1145–1179. See also Bryan S. Turner. "Simmel, Rationalisation and the Sociology of Money." *Sociological Review* 34(1986):93–114.

11. For a similar delineation, see Arnold Eisen. "The Meanings and Confusions of Weberian 'Rationality.'" *British Journal of Sociology* 29(1978):57–70.

12. I would like to thank one of my students, Michael Saks, for this point.

13. Kenneth R. Varney. "Automated Credit Scoring Screens Loan Applicants." *Washington Post,* January 15, 1994, pp. E1, E13.

14. Saul Hansell. "Into Banking's Future, Electronically." *New York Times,* March 31, 1994, pp. D1, D13.

15. Saul Hansell. "Into Banking's Future, Electronically." *New York Times,* March 31, 1994, p. D13.

16. Georg Simmel. *The Philosophy of Money.* London: Routledge & Kegan Paul, 1907/1978, p. 256.

17. Christopher S. Rupkey, "The 'Have It All Now' Generation." *New York Times,* May 13, 1979, p. 26.

18. Albert G. Crenshaw. "Americans Putting Brakes on Borrowing." *Washington Post,* March 8, 1991, pp. A1, A14.

19. Yvette Kantrow. "Fewer Paying Off Card Balances, ABA Survey Finds." *American Banker,* September 19, 1989, pp. 1, 22.

20. Walter L. Updegrave. "How Lenders Size You Up." *Money,* April 1987, pp. 145ff.

21. Walter L. Updegrave. "How Lenders Size You Up." *Money,* April 1987, p. 146.

22. Walter L. Updegrave. "How Lenders Size You Up." *Money,* April 1987, p. 147.

23. Jube Shiver, Jr. "Scoring System for Loan Seekers Stirs Debate." *Los Angeles Times,* October 30, 1988, p. IV5.

24. Albert B. Crenshaw. "Keeping Tabs on Card Holders." *Washington Post,* January 20, 1991, p. H4.

25. Albert B. Crenshaw. "Keeping Tabs on Card Holders." *Washington Post,* January 20, 1991, p. H4.

26. Gerri Detweiler. *The Ultimate Credit Handbook.* New York: Plume, 1993.

27. "Evaluating the Payments: More Is Better." *Chain Store Executive,* September 1992, p. 28.

28. Michael Quint. "D'Agostino to Accept Debit Cards for Purchases." *New York Times,* May 19, 1990, p. 43.

29. Roger L. Pierce. "Seeking New Opportunities in Tomorrow's Payment-Systems World." *American Banker,* July 5, 1990, p. 11A.

30. Stephanie Strom. "Holiday Shoppers Are Whipping Out the Plastic." *New York Times,* December 18, 1993, p. 45.

31. Robin Leidner. *Fast Food, Fast Talk: Service Work and the Routinization of Everyday Life.* Berkeley: University of California Press, 1993.

32. "EFT Experts Look Ahead With Costs on Their Minds." *American Banker,* May 20, 1991, p. 22A.

33. Beth Piskora and Jeffrey Kutler. "ATM, Debit Cards and Home Banking: Finally, Many Bank Customers Seem to Be Ready for the Future." *American Banker,* September 27, 1993, p. 1A.

34. "Road to Cashlessness Paved With Plastic." *Los Angeles Times,* December 20, 1993, p. C1.

35. Gerri Detweiler. *The Ultimate Credit Handbook.* New York: Plume, 1993, pp. 10, 39. Italics added.

36. "Hello, Central, Get Me 18005551696034858369394163859050488 7659876." *Consumer Reports,* August 1992, p. 7.

37. Adam Bryant. "It Pays to Stick to Basics in Credit Cards." *New York Times,* October 31, 1992, p. 35.

38. Personal communication from Gerri Detweiler, former executive director of Bankcard Holders of America.

39. Lewis Mandell. *The Credit Card Industry: A History.* Boston: Twayne, p. 79.

40. For a discussion of the advantages of another key element of the rationalization process, the fast-food restaurant, see George Ritzer. *The McDonaldization of Society.* Thousand Oaks, CA: Pine Forge Press, pp. 14–15.

41. Terry Galanoy. *Charge It: Inside the Credit Card Conspiracy.* New York: Putnam, 1980. In fact, Dee Ward Hock, the person responsible for the creation of Visa, actually envisioned an all-purpose card like Lifebank. (See Joseph Nocera. *A Piece of the Action: How the Middle Class Joined the Money Class.* New York: Simon & Schuster, 1994, p. 307.)

42. Terry Galanoy. *Charge It: Inside the Credit Card Conspiracy.* New York: Putnam, 1980, p. 215.

43. I would like to thank Meghan S. Lee for making this point.

44. Gerri Detweiler. *The Ultimate Credit Handbook.* New York: Plume, 1993, p. 227.

Chapter 7

1. David Rieff. "The Culture That Conquered the World." *Washington Post,* January 2, 1994, pp. C1–C4.

2. Stanley Lebergott. *Pursuing Happiness: American Consumers in the Twentieth Century.* Princeton, NJ: Princeton University Press, 1993; Richard W. Fox and T. J. Jackson Lears (eds.), *The Culture of Consumption.* New York: Pantheon, 1983.

3. Francis Williams. *The American Invasion.* New York: Crown, 1962, p. 63.

4. Steve Lipin, Brian Coleman, and Jeremy Mark. "Visa, American Express and MasterCard Vie in Overseas Strategies." *Wall Street Journal,* February 15, 1994, p. A10.

5. "Associations Explore International Waters for Cardholders." *Card News,* November 29, 1993, p. 6.

6. *Credit Card News,* August 15, 1993, p. 5.

7. Steve Lipin, Brian Coleman, and Jeremy Mark. "Visa, American Express and MasterCard Vie in Overseas Strategies." *Wall Street Journal,* February 15, 1994, p. A1.

8. "Credit Card Issuer's Guide: 1995 Edition." *Credit Card News*, August 15, 1994, p. 3.

9. *Credit Card News*, August 1993, p. 3; Richard Rolfe. "Europe's Grand Prix in Cards." *Credit Card Management*, August 1994, pp. 57–62.

10. "Associations Explore International Waters for Cardholders." *Card News*, November 29, 1993, p. 6.

11. "Credit Cards Deny Liability Overseas." *Sunday Times*, November 21, 1993, p. 1.

12. Rob Wells. "Japan to Enter Credit Card Market in U.S." *Washington Post*, March 6, 1994, p. H14.

13. "Firm Seeks Use Abroad of Yuan Credit Card." *South China Morning Post*, October 25, 1993, p. 2.

14. Jeffrey Kutler. "Visa Seals Debit Strategy by Purchasing Plus." *American Banker*, November 2, 1993, p. 15.

15. Roland Robertson. *Globalization: Social Theory and Global Culture*. London: Sage, 1992.

16. Mike Featherstone. "Global Culture: An Introduction," in Mike Featherstone (ed.), *Global Culture: Nationalism, Globalization and Modernity*. London: Sage, 1990, p. 1.

17. Arjun Appadurai. "Disjuncture and Difference in the Global Cultural Economy," in Mike Featherstone (ed.), *Global Culture: Nationalism, Globalization and Modernity*. London: Sage, 1990, p. 298.

18. See Georges Duhamel. *America the Menace: Scenes from the Life of the Future*. Boston: Houghton Mifflin, 1931; Francis Williams. *The American Invasion*. New York: Crown, 1962; Edward A. McCreary. *The Americanization of Europe: The Impact of Americans and American Business on the Uncommon Market*. Garden City, NY: Doubleday, 1964; J.-J. Servan-Schreiber. *The American Challenge*. New York: Atheneum, 1968; Peter Duignan and Lewis Gann. *The Rebirth of the West: The Americanization of the Democratic World*. London: Blackwell, 1992.

19. Georg Simmel. "Money in Modern Culture." *Theory, Culture and Society* 8(1991):27.

20. Georges Duhamel. *America the Menace: Scenes from the Life of the Future*. Boston: Houghton Mifflin, 1931, p. 215.

21. J.-J. Servan-Schreiber. *The American Challenge*. New York: Atheneum, 1968, p. 3.

22. Francis Williams. *The American Invasion*. New York: Crown, 1962, npi.

23. Francis Williams. *The American Invasion*. New York: Crown, 1962, npi.

24. Richard Kuisel. *Seducing the French: The Dilemma of Americanization*. Berkeley: University of California Press, 1993, p. 4.

25. Richard Kuisel. *Seducing the French: The Dilemma of Americanization*. Berkeley: University of California Press, 1993, p. 3.

26. Richard Kuisel. *Seducing the French: The Dilemma of Americanization*. Berkeley: University of California Press, 1993, p. 10.

27. Richard Kuisel. *Seducing the French: The Dilemma of Americanization*. Berkeley: University of California Press, 1993, p. 11.

28. For a discussion of Ford's assembly line as such a precursor, see George Ritzer. *The McDonaldization of Society*. Thousand Oaks, CA: Pine Forge Press, 1993, pp. 25–27.

29. Richard Kuisel. *Seducing the French: The Dilemma of Americanization*. Berkeley: University of California Press, 1993, pp. x, 4.

30. Richard Kuisel. *Seducing the French: The Dilemma of Americanization*. Berkeley: University of California Press, 1993, p. 4.

31. Richard Kuisel. *Seducing the French: The Dilemma of Americanization*. Berkeley: University of California Press, 1993, p. 36.

32. Richard Kuisel. *Seducing the French: The Dilemma of Americanization*. Berkeley: University of California Press, 1993, p. 11.

33. Richard Kuisel. *Seducing the French: The Dilemma of Americanization*. Berkeley: University of California Press, 1993, p. 13.

34. Richard Kuisel. *Seducing the French: The Dilemma of Americanization*. Berkeley: University of California Press, 1993, p. 13.

35. Simon Clarke. "The Crisis of Fordism or the Crisis of Social Democracy?" *Telos* 83(1990): 71–98.

36. Edward A. Tiryakian. "Pathways to Metatheory: Rethinking the Presuppositions of Macrosociology," in George Ritzer (ed.), *Metatheorizing*. Newbury Park, CA: Sage, 1992, p. 79.

37. There is an enormous primary and secondary literature on postmodernism. One good secondary source is Pauline Marie Rosenau. *Post-Modernism and the Social Sciences*. Princeton, NJ: Princeton University Press, 1992. For a recent effort to link Simmel's thinking to postmodernism, see Deena Weinstein and Michael A. Weinstein. *Postmodern(ized) Simmel*. London: Routledge, 1993.

38. Jean Baudrillard. *Simulations*. New York: Semiotext (e), 1983.

39. Jerald Hage and Charles H. Powers. *Post-Industrial Lives: Roles and Relationships in the 21st Century*. Newbury Park, CA: Sage, 1992.

40. David Harvey. *The Condition of Postmodernity: An Enquiry into the Origins of Cultural Change*. Oxford: Basil Blackwell, 1989.

41. David Rieff. "The Culture That Conquered the World." *Washington Post*, January 2, 1994, pp. C1–C4.

42. One author who equates the two defines Americanization as anti-Americanism: "a catchall for anything of which the speaker morally and emotionally disapproves." See Edward A. McCreary. *The Americanization of Europe: The Impact of Americans and American Business on the Uncommon Market*. Garden City, NY: Doubleday, 1964, p. 1.

43. Richard Kuisel. *Seducing the French: The Dilemma of Americanization*. Berkeley: University of California Press, 1993, p. 8.

44. Richard Kuisel. *Seducing the French: The Dilemma of Americanization*. Berkeley: University of California Press, 1993, pp. 8–9.

45. In any case, the distinction between high and low culture has come to be viewed as increasingly valueless. See, for example, Pierre Bourdieu. *Distinction: A Social Critique of the Judgment of Taste*. Cambridge: Harvard University Press, 1984.

46. David Rieff. "The Culture That Conquered the World." *Washington Post*, January 2, 1994, p. C4.

47. Francis Williams. *The American Invasion*. New York: Crown, 1962, pp. 11–12.

48. Richard Kuisel. *Seducing the French: The Dilemma of Americanization*. Berkeley: University of California Press, 1993, p. 63.

49. David Rieff. "The Culture That Conquered the World." *Washington Post*, January 2, 1994, p. C4.

50. Richard Kuisel. *Seducing the French: The Dilemma of Americanization*. Berkeley: University of California Press, 1993, p. 13.

51. Richard Kuisel. *Seducing the French: The Dilemma of Americanization*. Berkeley: University of California Press, 1993, p. 127.

52. "French 'Cast Members' Get Used to the Rules in a Magic Kingdom of Jobs." *Chicago Tribune*, January 31, 1992, p. 2.

53. Marjorie Robins. "Awfully American for Grown-ups." *Los Angeles Times* May 3, 1992, p. L1.

54. Richard Kuisel. *Seducing the French: The Dilemma of Americanization*. Berkeley: University of California Press, 1993, p. 228; Scott Kraft. "Agog at Euro Disneyland." *Los Angeles Times*, January 18, 1994, p. H5.

55. Peter Gumbel and Richard Turner. "Fans Like Euro Disney but Its Parent's Goofs Weigh the Park Down." *Wall Street Journal*, March 10, 1994, pp. A1, A12.

56. Roger Cohen. "Euro Disney in Danger of Shutdown." *Washington Post*, December 23, 1993, p. D3.

57. Brian Coleman and Thomas R. King. "Euro Disney Rescue Package Wins Approval." *Wall Street Journal*, March 15, 1994, pp. A3, A6; "Fairy Tale Ending?" *Time*, June 13, 1994, p. 20.

58. Scott Kraft. "Agog at Euro Disneyland." *Los Angeles Times*, January 18, 1994, p. H1.

59. Francis Williams. *The American Invasion*. New York: Crown, 1962, p. 146.

60. James Sterngold. "Tokyo's Magic Kingdom Outshines Its Role Model." *New York Times*, March 7, 1994, pp. D1, D7.

61. Cited in Richard Kuisel. *Seducing the French: The Dilemma of Americanization*. Berkeley: University of California Press, 1993, p. 230.

62. Arjun Appadurai. "Disjuncture and Difference in the Global Cultural Economy," in Mike Featherstone (ed.), *Global Culture: Nationalism, Globalization and Modernity*. London: Sage, 1990, p. 307.

Appendix

1. Robert Mitchell. "Debit's Troubling On–Off Switch." *Credit Card Management*, July 1994, p. 44.

2. Peter Lucas. "Crediting Debit." *Credit Card Management*, February 1994, p. 18.

3. Barton Crockett. "Banks Unlikely to Find a Bonanza in Debit Cards." *American Banker*, September 2, 1992, p. 10.

4. Yvette Kantrow. "Visa and MasterCard Battle for Debit-Card Supremacy." *American Banker*, August 26, 1992, pp. 1, 9; Michael Quint. "MasterCard and Visa in a Debit-Card Battle." *New York Times*, May 5, 1992, pp. D1, D20.

5. "This Debit Card Dies Aborning." *Business Week*, May 21, 1990, p. 52.

6. Patricia A. Murphy. "Regional Networks Drive Debit Growth." *ABA Banking Journal*, September 1992, pp. 68ff.

7. Patricia A. Murphy. "Regional Networks Drive Debit Growth." *ABA Banking Journal*, September 1992, pp. 68ff.

8. Based on Sandra Lowe. "Americard Banking Cashes In on Debit Card System." *San Antonio Business Journal* 6 (1992):1.

9. S. J. Diamond. "Debit Cards Pay Off—and Do It Really Fast." *Los Angeles Times*, April 22, 1985, p. IV1.

10. Jane Bryant Quinn. "The Era of Debit Cards." *Newsweek*, January 2, 1989, p. 51.

11. Leonard Sloane. "Debit vs. Credit Cards: Pay Now, or Later." *New York Times* March 21, 1992, p. 52.

12. "Fast Food Market Showing Some Advantages of Debit Over Credit." *Card News*, June 1, 1992, pp. 5–6; "POS Debit to Become Universal Faster Than Expected." *Card News*, December 28, 1992, pp. 5–6.

13. "The Case for National Debit." *Chain Store Executive*, September 1992, p. 24.

14. Jan Jaben. "Debit Card/POS—An Uphill Climb." *U.S. Banker*, April 1988, pp. 43–45; Suzanne Woolley. "The Dawn of the Debit Card. Well, Maybe." *Business Week*, September 21, 1992, p. 79.

15. "Prepaid Cards Making Their Way Around the Globe." *Card News*, April 20, 1992, pp. 1–4; "Prepayment to Nirvana." *The Economist*, November 19, 1989, p. 90.

16. Nora Zamichow. "Transit Card Plan to Debut Amid Doubts." *Los Angeles Times*, November 17, 1992, pp. B1, B4; Glenn Rifkin. "Electronic Toll-Taking Is Being Put to the Test." *New York Times*, September 9, 1992, pp. D1, D4.

17. Linda Punch. "Is Prepaid Debit Coming of Age?" *Credit Card Management*, October 1992, pp. 10ff.

18. Gary H. Anthes. "Food Stamp Program Soon to Be Electronic." *Computerworld*, January 13, 1992, pp. 51, 55.

19. "Fast Food Market Showing Some Advantages of Debit Over Credit." *Card News*, June 1, 1992, p. 5.

20. Jeffrey Kutler. "Visa Starts Push for Smart Card to Replace Cash." *American Banker*, March 22, 1994, p. 1.

21. Suzanne Woolley. "The Dawn of the Debit Card, Well, Maybe." *Business Week*, September 21, 1992, p. 79.

22. American Bankers Association. *Bank Card Fact Book*. Washington, DC: American Bankers Association, 1990, p. 23.

23. Karen Gullo. "Electronic Bill Payment: Low-Cost Systems Explored." *American Banker*, January 27, 1992, p. 3.

24. Michael Quint. "Banks' Plea: Drop That Checkbook." *New York Times*, March 7, 1992, pp. 39, 49.

25. Michael Quint. "Banks' Plea: Drop That Checkbook." *New York Times*, March 7, 1992, p. 49.

26. Karen Gullo. "Electronic Bill Payment: Low-Cost Systems Explored." *American Banker*, January 27, 1992, p. 3.

27. The Bureau of National Affairs. "White House Looking at Electronic Benefit System Deployment by 1996, Official Says." *Daily Report for Executives*, December 3, 1993, p. A231.

28. The Bureau of National Affairs. "White House Looking at Electronic Benefit System Deployment by 1996, Official Says." *Daily Report for Executives*, December 3, 1993, p. A231.

29. "Electronic Funds Transfer Expected to Grow in Medicaid Program, IG Reports." *Daily Report for Executives*, July 15, 1992, pp. A12, A13.

30. Stephen Barr, "Adding Dignity to Aid with New Technology." *Washington Post*, June 4, 1993, p. A23.

31. "Maryland Switches to Bank Cards for Distributing Welfare Benefits." *New York Times*, May 13, 1991, p. 39.

32. Yvette D. Kantrow. "Banc One to Launch Health Care Payment Net." *American Banker*, March 17, 1992, pp. 1, 22.

33. Jane Bryant Quinn. "Automated Monthly Payments Offer Convenience and Savings." *Washington Post*, October 13, 1991, p. H3.

34. "A Call to Cut Check Use." *New York Times*, May 27, 1988, p. D6.

35. Gary Legg. "Smart-Card Applications' Hidden Problems Add to Designers' Challenges." *EDN*, March 2, 1992, pp. 83–90; Jeffrey Kutler. "Is Banking Finally Ready for Smart Cards?" *American Banker*, July 7, 1992, pp. 1, 7; " 'Smart Card' Keeps Track of Betting." *New York Times*, August 20, 1988, p. 34.

36. James Bates. "Banks in the '90s Appear Headed Back to Basic." *Los Angeles Times*, April 17, 1991, p. A14.

37. James Bates. "Banks in the '90s Appear Headed Back to Basic." *Los Angeles Times*, April 17, 1991, p. A14.

38. "A History of Debit and Credit: How Plastic Cards Changed Our Lives." *Chain Store Executive*, September 1992, p. 22.

39. Lauri Giesen. "The Private Sector Takes on the Fed for ACH Transactions." *Magazine of Bank Administration*, July 1992, pp. 61–63.

40. These data and other information on ACHs come from data provided by National Automated Clearing House Association.

41. "Use of ACH on Rise in the Midwest." *ABA Banking Journal*, December 1988, p. 66.

42. Barton Crockett. "Bankers Create Group to Promote Wider Use of EDI." *Network World*, February 20, 1989, p. 6.

43. Edward J. Joyce. "Tales of EDI Trailblazers." *Computer Decisions*, February 1989, p. 65.

44. Sharen Kindel. "The Esperanto of Documents." *Financial World*, July 7, 1992, p. 64.

45. Richard R. Oliver. "The All-Electronic ACH." *EDI Forum* 5(1992): 21–23.

46. Ned C. Hill and Daniel M. Ferguson. "Introduction to EFT and Financial EDI." *EDI Forum* 5(1992):12–20.

47. Sheila O'Heney. "Fedwire Goes With the Flow." *Computers in Banking*, October 1988, pp. 44ff.

48. Karen Gullo. "Global Electronic Payments Show Early Signs of Growth." *American Banker*, January 8, 1992, p. 3.

49. NACHA. "Cross-Border Payments." Unpublished document.

50. Ian Lynch. " 'If You Build It, He Will Come': Cross-Border EDI/EFT in Europe." *EDI Forum* 5(1992):99–102.

51. Wayne Eckerson. "Bank Holding Company Sees Paperless Future." *Network World*, April 17, 1989, pp. 23, 27.

52. Gerri Detweiler. *The Ultimate Credit Handbook*. New York: Plume, 1993, p. 277.

53. Kirk Johnson. "One Less Thing to Believe In: High-Tech Fraud at an ATM." *New York Times*, May 13, 1993, pp. A1, B9.

54. Jerry Knight. "On PINs and Needles Over ATMs." *Washington Post*,

May 21, 1993, pp. G1, G8; "2 Sentenced in $100,000 Bank Machine Fraud." *New York Times*, December 21, 1993, p. B5.

55. Jerry Knight. "On PINs and Needles Over ATMs." *Washington Post*, May 21, 1993, p. G8.

56. Bill Miller. "Instant Banking Inspires Abductions." *Washington Post*, September 29, 1993, p. D1.

57. Jon Jeter. "Teen Charged in 3 Rapes and Robberies by ATM." *Washington Post*, October 7, 1993, p. D1.

58. Michelle Singletary. "Crooks Are Turning ATM Trash into High Speed Cash." *Washington Post*, June 7, 1994, pp. D1, D7.

59. Don Terry. "Police Station Becomes a Cash Station." *New York Times*, April 1, 1994, p. A12.

60. Saul Hansell, "Bank Says Cash Machine Problems Are Fixed." *New York Times*, February 19, 1994, pp. 37, 46.

61. See, for example, S. J. Diamond, " 'Fraudbusters' Go After Illegal Use of ATMs." *Los Angeles Times*, August 25, 1986, p. IV1.

62. Gerri Detweiler. *The Ultimate Credit Handbook*. New York: Plume, 1993.

63. Jeffrey Rothfeder. *Privacy for Sale: How Computerization Has Made Everyone's Life an Open Secret*. New York: Simon & Schuster, 1992, p. 94.

Index

AAdvantage card, 39
Addiction, 65, 69
Advertising, reliance on, 129–132
"Affinity cards," 45, 77, 113
Agency-structure integration, 16
Airplanes, 31–32
Alcoholics Anonymous, 67, 79–80
American Airlines, 39, 122
American Bankers Association (ABA),
    61–62, 65, 103, 184
"American Dream," 157–158
American Express, 26–28, 34, 36–37,
    39, 40–44, 46–47, 49–50, 75, 95,
    118, 121–123, 131–133, 148, 158,
    160–161, 172, 174
    "Charge Against Hunger," 133
    Corporate Purchasing Card, 44–45
    Gold card, 41, 49–50, 133
    Global Assist, 47
    Optima card, 133
    Optima True Grace card, 95
    Platinum card, 41, 50
American Invasion, The, 164
Americanism, 163
Americanization, 22, 173–175, 177, 196
Amoco, 34
Amusement parks, 32–33, 170
Annual fees, 3, 13, 27, 35–38, 41, 44,
    46, 48–51, 52–53, 94, 96, 104, 113,
    131, 137, 151
Annual percentage rate (APR), 53,
    94–95
Annunzio, Frank, 93

Anti-Americanism, 171–175
Apple Computer, 40
Arby's, 49
Arizona Clearing House Association,
    189
Asia, 160
Assembly-line technology, 164
ATM cards, 55–57, 98–99
AT&T, 27, 38–41, 78, 88, 104, 131
Automated clearinghouses (ACHs), 55,
    179, 184, 188–192, 195–196
    cash concentration(s), 190, 192
Automated payments, 63, 187
Automatic teller machines (ATMs), 54–
    56, 70, 88, 147, 155, 170, 183–184,
    188, 192–196
Automobile(s), 31, 48

Balance, average daily, 76–77, 94–95
Banc One, 185–186
BankAmericard, 27, 37
"Bank card," 36–38, 41–42, 61–62
Bankcard Holders of America, 68, 71,
    94
Bank of America, 37
Bankruptcy, 6, 18, 46, 51, 65, 67–68,
    70, 73, 79, 97, 116, 140, 142
Banks, 6–7, 9–11, 39, 45, 48, 59, 61–62,
    69–70, 78–79, 82, 93, 101, 105,
    131, 139, 143, 153, 176, 182, 185,
    187
Bank statements, 59, 62
BarclayCard, 161, 171

Berger, Peter, 29
Best Western, 31
Better Business Bureau, 113
Big Mac, 33, 172
Blumer, Herbert, 20
Boesky, Ivan, 176
Bourdieu, Pierre, 32
British Petroleum (BP), 34
Bureaucracy, 21
Burger King, 131
Busch Gardens, 168
Bush, George, 103
Business Week, 117
Buyer-protection programs, 48, 77

Canada/Canadians, 42–43, 191,
Capitalism/capitalist society, 17–19, 21,
    42, 82, 97
  exploitation in, 18
  and point of diminishing returns, 19
Carte Blanche, 36, 171
Cash, 24–25, 28, 54, 56, 59–60, 62, 75,
    83–84, 143, 145–147, 152, 154–
    156, 192, 196
  advances, 10, 57, 70–73, 76, 94, 105
  crime and, 83–84
  economy, 60, 147
  fees, 71
  transactions, 62–64, 107
Cashless society, 109
Cash on delivery (COD), 74
Catalogs, 9
CBS, 118
Chain stores, 32
Character and Social Structure, 16, 21
"Charge cards," 36, 41, 49, 75, 140
  decline of, 41–42
Charge It, 153
Checkbooks, 63
Checking account(s), 54, 62–63, 141,
    146, 154, 180–181
"Checkless society," 189
Checks, 24, 32, 54, 56, 75, 87, 143, 147,
    152, 181, 182, 185–187, 190, 196
  bounced, 63, 143
  fees, 63
  and float, 181
  transactions, 62–64, 189

Chemical Bank, 47
China/Chinese, 157, 160–161, 171
Chronic overspender, 80 (*see also* Com-
    pulsion/compulsive overspending)
Cigarette industry, 17
Cirrus ATM cards, 162
Citibank, 35, 39–41, 47, 77
  "Citidollars," 47
Citicorp, 38, 41, 108, 115–116, 184
Clayton, Gary E., 6
Clearing House for Interbank Payment
    Systems (CHIPS), 191
Coca-Cola, 1, 158, 172–174, 195
"Coca-colonization," 173
Collections business, 65
Communist society, 18, 157
Compression, 169–170
  of space, 169–170
  of time, 169–170
Compulsion/compulsive overspending,
    69, 79
Computer banking, 155
Computers, 31
Conflict theory, 15
Consumer Credit Protection Act, 101–
    102
Consumer culture, 21
Consumer debt, 64–68
  as personal trouble, 65–68
  as public issue, 64–65
Consumerism, 2, 68–69, 106, 152, 165,
    170–171, 176
Consumer Protection Act (1968) (also
    known as Truth-in-Lending Act),
    52
Consumer Reports, 110, 123
Consumer society, 3, 9, 12, 82, 97
Consumers Union, 110, 119
Consumption, 145–146
Corbey, Robert, 111
CoreStates Financial Corp., 192
Courtesy cards, 34
Credco, 123
CREDEBELS, 53–57, 59, 63, 84, 107–
    109, 116, 136–137, 146, 154, 163,
    170–171, 177, 179–184, 191–193,
    195–196
  fraud, types of, 193–195

CREDEBELS *(continued)*
  personal troubles and public issues
    with, 192–196
Credit,
  denial of, 110
  letters of, 10
Credit and Charge Card Disclosure
    and Interest Rate Amendment,
    104
Credit approval, computerized, 150
Credit bureaus, 42, 52, 102, 109–110,
    113, 115–117, 119, 123–126, 134,
    142, 149, 152, 155 (*see also* Equifax;
    Trans Union; TRW)
Credit Card News, 48, 71
Credit card(s),
  "accidental revolvers," 49
  advantages of, 3–5
  advertising of, 14, 19
  as an American icon, 27–28
  Americanization of, 162–171
  balances, 36, 41, 53, 65
  bills, 12
  biometric information, 99–100
  brand loyalty, 15
  card activation, 101
  Central Deposit Monitoring, 100
  and charities, 43
  co-branded, 35, 39–41, 48, 77, 131
  combination users, 34
  company card, 75
  convenience users, 34, 142
  corporate/business, 44–45
  counterfeiting of, 88–89
  country-club billing, 148, 153
  customer liability, 52
  debt, 59–82
  delinquency, 65, 70
  descriptive billing, 148, 153, 155
  discrimination and, 25, 52, 150
  encrypted code, 99
  fees, 76, 85, 88, 94, 96, 99
  fraud, 85–106, 151, 176
  fraudulent applications, 89–90, 100–
    101
  global spread of, 159–162
  growth/expansion of, 23, 25–27, 42–
    51

health care, 185
history of, 31–57
information, stolen, 86–88
international use of, 46
Issuers Clearinghouse Service, 100
late charges, 151
legislation, 51–53
malignant effects of, 172–175
marketing of, 13–14, 17, 19
and mass media, 92–93
minorities and, 25
myths, 28–30
negative view of, 29
"nonbanks" and, 27, 38–41, 131
personal identification number(s)
    (PIN), 98–99
pharmacy, 185
positive view of, 28–29
preapproved, 120, 135, 142, 145
prescreening, 155
problems with, 5–7, 12, 29–30
records, access to, 107–108
secured, 44, 96–97, 103, 105
signed, 98
simulations, 170
and small businesses, 45
sociological theory of, 15–23
stolen, 85–86
and students, 12–15, 43, 62, 71, 82,
    132
universal cards, 34–38
unsecured, 44
user's photograph, 99
Credit checks, 116
Credit doctors, 103, 105
Credit histories, 116, 118
Credit limits, 61, 69, 76, 100, 137–138,
    146, 148, 176
Credit lines, 61
Credit rating, 118, 154
Credit record(s), 112, 124, 142
Credit repair clinics, 103
  fraudulent, 91–92, 105
Credit reporting agencies, 109–113,
    124 (*see also* Credit bureaus)
Credit reports, 110–113, 123–124
Credit scoring, 139–142, 152
Creditworthiness, 152

Crime, 2
    ATM-related, 176, 193–194
    cash-based, 5
Critical school, the, 21–22
Critical theory, 21
Cross-merged files, 112
Customs Service, U.S., 191

Dean Witter, 38
Debit cards, 53–57, 60, 84, 98, 99, 107,
    136, 143, 147–148, 179–185, 192,
    196
    account balance, and, 57
    as "electronic checks," 143
    fees with, 182
    and float, 180
    liability with, 182
    loss of, 195
    "off-line," 180
    "on-line," 180
    as "plastic checks," 54
    prepaid, 182–183, 185
Debt(s), 9–14, 18, 20, 26, 37, 46, 51–
    52, 69, 97, 105, 137–139, 176
    consumer, 68–69
    credit card companies, 69–71
    federal, 6
    limit, 176
    responsibility for, 68–71
Debtors Anonymous, 67, 79–80
Dehumanization, 2, 21, 134–135, 149–
    150, 153, 166, 177, 195–196
Depression
    economic, 17
    individual, 17, 69
Detweiler, Gerri, 95, 149
Dezalay, Yves, 162
Diners Club, 25, 36, 130, 160–161, 171
Direct deposit, 55, 189, 190
Discover, 14–15, 26, 38, 43, 149, 171
Disney, 174–175
Disneyland, 31–32, 65, 158–159
Distinction: A Social Critique of the Judg-
    ment of Taste, 31
Drive-through window(s), 142
Duhamel, Georges, 163
DuPont, 191

Economies of scale, 166
Eiffel Tower, 175
Electronic benefit transfers (EBTs),
    183, 185–186
    Medicaid, 185
    of welfare benefits, 185
Electronic data interchanges (EDIs),
    55, 190–192
Electronic data transfers, 186
Electronic Funds Association, 193
Electronic funds transfers (EFTs), 53,
    55–57, 60, 84, 107, 137, 143, 171,
    179–180, 184–188, 191–192, 195,
    196
    by computer, 196
    by telephone, 196
Electronic Funds Transfers Act (1978),
    53
Electronic Funds Transfer
    Association (EFTA), 54–55,
    184–185
"Electronic purse," the, 183
Enhancements, 46–48, 50–51
"Ethnoscape," 163
Euro Disney, 174–175
Europe, 160, 169, 182, 192
Equal Credit Opportunity Act (1974),
    52
Equifax, 110, 112, 115–116, 120–121,
    123–124
Expansion, 129, 132–133

Fair Credit and Charge Card Disclo-
    sure Act (1988), 53
Fair Credit Billing Act (1974), 52
Fair Credit Reporting Act (1971), 52,
    118, 124
Fast-food industry, 18, 32–33, 49
    similarities to credit-card industry,
    129–133
Fast-food restaurants, 60, 129–156,
    158–159, 183
Featherstone, Mike, 162
Federal Reserve Board, 24, 189, 191
Federal Trade Commission (FTC),
    110, 118–119
Fedwire, 191

Finance charges, 52
  minimum, 53
Financial Institutions Regulatory and
    Interest Rate Control Act (1978),
    52
"Finanscape," 163
Fioretto, Jeanne, 79
Ford, 39–40, 172
Fordism, 164, 166–167
  post-Fordism, 167
France, 46, 159–160, 163–166, 172–
    175
Franklin National Bank, 37
Fraud, 2, 12, 75, 176
  protecting customers, 101–106
  weapons against, 98–106
French, the (*see* France)
Frequent-flyer miles, 48
  cards, 55

Galanoy, Terry, 3, 18, 68, 75, 81, 97,
    108, 153
General Electric, 39–40
General Motors, 27, 39–41, 78, 104,
    121, 131, 150–151, 159
  GM card, 35, 121
Gerhard, Martin, 6
Germany, 46, 160
Gerth, Hans, 16, 21
Giant Food, 49
Gitlin, Todd, 175
Globalization, 22, 162, 165, 167, 196
Government, federal, 8–9, 24, 45, 51–
    53
  budget deficit, and the, 176
  (*see also* Credit cards, legislation)
Grace period, 34, 51, 53, 56, 94–95,
    105, 151, 180–181
Great Britain, 159, 161, 164, 171–172
Great Wall credit cards, 161, 171
Greenwood Trust, 38
Gross domestic product (GDP), 6
Gross national product (GNP), 6
Guide to Everyday Economic Statistics, A,
    6

Hansell, Saul, 181

"High" vs. "low" culture, 31, 168, 172
Holiday Inn, 31–32, 158
Home mortgages, 64, 66
Homogenization, 2, 22, 172–175, 177,
    196
Hong Kong, 88, 161
Household International, 121
Hoyos, Oscar, 44
Huntington Bancshares, 135–136, 150

Indebtedness, 2, 7–9, 11, 17, 19–20, 36,
    62–63, 69, 71, 81
Individualism, 3, 8
Individual Retirement Account (IRA),
    67
Inflation rate, 9, 13, 75, 138, 176
"Information highway," 147
Innovation, lack of, 129–130
Interest payments, 72
Interest rates, 2, 9–10, 27, 35–37, 41,
    44, 48, 51–52, 64, 65, 69, 71, 75–
    78, 85, 88, 93–94, 96, 99, 103–105,
    113, 131, 137, 151, 187
Interlink debit cards, 162, 181
Internal Revenue Service (IRS), 111

Japan, 46, 159–160, 175, 182–183
  Disneyland, 175
Japan Credit Bureau (JCB), 160–161,
    171
Joe Camel, 17

Kroc, Ray, 130
Kuisel, Richard, 164–165, 170–174
Kurtzman, Joel, 24

Labor market, 18–19
Late fees, 94
Legislation (*see* Credit cards, legisla-
    tion)
Levi's, 1, 158
Levittown, New York, 31
Lifebank, 153–154
"Lifestyle" card, 45
  American Sociological Association,
    45
  Catholic Charities, 45

"Lifestyle" card *(continued)*
  Caritas card, the, 45
  Sane/Freeze, 45
  Sierra Club, the, 45
Loans
  automobile, 11, 64, 135
  consolidation, 13, 72–73
  consumer, 21
  home equity, 10–11, 64–65, 73, 78,
    104–105, 135, 176
  mortgage, 11, 78, 135
Lotus Development Corporation, 115
Louvre, the, 175

Macau, 161
Macro-micro relationships, 16–17,
  21–23
Macroscopic theories, 15–16
Maestro, 148, 162, 181
Mall of America, 33, 158
Mandell, Lewis, 130
Marketplace, 115
Marlboro, 1
Marriott, 122
Marx, Karl, 18, 20–22
Marxian theory, 18, 20
Mass culture, 21
MasterCard, 3, 26–28, 33–34, 36–38,
    39, 41, 44–46, 49, 54, 56, 60, 62,
    70, 82–83, 85, 87–88, 98, 100, 131,
    133, 140, 158, 160, 162, 180, 181,
    196
Master Charge, 27, 37
Master Debit, 181
Materialism, 3
Mathews, Jay, 95
MBNA, 113
McDonaldization, 130
  of banking, 135–136
McDonaldization of Society, The, 18
McDonald's, 1, 31–32, 130–131, 134,
    136, 138, 158, 172
  Hamburger University, 144
MCI, 88
"Mean machinations," 20, 83–84, 92,
    113, 176
  by card users, 97–98
  by credit card companies, 92–97, 106

excessive fees, 93–94
excessive interest rates, 93–94
exploitive billing practices, 94–97
Mellon Automated Clearing House
    Association, 189
Microscopic theories, 15–16
Milken, Michael, 176
Mills, C. Wright, 16–18, 21–22, 175
Minimum payment, 14, 72, 76, 94–95,
    104
Mobil, 35
Modernism, 167–170
Modernization, 164–165, 167
Money, 2, 19, 21, 23
  alienating and separating effect of, 3
  circulation of, 59–60
  computerization of, 196
  history of, 23–25
Money Access System (MAC), 181,
    192
  Medical Payment Service, 192
Money economy, 19–21, 83
  problems associated with, 19–21
Monthly payments, 10, 12
Mortgage(s), 10
Mortgage companies, 6–7
Motel chains, 32–33, 158–159
Movie theaters, 49
Mundis, Jerrold, 74–75

National Association of Secondary
    School Principals, 15
National Audubon Society, 113
National Automated Clearing House
    Association (NACHA), 55, 189,
    191
National Criminal Information Center,
    118
National Foundation of Consumer
    Credit, 80
Nationsbank, 47–48
Neo-Marxian theory, 18–19, 21
New York Telephone (Nynex), 99
Nintendo, 65
No-fee cards, 50
Nonprofit consumer credit counseling
    centers, 78
Nordstrom, 35

Northwest Airlines, 33
NYCE, 181

Optima, 27, 49, 171
Overdraft lines of credit, 62
Overdraft protection, 62–63
Overeaters Anonymous, 79
Overspenders Anonymous, 79
"Owner's Guide to a Chase Credit Card," 14

Parking facilities, 49
Pepsi, 195
Personal computer banking, 184
Personal identification number (PIN), 182, 193
"Personality" cards, 45
    Elvis Presley, 45
    New York Giants, 45
"Petty products," 172
Pharmacies, 54
Phenomenology, 15
Pizza Hut, 49
Plus ATM Network, 161–162
"Point-of-sale system" (POS), 180, 182, 184, 192
Popular culture, 31
Postal Service, 119
Postmodernism, 31, 168–170
"Postrational" society, 167
Premodernism, 173
"Prescreening," 120
Price protection, 47
Prime rate, 40, 104–105
Privacy
    invasions of, 2, 12, 20, 107–127, 151, 177
    protection of, 125–127
Privacy Protection Commission, U.S., 122
Privacy Times, 115
Private investigators, 117
Prodigy, 185
"Product benefit cards," 39–41 (*see also* Credit cards, co-branded)
Psychosis, 17

Quayle, Dan, 117

Rather, Dan, 118
Rationalization, 21–22, 129, 133–156, 158, 165–167, 169–170, 173, 177, 195–196
    calculability, and, 21, 133–135, 137–142, 152, 165, 195
    coping with, in the credit card industry, 155–156
    efficiency and, 21, 134, 142–144, 152, 195
    "iron cage" of, 21, 134, 154–156, 177
    irrationality of, 134–135, 137, 149–151, 153, 196
    personal troubles of, 151–155
    predictability and, 21, 144–146, 152–153, 166, 196
    quantification and, 137–141, 152
    substitution of nonhuman for human technology and the, 21, 134–135, 146–149, 152–153, 166, 196
    technological control and, 21
Rebates, 27, 41, 46, 48, 50, 77
Recession(s), 17, 26, 77, 145
Reducing Crime by Eliminating Cash, 83–84
Relativism, 169
"Representations," 169
Revolving credit, 34, 41, 51, 64, 92, 96, 105, 180
Ronald McDonald House, 133
Rothfeder, Jeffrey, 123
Roy Rogers, 144
Russia, 157

Savings, personal, 6–12, 17, 46, 93, 138, 141, 146, 176
Scholastic, Inc., 14
Schrage, Michael, 81
Schwarzenegger, Arnold, 33
Sears, 38
Secrecy problems, 20, 107–127, 151
    computerized databases, 121–123
    coping with, 123–125
    erroneous credit records, 109–113
    excessive data collection, 116–117
    illegitimate access to credit records, 117–119
    lack of, 20

Secrecy problems (*continued*)
  nondisclosure of affinity card terms, 113–116
  nondisclosure of credit terms, 109
  sale of credit and lifestyle information, 119–121
Seducing the French: The Dilemma of Americanization, 164
Segmentation, 169
"Sensitizing concepts," 20
Servan-Schreiber, J.-J., 163
Service (gas) stations, 31, 33, 62–63, 86
Share Our Strength (SOS), 133
Shell, 27, 40, 47
Shopaholics Anonymous, 79
"Shopping buddies," 79
Shopping malls, 31–33, 82, 158–159
Siler, Charles, 25
Simmel, Georg, 2–3, 19–22, 59–60, 64, 83–84, 92, 107–108, 133, 138, 163, 175
  theory of money and secrecy, 108
Simulations, 168–170
"Sin tax," 81
"Skimming," 88–89
"Smart cards," 55, 100, 119, 146–147, 183, 187
Smart telephones, 184
Social Meaning of Money, The, 138
Social problems, 16, 29–30
Society for Worldwide Interbank Financial Telecommunications (SWIFT), 191
Sociological Imagination, The, 16
Sohio, 34
Spence, Craig, 107
SpenderMender, 79
Spending limits, 28, 146
Sprint, 149
Steinem, Gloria, 132
Structural functionalism, 15
Suburbs, 32
Supermarkets, 48, 54, 70
Sweden, 172
Symbolic interactionism, 15
Symbolic Interaction: Perspective and Method, 20

Tax(es), 8
Tax Reform Act of 1986, 139
Taxis, 49
Teaser rates, 105
"Technoscape," 163
Telemarketers
  abuses by, 90–91
  "laundering" of drafts, 91
Telephone banking, 135–136, 155
Telephone bill-paying, 143, 184, 187
Telephone cards, 55, 88
  fraud and, 88
  "shoulder surfers," 88
Television, 31–32
  advertisements, 70, 81
  home shopping networks, 9
"Temptation to imprudence," 20, 59–82, 176, 192, 193
  of credit cards, 60–62
  danger signs of, 72–73
  of debit cards, 62–63
  electronic funds transfers, 63–64
  getting outside help, 78–81
  how to overcome, 71–81
  stopping credit abuse, 73–76
  what the credit card industry could do, 81–82
  what the government can do, 81
Theft, 75
Theme park, 158–159
"Third cultures," 162–163
Tianamen Square, 157
"Toyotaization," 163
Transaction fees, 51, 63
Trans Union, 110, 112, 121, 123
Travel accident insurance programs, 48
"Travel and entertainment cards," 36–38, 44
Traveler's checks, 32, 36
Truth-in-Lending Act, 104 (*see also* Consumer Credit Protection Act)
Truth-in-Lending Simplification and Reform Act (1980), 53
TRW, 92, 110, 114–115, 121, 123
Turner, Bryan S., 21

Unemployment, 51
United Kingdom, 46, 160

"Value-added" cards, 46–47
Visa, 3, 15, 26–28, 34–39, 41, 44–46,
    49, 54, 82–83, 85, 87, 88, 100, 131,
    133, 140, 143, 144, 147, 158–162,
    171, 179–181, 183, 188–189, 196
Visa Check, 54, 161, 181
Visa Debit, 181
Visa Germany, 160
Visa International, 159–160
Visa Internet, 148
Visanet, 147
Visa U.S.A., 91
Volvo, 172

Wages, 18, 73
Waldenbooks, 117
Wal-Mart, 144
Walt Disney, 1
Ward, Pam, 65–67
Ward, Peter, 65–69
Warwick, David, 83–84
Weber, Max, 21–22, 133–134, 154, 156,
    177
Wendy's, 131
William, Francis, 158, 164, 173, 175

Zelizer, Viviana, 138

(acknowledgments continued from p. xvi)

San Francisco Chronicle for Katy Butler, "Big Spenders Learn to Set Limits," *San Francisco Chronicle*, September 17, 1991, p. A1.

The Society for the Advancement of Education for Elgie Hostein, "The Hidden Costs of Credit Cards," *USA Today*, November 1989, p. 82.

South China Morning Post for "Firm Seeks Use Abroad of Yuan Credit Card," *South China Morning Post*, October 25, 1993, p. 2. © 1993 *South China Morning Post*. Reprinted by permission of the Editorial Library.

Time Inc. for Janice Castro, "Charge It Your Way," *Time*, July 1, 1991, p. 51; Andrew Tobias, "Beware the Plastic Loan Shark," *Time*, January 10, 1994, p. 20; Michael G. Riley, "Sorry, Your Card Is No Good," *Time*, April 9, 1990, p. 62; Richard Lacayo, "Nowhere to Hide," *Time*, November 11, 1991, p. 36. Copyright © 1990, 1991, 1994 by Time Inc. Reprinted with permission. Also for: Julia Lieblich, "Credit Card Wars on Campus," *Fortune*, April 10, 1989. © 1989 Time Inc. All rights reserved. Also for Walter L. Updegrave, "How Lenders Size You Up," *Money*, April 1987, pp. 146, 147, reprinted from the April 1987 issue of *Money* by special permission; copyright 1987, Time Inc.

Tribune Media Services for "Dennis Romero, "Piling Up Debit: Easy Credit Luring College Students," *Chicago Tribune*, December 20, 1993, p. C1. Reprinted by permission: Tribune Media Services.

Eric Tyson for "Credit Crackdown: Control Your Spending Before It Controls You," *The San Francisco Examiner*, November 28, 1991, p. E1. Copyright 1991 by Eric Tyson, *San Francisco Examiner* columnist and author of *Personal Finance for Dummies*.

U.S. News & World Report for Margaret Mannix, Diane Duke, and Marc Silver for "Match That Price," *U.S. News & World Report*, April 15, 1991, p. 74.

The Washington Post for Stephen Barr, "Adding Dignity to Aid with New Technology," June 4, 1993, p. A23; the following articles by Albert Crenshaw: "Battling the High Costs of Borrowing" (January 27, 1992, p. A1), "Checking the Credit Bureau Industry" (June 9, 1991, p. H3), "A Crash Course in Credit" (November 7, 1993, p. H3), "Complex Charges on Credit Cards Can Push Rates Higher, Study Says" (June 19, 1992, pp. C1, C4), "Credit Card Holders to be Warned of Lists" (May 14, 1992, p. D14), "Credit Card Rate Spreads Keep Growing" (October 13, 1991, p. H3), "Credit Cards in Combat" (July 11, 1991, p. A33), "Keeping Tabs on Card Holders" (January 2, 1991, p. H4), "Rising Debit Card Use Heralds Change in Spending Habits" (September 18, 1991, p. D1); Jerry Knight, "On PINs and Needles over ATMs," May 21, 1993, p. G8; Celia Cassidy, "Chaarrge!: America's Card-Carrying Teens," June 25, 1991, p. D5; Michael Isikoff, "Theft of U.S. Data Seen as a Growing Threat," December 28, 1991, pp. A1, A4; Serge F. Kovaleski, "Credit Scam Targets Mailboxes," December 2, 1993, p. A4; Daniel Mendel-Black and Evelyn Richard, "Peering Into Private Lives," January 20, 1991, p. H1; Bill Miller, "Instant Banking Inspires Abductions," September 29, 1993, p. D1; Mark Potts, "The Ghosts of Debt to Come," January 1, 1993; William F. Powers, "For More Customers, Electronic Money Is the Way to Pay," January 19, 1994, p. 7; Michael Shrage for "It's Time to Put a Transaction Tax on Credit Card Purchases," October 12, 1990, p. F3; David Warsh, "Credit Rate Cap Is One Way to Treat an Addiction," November 27, 1991, p. C3. © 1990, 1991, 1992, 1993, 1994 The Washington Post. Reprinted with Permission.